Casino and Museum

Casino and Museum

Representing Mashantucket Pequot Identity

John J. Bodinger de Uriarte

The University of Arizona Press   Tucson

The University of Arizona Press
© 2007 The Arizona Board of Regents
All rights reserved

Library of Congress Cataloging-in-Publication Data
Bodinger de Uriarte, John J. (John Joseph), 1959–
   Casino and museum : representing Mashantucket Pequot
identity / John J. Bodinger de Uriarte.
     p. cm.
   Includes bibliographical references and index.
   ISBN-13: 978-0-8165-2545-4 (hardcover : alk. paper)
   ISBN-10: 0-8165-2545-5 (hardcover : alk. paper)
   1. Pequot Indians—Gambling. 2. Gambling on Indian
reservations—Connecticut. 3. Casinos—Connecticut.
4. Pequot Indians—Museums. 5. Mashantucket Pequot
Museum & Research Center. 6. Mashantucket Pequot Tribal
Nation. I. Title.
  E99.P53B63 2007
  305.897'344—dc22   2006028666

Publication of this book is made possible in part by a grant
from Susquehanna University.

Manufactured in Canada on acid-free, archival-quality paper
containing a minimum of 10% post-consumer waste.

12 11 10 09 08 07   6 5 4 3 2 1

For Jacob and Leah

Contents

List of Figures   ix

Acknowledgments   xi

Introduction   3

1   Coming to Ground   13

2   Tribal Renaissance   40

3   "The Wonder of It All"   63

4   "Discover a Nation in Your Own Backyard"   103

5   A Tribal Portrait   161

Conclusion   209

Notes   219

Bibliography   225

Index   235

Figures

1.1   View of the Grand Pequot Tower   14

1.2   The Mashantucket Pequot Museum and Research Center   17

3.1   The Grand Pequot Tower   64

3.2   *The Rainmaker*   66

3.3   The concourse   79

3.4   The casino level of the Foxwoods Resort Casino   85

3.5   A glass-walled gaming room   87

3.6   An exhibit in the casino's first museum   95

3.7   Cinetropolis   97

4.1   The Mashantucket Pequot Museum and Research Center observation tower   104

4.2   Map of the museum and research center's public spaces   107

4.3   A side view of the Gathering Space   109

4.4   Underhill's portrayal of the attack on the Pequot Fort at Mystic   110

4.5   The entrance to the Mashantucket Pequot Tribal Nation gallery   111

4.6   The model of the reservation in the Tribal Nation gallery   114

4.7   The Tribal Nation gallery   116

4.8   The Dream Catcher   118

4.9   The escalator into the glacial crevasse   124

4.10   A scene from the Pequot Village   130

4.11   A detail from the caribou hunt diorama   131

4.12   A caribou hunter   132

4.13   Life-casts from the four seasons dioramas   133

4.14   Figures harvesting in the cornfield   134

x   Figures

4.15   A scene from the Pequot Village   135

4.16   A cut-away wigwam   136

4.17   Figures working on the postcontact village palisade   137

4.18   The Pequot Austin George, a Union soldier in the Civil War   145

4.19   The Pequot Peter George, a whaler   146

4.20   The Mashpee Meetinghouse   147

4.21   The farmstead in the gallery   148

4.22   An exterior view of the farmstead   150

4.23   The trailer home in the gallery   158

5.1   The final gallery: A Tribal Portrait   163

5.2   Another view of A Tribal Portrait   166

5.3   Chief Nathan Young   168

5.4   Alice R. Kirchner   172

5.5   *The Vanishing Race—Navaho*, by Edward Curtis   177

5.6   Jean Merrill, Joy Hale, and Joshua Hale   188

5.7   Matthew Pearson   190

5.8   Arline Phelmetta and Eunice Mitchell   196

5.9   Gary Brend   198

5.10   Michael Holder and sons   199

5.11   Carolyn Colebut and Steven Colebut   200

5.12   Vernon Colebut   201

Acknowledgments

I owe many thanks; without the support of numerous individuals and institutions this book would not have been possible. First, I would like to thank the Mashantucket Pequot Tribal Nation, the Mashantucket Pequot Museum and Research Center, and Design Division, Inc.

The Mashantucket Pequot Tribal Nation allowed me to work on the museum project and provided the grant-proposal writing contracts that originally made it possible for me to do my fieldwork. I also thank them for granting permission for me to reproduce images from Foxwoods Resort Casino materials. Special thanks are due to Bruce MacDonald and Carol Boyd for securing and providing photographs used here.

At the Mashantucket Pequot Museum and Research Center I am particularly grateful to Kevin McBride for encouragement and the free exchange of ideas about the museum and its projects, to Terry Bell, and to Jack Campisi for providing my first introduction to the museum. Thanks also to Robert Halloran, Russ Handsman, David Holahan, Gabriella Kaye, and Trudie Richmond.

Lauri Halderman and Mike Hanke of DDI were very supportive of my work, and I owe DDI particular thanks for making it possible for me to continue my fieldwork and to contribute to the final exhibitions for the museum.

Photographer David Neel has been extremely generous and helpful in answering questions and supplying images for use in this book and elsewhere. I am grateful for the opportunity to speak and correspond with him. I deeply appreciate his permission to use his photographs here.

xii Acknowledgments

I am indebted to Pauline Turner Strong for her encouragement and her consistent efforts to challenge my thinking and writing throughout my graduate career and beyond. Over the course of this study I have talked with countless friends and colleagues at the University of Texas and elsewhere who have offered encouragement, criticism, and new ideas and works to pursue and who have endured my fascination with Mashantucket, casinos, and museums. I cannot possibly name everyone, but I would like to especially acknowledge Melissa Biggs for her sharp wit and perceptive critique and James Brow, Doug Foley, Howard Lutz, Guha Shankar, Katherine Spilde, Katie Stewart, and Terry Winegar. I thank Susquehanna University for supporting the production of this book.

At the University of Arizona Press, thanks to Christine Szuter for her continued encouragement, to Allyson Carter for her enthusiasm and support, and to Mary M. Hill for her careful copyediting. The considered and insightful suggestions of the anonymous reviewers were invaluable. All errors, overstatements, and idiosyncrasies are my own.

Finally, but by no means least, I thank my mother and my sister for their love and support; my extended family for their belief and patience; and Anne, Jacob, and Leah for making it all worthwhile.

Casino and Museum

Introduction

Foxwoods Resort Casino, the main business enterprise of the Mashantucket Pequot Tribal Nation, is the largest casino in the Western Hemisphere. Located near Ledyard, Connecticut, Foxwoods offers a densely scripted public site where Las Vegas–style narratives mix with generalized Native American and specific Mashantucket Pequot representations. The immersive environment of Foxwoods resembles many media-saturated public spaces. The elements that make up the total milieu, rather than being consciously engaged on a piece-by-piece basis, become part of the affective environment, part of the unquestioned "common sense" of the interior and its theme. The tribal nation is also home to the Mashantucket Pequot Museum and Research Center (MPMRC), a state-of-the-art 193-million-dollar public facility constructed to present the history and contemporary community of the Mashantucket Pequots.

This work explores these enterprises in part as self-representational and authenticating industries that use display; photographs; narratives of the exotic, the essential, and the real; geographic location; and architectural design to present and articulate representations of Native American and Mashantucket Pequot identities. This study focuses on the play between the referential "fact" of the Mashantucket Pequots as a federally recognized and identified tribal nation and the public performance of that identity as represented in displays and historical narratives constructed on the reservation. It sets out to investigate the productive space between reference and performance—between naming something and experiencing what that name means—and the articulation and strategic use of this space at

Mashantucket. Field research included work with the Mashantucket Pequot Tribal Nation, the MPMRC, Design Division, Inc., and the Connecticut River Museum.

As counterindicative and countersupportive structures, the museum and the casino generate both economic and symbolic capital. The casino provides a stream of income for tribal development while it simultaneously raises questions in the surrounding and national public centered on issues of authenticity, identification by phenotype, and perceptions of the Pequots as "not only nouveau riche, but nouveau Indian" (Kroft 1994). Many studies of contemporary Indian gaming either examine economic impact or trace the history of a particular tribal nation as a means to legitimate (or call into question) their legal and cultural identity. I take both of those issues as given—Indian gaming has enormous economic impact, and the Mashantucket Pequots have an authentic legal and cultural identity as an Indian nation.

The success of Foxwoods and the questions raised about its owners frame the authentic in terms of appearance or expectation, as nostalgia mixing with an existing archive of popular Indian images and understandings. In part these questions focus on the relatively rapid repopulation of the reservation and the cultural, political, and economic renaissance of its assembled community. As the casino's companion enterprise, the museum focuses on presenting a validating and authenticating historical and ethnographic narrative that firmly locates the Mashantucket Pequots in the space and time of Mashantucket and New England.

Native self-representation powerfully challenges the effects of centuries of images and understandings of Indianness forged in the U.S. public sphere. Across Native America the development of public terrain—spaces that attract large numbers of mostly non-Native patrons and visitors—for cultural representation is an important issue. Indian gaming provides a potential source of capital for accelerated and energized participation in this development. Indian gaming enjoys and depends on a substantial patron base; the National Indian Gaming Association (2004:7) estimated more than 114 million visits to Indian casinos in 2003 alone.

The public spaces constructed for gaming often house other immediate commercial concerns that support the gaming "experience," including restaurants, shops, theaters, and entertainment. Casino spaces provide important new forums for the representation of public identities in "Indian country."[1]

The construction of museums and cultural centers is a key parallel enterprise for many tribal nations. Often funded by new monies made available through gaming profits, this construction also reflects the passage and implementation of the 1990 Native American Graves Protection and Repatriation Act (NAGPRA). The act created a means for the return of human remains, funerary and sacred objects, or objects of cultural patrimony to culturally affiliated Indian tribes or lineal descendents. These objects, then, can move from museums and collections reflecting dominant anthropological, historical, or national narratives to institutions or collections reflecting Native understandings or telling Native stories. Increasingly, museums are recognized as important public sites for the potential unsettling of dominant and popular representational narratives about Indian histories and peoples.[2]

Two modes of understanding identity frame this productive space: identity as evidential—knowledge or understanding based on structures of naming, defining, or categorizing—and as evocative—knowledge or understanding based on something sensed or felt. This distinction points to a key issue in Native America specifically focused on Indian identity. On the one hand, Indian identity is often understood as a specific or fixed category (or set of categories) that can include federal recognition, a government-to-government relationship between Indian tribes and the U.S. government that recognizes their sovereignty or the right to tribal self-government and protects them from decisions made about their lands or people without their consent. On the other hand, Indian cultural identity is fluid, nuanced, practiced, and felt—something not fully captured by fixed points of meaning.

Popular representations of Indians, thematic representations of Indians, and historical representations of Indians all contribute to the formation of the American Indian subject in the popular imaginary. Control over who will be able to tell foundational and popular stories about Indians and how is a strategic battleground for many Native Americans, and the stakes are high. The range and power of representations run from romanticized and warm-toned photographic images of the "noble but doomed savage" to cases brought for federal recognition through the Bureau of Indian Affairs or argued in the courts. Representations depend on and support particular ways of being "seen," of being understood as occupying recognizable locations, designations, or identities. The active participation in and control of such representations inextricably links the politics, culture, and economy of Native America. The means to self-representation—or the control of foundational public stories of origin and place in political and cultural histories—has far-reaching repercussions and force.

While Foxwoods puts forth a densely scripted public space, the casino's profits support a powerfully private and insular gated community. Mashantucket presents a difficult field site, one that problematizes traditional power relationships between U.S. anthropologists and their Indian "others." Mashantucket ways of being include new and revitalized cultural forms and practices, successful entrepreneurship, and the flexing of political muscle in local, state, and federal arenas. The ethnographic subjects at Mashantucket have more than enough power and security to avoid or deflect investigation or the kind of access and cooperation necessary to provide rich ethnographic detail and a sense of lived Pequot lives.

Instead, this study proposes a careful hermeneutics of the casino and museum as productive spaces that offer constructed public representations of Mashantucket Pequotness and Indianness for consumption by a large visiting (and overwhelmingly non-Native) population. Accordingly, this exploration maintains the perspective of an informed patron throughout this work. I work in public spaces with public narratives, and the examples on which I focus include artifacts, galleries, buildings, texts, and public casino spaces chosen from an array of possible combinations of object, location, and intensifying text or performance.

Different Ways In

This investigation also works photographically through the public spaces at Mashantucket to create an observational record. I am an anthropologist and a photographer, and my textual narrative merges with a series of photographs I took at the museum. Beyond merely illustrating the text, the photographs extend a different modality for experiencing immersive Mashantucket public spaces. Neither purely referential nor interpretive, they provide a means of exploration, making spatial and formal "sense" of the museum exhibitions and navigating its galleries and public spaces. This photographic record combines with those created by the Mashantucket Pequots and others for public consumption. It joins works by David Neel, selected from the museum's final gallery; a photograph by Edward S. Curtis; and images from advertising, informational brochures, and public relations materials for Foxwoods and the MPMRC. The photographs offer a way to *see* the spaces; as photographs, they also record acts of viewing.

Photographs fix time and space in condensed and portable representations that can be used in different narratives to mean different things, and they offer a critical introduction and insight into representational practices at Mashantucket. Photographs mix a sense of the evidential—the photograph as mechanical record—with the evocative—the photograph as location for imagination and felt connection. They furnish powerful illustrations of the productive zone between reference and performance. In this work photographs are both a method of and a focus for investigation. They also allow the reader to alternate between the book's descriptive and analytical work. The analysis below circles to center on photographs of American Indians in history and in the MPMRC final gallery as one way to explore the interrelationship between a representation as evidential record and evocative artifact, as a context-reliant interpretive image, and as an object able to shift through a number of different values and meanings during its own "social life" (Appadurai 1986).

8 Introduction

As the second strategy, the observing and visual "recording" perspective of the photographer couples with the ambulatory "reading" perspective of a museum visitor. Comprehending the Foxwoods Resort Casino and the MPMRC requires recognition that their parallel and complementary immersive public spaces have representation as a principal product. The casino and (especially) the museum are rich *display environments*, what John Dorst defines as "physical space[s] in which material elements have been selected and arranged primarily for the purpose of being looked at" (1999:119). The display environments at Mashantucket speak, record, and categorize while simultaneously acting, producing, and institutionalizing.

The idea of "looking at" is critical for an exploration of Mashantucket. The practice of looking unites all the public representational efforts and determines many of the public challenges to Mashantucket Pequot identity. The two towers—the Grand Pequot Tower of the Foxwoods Resort Casino and the observation tower of the MPMRC—speak powerfully to the idea of looking, to scanning the surround and noticing the size of the host's footprints inscribed thereon. The entire structure of a museum narrativizes "looking at," directing gaze through narrative and exhibition design. The MPMRC's closing gallery, with its collection of contemporary photographic portraits of tribal members, presents one of the more potent locations for looking in the museum. All photographs are products of a particularly mechanized looking, of a formal apparatus for looking and capturing for the gaze—the portrait subjects in the gallery are arranged so that most "look through" their photographs, back to the imagined audiences of the museum.

Authenticity and the practices of authentication are key to understanding issues raised in this study. Representation, the formation of oppositional narratives and the use of popular and counterpopular iconics, can be thought about in terms of seeing, looking, and the act of recognition. Here recognition is a multivalent term—we can think about it in its legal and federal sense, but we can also think about it in a popular sense, in terms of seeing and fitting something seen into an existing or held set of hegemonic categories or possibilities. Here I follow Raymond Williams's understanding of hegemony not as direct political control but as "a more general predominance that includes, as one of its key features, a particular way of seeing the world and human nature and relationships" (1977:145). Part of what happens in Mashantucket challenges this existing set of popular categories in part by constructing new ones, in part by reinscribing existing ones with new images or narratives and firmly locating these representations *in place*.

In the casino looking is part of a larger order of consumption. The spaces serve as intensified areas of display, but, as in other casinos, the looking intends to spark engagement. The patron oscillates between viewing and participating roles, and the lines between casinos as a place to look and a place to be looked at are purposefully obscured. In many ways, casinos present the ultimate performance space of consumer culture, where the differences between symbolic capital and economic capital blur, as does the distinction between audience and actor. There are few, if any, private spaces in a casino. All transactions occur in public—from penny-ante slots to high-stakes table games—mostly in front of strangers, part spectacle and part participation.

This project's third strategy investigates how the Mashantucket Pequots use the casino and the museum as public theaters to mount narratives that oppose existing hegemonic discourses of Native American identity, expressed in the registers of race, ethnicity, capital success, and New England history (Chambers 1991). The representational spaces at Mashantucket depend too heavily on traditional casino and museum industry design and effect to be considered clearly counterhegemonic or resistant structures. Nevertheless, different texts and displays skillfully and tactically counter master narratives of "Indianness" extant in the public imaginary. While examples of these representational tactics exist throughout the casino and the museum, the final museum gallery, with its composite portrait of the tribal nation, advances the most compelling display of oppositional discourse. Here the Mashantucket Pequots concentrate and present their contemporary public "face"; here they cement their projection as a coherent tribal nation with a coherent tribal identity, an identity that rebuts challenges made in popular understandings of race and ethnicity. The portrait project is ongoing, and the density of the group's representation changes as new photographs are added.

The Mashantucket Pequots create and mobilize self-representations in several central spaces, and these spaces offer infinite points for focus and understanding. This study moves between these different levels as a strategy for understanding poetic expression as a means of self-identification and self-representation. As a form of mimesis the study enacts its own kind of experiential immersion, thickly accreting data and mixing ideology with sensory experience, drawing its focus closer as it moves deeper into representational space. As in the museum, the final chapter culminates in the images found in the closing gallery. John Berger's concept of a "radial system of presentation" for photographs—the photograph-as-artifact seen "in terms which are simultaneously personal, political, economic, dramatic, everyday, and historic" (1980a:63)—provides a means for approaching the entire practice of representation at Mashantucket. Each artifact, building, representation, or industry offers a complex set of interconnected influences and understandings. A radial reading must include a consideration of contextualization, the saturation and overlap of space and time, and the products and industries of identity representation. Here the casino and the museum share the largest porous boundary of mutual influence.

The study traverses three fields of experience. The first explores the relationship between the referential meaning of "Indian" and the performative meaning of "Indian." This relationship creates a dialectic between meaning as an assembly of evidential data and meaning as felt through the use of these data as the basis for the experience of sensual immersion. The casino is a particularly rich site for this kind of interplay, but the museum's use of this dynamic is no less fundamental.

The second field of experience recognizes the Mashantucket Pequots' skillful use of tactical opposition and appropriation. As representational spaces the casino and the museum appropriate industries, technologies, knowledges, and existing archives and genres for rereading and incorporation. Appropriation is a poetic shift, a way of generating new performative meaning in referential relationships by shifts in position and emphasis. At Mashantucket appropriation is a means of production.

The practice of appropriation speaks to the relationship between the hegemonic and the oppositional, between stabilizing tradition and tactical engagements designed to destabilize traditional practices, taking advantage of fissures or tensions in existing and persuasive discursive structures. As Ross Chambers notes, such "oppositional behavior, particularly discursive, has particular potential for changing states of affairs by changing states of mentalities" (1991:47). The project of identity politics and identity representation at Mashantucket inhabits the tense plain between the hegemonic and the oppositional. While most obvious in the public spaces of museum and casino, it is no less true in the politics of Mashantucket. Enormous, fundamental stress is placed on achieved federal recognition—key to identity confirmation and to providing the opportunity for participating in the gaming industry. This opportunity presents the most powerful option available to grow Native economic and political power. Some Native activists argue that federal recognition and state gaming compacts compromise the ideal of Native sovereignty; others see an opportunity provided, within existing political and legal structures, for material and political advantage.

Finally, Mashantucket furnishes a unique space in which to consider Benedict Anderson's concept of "imagining the nation," where the immediate and lived experience of national citizenship is an act of imagination, an in-filling of framework and designation with a performance of belonging. The museum and the casino offer prime sites for understanding the revitalized formation of a national community—how public spaces of representation, both formal and vernacular, are mobilized to support the parameters of community as a simultaneously inclusive and exclusive construct. Understanding the complex institutional spaces and relationships at Mashantucket provides awareness and raises questions about the interplay between the politics and poetics of self-representation that extend beyond the reservation.

This book explores the ways in which the poetics of museum spaces and spectacular public displays as well as past and present narratives surrounding Native American cultural practices and economic pursuits contribute to the contested construction and emergence of an "authentic" "Indian" subject in discourses that include anthropology, photography, theories of imagining the nation and the creation of tradition, and issues of representational practice, particularly in museum exhibitions. In part this study is a celebration of the (micro–)Mashantucket Pequot and the (macro-)Indian ability to both create and control public narratives about identity.

1 Coming to Ground

Connecticut had seen better days. I was driving through its rolling farmlands and forests, occasionally passing through weary cities and old industrial towns, their mills long since closed. While the state boasts the highest per-capita income in the United States, much of that has its origins elsewhere. Rising unemployment brought Connecticut to its economic knees in the 1980s; by the early 1990s the state was increasingly frayed and economically depressed.[1] Recent growth in software, pharmaceutical, and tourist industries has given the economy a much-needed boost, but the road to full economic recovery is long.

New England was one leading edge for the European invasion and occupation of America, and it was surprising to see that not everything is part of the Boston-to-Washington urban corridor. In Connecticut major cities are relatively close to less-developed areas, and state highways are often bordered by dry-stone walls, farmland, second-growth forests, and outcroppings of blasted stone ledge.

Approaching Mashantucket from I-395, the highway is marked with occasional brown "historical site" signs for the Mashantucket Pequot and Mohegan reservations. The route to Mashantucket passes the Mohegan Sun Casino and cuts above the towns of Mohegan and Uncasville. It is a small, scenic, two-lane highway through gently rolling hills and woods. Then, as one tops a low incline, the Grand Pequot Tower rises from the woods: twenty-five gleaming stories of tinted glass and concrete topped with different sections of bright turquoise roof.

A series of white dish antennae—aligned like phototropic blossoms to face invisible satellites for simulcast national and international sports events—marks

Figure 1.1 View of the Grand Pequot Tower, including the earlier phases of the Foxwoods Resort Casino. (Photograph provided by the Mashantucket Pequot Tribal Nation)

the adjacent lower rooflines. At the edge of the highway a large sign announces the entrance to Foxwoods Resort Casino, the main industry of the Mashantucket Pequot Tribal Nation. Faced with this Oz-like construction across a sea of trees, one might ask, "How did that get here?"

Key Backgrounds: Mapping the Site as Legislated Location

The last few decades have seen the renaissance of several Native American communities in the United States that have managed to revitalize marginal or depressed reservation economies and social infrastructures. Many have done so by mounting successful legal challenges, resulting in the return of reservation lands to Indian nations. And the operation of high-stakes bingo concerns on reservations following the decision of *Seminole Tribe of Florida v. Butterworth* in 1983 has opened up new and potentially lucrative industries for Native Americans.[2] The 1987 *California v. Cabazon Band of Mission Indians* decision effectively expanded the possible scope of gaming offered by federally recognized tribal nations.[3] With the passage of the Indian Gaming Regulatory Act (IGRA) on October 17, 1988, casino-style gambling became the latest and most profitable option for economic development on many Indian reservations.

In large part, the IGRA was passed to provide economic stimulus and development for many Indian nations. Forced removal, colonization, dispossession, and marginalization left the overwhelming majority of Indian reservation communities with a significant lack of resources and economic control. The virtual absence of vibrant economies on reservations and a dependence on federal aid programs led to Native Americans being what Eve Darian-Smith identifies as "the poorest and most deprived ethnic community in the US" (2004:95). When the IGRA was passed the 350 recognized reservation tribes in the United States were living in conditions of harsh poverty and despair, with an unemployment rate twice the national average. The tribes have the lowest level of educational attainment and a high incidence of alcoholism, drug abuse, domestic violence, and infant mortality.[4] Congress and many Native Americans saw the IGRA as a way to reduce the need for federal aid and to increase economic self-sufficiency. This self-sufficiency was not without its price. The act promoted entrepreneurship while reducing federal support for Indian people, a policy that has been referred to as "termination by accountants" (Morris 1992).

The IGRA was also a reaction to the gains made by the *Seminole* and *Cabazon* decisions. Indian gaming was a growing concern, and the issue of regulation was increasingly important. Under the act the administration created three classes of regulated gaming. Class I covers social or traditional forms of Indian gaming; Class

II covers bingo and related games; and Class III covers all forms of gaming that are not Class I or Class II, including slot machines and blackjack.[5]

The IGRA presents Native peoples with a new strategy to achieve economic independence, and it has had some phenomenal successes. Indian gaming has become the fundamental economic development initiative for Indian nations in the United States. By 2004 224 federally recognized tribes participated in either Class II or Class III gaming, with 249 tribal-state gaming compacts in 29 states. Approximately 65 percent of the Indian tribes in the continental United States generate governmental revenue through gaming (National Indian Gaming Association 2004:6).

Foxwoods and the Mashantucket Pequot Tribal Nation provide the most remarkable example of Indian gaming. By its fourth year of operation Foxwoods was grossing over $1 billion a year. The entire complex—gaming and public areas, hotels, and restaurants—includes 4.7 million square feet; 340,000 of them are devoted to gambling. Foxwoods employs over 11,500 people, and, after the federal government, the Mashantucket Pequot Tribal Nation is first in direct financial contributions to the state. In 1995, through its negotiated deal for the state monopoly on operating slot machines, the casino paid Connecticut $134 million and donated an extra $15 million to balance its budget. In June 2005 total Mashantucket Pequot financial contributions to Connecticut reached $2 billion.

The Mashantucket Pequots most visibly exemplify Indian peoples who have negotiated and overcome legal, logistical, and other hurdles to establish themselves as a potent economic, cultural, and political force not only in the local economy of New England but also in the larger nationally imagined and real spaces of "Indian country." A key component of this effort, the MPMRC, was completed on the reservation in 1998 and funded almost entirely by Foxwoods profits. It is the largest Native-owned and -operated museum facility in the Americas.

The two main commercial structures of the reservation, the museum and the casino complex, overlap in their articulation of representational space. While the

Figure 1.2 The Mashantucket Pequot Museum and Research Center. (Photograph provided by the Mashantucket Pequot Museum and Research Center)

casino is crucial as an economic generator, the museum is an important site wherein the Mashantucket Pequots display public representations of their identity, history, and culture. Furthermore, the MPMRC's significant independent funding ensures its ability to successfully enact the scope of its vision and projects.

While the museum is part of the Foxwoods destination resort, it also illustrates how the Mashantucket Pequots appropriate the discourses and practices of museum curatorship and science, including those of anthropology and archaeology, to further substantiate their claims to a historical continuity with both Mashantucket Pequot ancestors and the larger community of American Indian peoples.

Accordingly, the scientific research and entertainment industries of the Mashantucket Pequot Tribal Nation provide key sites at which to analyze the articulation, representation, and materialization of Native American identity—racial and national, individual and collective—within the local community and the corresponding resonance of these constructions with popular understandings of "Indianness" in the national imaginary. I understand "identity" here as an ongoing, dynamic, and public social process. Crucially, Indian identity in Mashantucket involves the representation of self and group to the reservation and local communities and the world beyond as the cohesive yet contingent projection of membership in a community or, in a Weberian sense, an imagined "belonging together" (e.g., Brow 1988, 1990, 1996).

But the success of the Mashantucket Pequots has come at a significant price. This emerging Indian nation has become a lightning rod for a number of volatile issues in "Indian country," the regional political economy, and the United States. The legitimacy of Mashantucket Pequot self-identification as an Indian tribal nation has been challenged on grounds that include cultural practices, phenotypical appearance, and blood-quantum reckoning. More specifically, the "racial identity" of the Mashantucket Pequots endures as a key issue for public discourse surrounding the tribal nation's claims to Indian legitimacy.

Paradoxically, these external and often pejorative constructions, particularly blood-quantum reckoning, have provided the Mashantucket Pequots and other Native Americans with the means of asserting claims to federal recognition and tribal sovereignty, making accessible resources not available to other subjugated groups in the United States. Mashantucket Pequot self-definition and autonomy must therefore be understood as often antagonistic but always related processes of contestation between local definitions and discourses of self and dominant narratives of racial essence and cultural stereotype that pervade the historical encounters between a majority "America" and its Indian "other."

My work contends that the politics and poetics of the Mashantucket Pequot museum and Foxwoods reflect both the Mashantucket Pequots' engagement with making history and particular manifestations of history-making practices in Indian country. Mashantucket provides a high-profile example for comprehending the dynamics of local community formation and for understanding the entangled and continually transforming histories of the United States and Indian nations in the making.

Self-Reflection, Self-Construction

My interest in this subject is threefold, and it includes (1) the formation of self-represented identities in the face of challenge, especially where this challenge is articulated in terms of appearance and a conformity with established public notions of ethnicity, race, or nationality; (2) the practice of representation—how representational structures are designed and what strategies they employ to present their narratives to the public; and (3) the practice of self-representation, specifically individual, ethnic, racial, or national identity, in the public spaces of casinos and entertainment complexes. Critical to these issues is their formulation and presentation to the public: museums and casinos offer intensified registers for mixing the factual and material with the fantastic.

I am a white Mexican American. While many of the cultural practices I was raised with were particularly marked as Mexican American, both self-constructed and by language, family, and an understanding of the national histories of Mexico and the United States, the environment for my formative years was primarily white, lower middle class. When my father was part of our nuclear family we lived in a predominantly white suburb in Orange County, California. My parents divorced, and my mother returned to college in the early 1970s; we dropped in our economic bracket at the same time that we (my mother, my sister, and I) entered a long period of immersion in the academic sphere.

Part of any such immersion in the 1970s necessarily included an awareness of student-based political activism focused on civil rights, women's rights, the war in Vietnam, and the rights of minorities, primarily blacks, Chicanos, and Indians. I grew up knowing about these different and overlapping communities of activism and being able to navigate between some of them and the rest of my life as a suburban adolescent and teenager. In large part this was due to my ability to "pass," to construct my identity as necessary to hang out either with the Chicano activists or with my cronies trading Hot Wheels in the playground of an overwhelmingly white middle school.

While I learned to appreciate what Karen Blu calls a "voluntaristic attitude of identity" (1980:209), I also found myself defending one or another self-identification depending on the challenge offered and my own investment in making a statement. My ability to engage in such statements involved navigating the contradictions of a racial-as-biological versus ethnicity-as-cultural argument of identity. Sometimes the arguments I made simply did not matter because I did not have the other credentials deemed necessary for a complete marginalized identity—I lacked the phenotypical features that would (popularly) mark me as Mexican American from a distance.

In college my studies centered on anthropology, sociology, and English, and I used these perspectives to explore the practices of textual representation. My reading worked to combine and compare anthropological, historical, and fictional literatures focused on and by American Indians. I was particularly intrigued by tensions and contradictions between my own "popular cultural" understandings and the anthropological and historical accounts of Native America.

I moved to San Francisco after college and began a career in photography, first as a self-funded documentary photographer, then in advertising. The work was demanding, and the amount of effort necessary to create a photograph for advertising was surprising at first. I worked during the ten years prior to the advent of digital imaging and image-manipulating software. All lighting effects were created at the film's exposure, and all errors or special effects were expensively corrected or produced by hand; the professional emphasis was on creating an ideally exposed sheet of film either in the studio or on location. I worked for a number of years producing and shooting car photography—large, "perfect" images of spotless, gleaming cars parked against mostly natural and dramatic backgrounds.

Working in photography trained my visual acuity and instilled in me a keen sense of the image, both as an artifact and as a form of highly selective representation. The interface between an advertising image and its consuming public represents a complex and negotiated intersection of technology; social, cultural, and political influences; personalized aesthetics; and individual agencies. This complexity persists even when the intersection between the photographer and the consuming public is more obvious, as in a gallery exhibition or a photo documentary. While it is seductive to imagine that a visitor alone in a photo gallery enjoys an unproblematic relationship with the images, issues of unstated mediation are critically important, perhaps even more so because the act of public display suggests a certain relationship made plain: the apparent removal of some mediating levels implies the removal of all. The beguiling "clarity" of a gallery experience makes problematic contextualizing or understanding additional relational nuances between the photographer and the photographic subjects; the gallery itself; the presented work as an element of the photographer's overall work; the relationships between the photographer and the gallery; the technological mediations of film, camera, optics, and printing; and the imagining of a projected audience.

One question in my own documentary work centered on how to present a group of images that revealed something more about photographic "subjects" and their collaborative relationship with the camera. Principal questions included the following: How could the collaborative relationship of photo making be made plain in a final image? At what point, if any, could a photograph of another person be a realization of the subject's self-representational desires or agency? What would the shape of a truly collaborative photographic project, one that had self-representation as a goal, take, and how would it work? Imagining these processes of negotiation and my experiences in photographic work were partly responsible for my return to anthropology.

Working in Native America, Working in Mashantucket

When I chose to work in Mashantucket I also chose to participate in the history between Indians and those—significantly, anthropologists and "Indian photographers"—who would make them the object of study or representation. U.S. anthropology and Indian photography "speak for" a historically marginalized people in professional practices that grew out of the manipulative power/knowledge relationships of colonialism and market economics in North America. Murray L. Wax notes: "Without political or military power, or the competencies needed for confronting government bureaucrats, [Indian peoples] were easy targets for manipulation" (1997:55).

Vine Deloria raised these issues, specifically as they related to the relationship between Native Americans and anthropologists, in *Custer Died for Your Sins: An Indian Manifesto* in 1969. A scathing critique of the anthropological community for its objectified treatment of Native Americans and the implications of a Native American–focused anthropology in "real-world" and academic politics, *Custer* focused on the power differential between Indians and "anthros" and fundamentally influenced the anthropology practiced in Native America.

Years later, Gerald Vizenor also examined relationships between Indians and "anthros" and the power that anthropologists hold in defining "culture," particularly Indian culture: "Everything in anthropology is an invention and an extension of the cultural colonialism of Western expansion. . . . Culture doesn't exist, they [anthropologists] invented it. . . . And the people who have that kind of power control culture, because they control the definitions, the symbols, and the masks that they've constructed about culture" (1990:161). Representation is key to the relationship between Indians and "anthros" and the privileged and sometimes arrogant position that anthropologists have taken in speaking "for" their Indian "subjects."

Mashantucket powerfully subverts this traditional power relationship. First and foremost, the financial resources available to the Mashantucket Pequot Tribal Nation allow the Mashantucket Pequots to create a reservation community that more closely resembles an affluent gated community. The tribal nation strictly controls access to its buildings and residential neighborhoods. It hires and controls its own public relations staff and maintains a powerful lobbying office in Washington, D.C. The Mashantucket Pequots create, promote, and disseminate their public story with financial and political clout.

Second, the community at Mashantucket is remarkably diverse and has assembled in response to two important factors. The current Mashantucket community traces its roots to the reservation repopulation effort initiated by Richard "Skip" Hayward in the early 1970s after the death of his grandmother, one of the last two reservation residents. Hayward wanted to establish a self-sufficient community to secure the reservation for future generations. The return of members from an existing diffuse network of identified and potential tribal members reflects clear decisions to participate in projects of community renewal, self-sufficiency, and economic growth. The historically dispersed Mashantucket Pequots have intermarried with other peoples over time, and the current population presents an ethnically, culturally, and racially diverse public face. Understanding race as a location for challenges to authenticity or as a rebuttal to such challenges is fundamental to any understanding of the Mashantucket Pequots. This initial call to the reservation eventually became an opportunity to participate in the rapidly expanding casino and hotel complex at Foxwoods. These conditions significantly affect the relationship between anthropologists and the reservation tribal community: Mashantucket presents neither a clear, geopolitically located community nor a traditionally powerless one.

Third, from almost the beginning of the tribe's renaissance the authenticity of members' tribal and Indian identities has been challenged, primarily as a means to contest their rights to self-determination or their ability to own and operate a casino. Challenges have been mobilized by competing casino operators, local politicians, and different activists from surrounding communities. Thus, many of the identity assertions or self-representations at Mashantucket are recent and strongly counteroppositional.

Entering Mashantucket, I entered a highly contested space of self-representation and identity assertion. The following analysis is not meant to provide a definitive discussion of the Mashantucket Pequots, their identity as a tribal nation, or the validity of their ethnicity or national identity claims. This study aims to provide a critical analysis of *how* the Mashantucket Pequots represent themselves in the public sphere. This includes not only their considerable casino and museum clientele but also the discursive arenas of regional, state, pan-Indian, and national identity. Accordingly, much of the material from which I work is public material made freely available by the Mashantucket Pequots. In addition to understanding *how* self-representations are conducted at Mashantucket, I focus on the experience of immersion in the reservation's different display environments, closely observing public self-representations in the museum and casino, recordings transcribed in these spaces, and informal conversations in these spaces and in the workspaces of the MPMRC. I combine this attention with participant observation in three roles at the MPMRC: I began as an intern performing research for the exhibitions in August 1997; I was later hired as a grants proposal writer for the Mashantucket Pequot Tribal Nation; I also worked as a researcher, writer, and photographer for the museum's exhibition designers—Design Division, Inc. (DDI). While my field experiences and their challenges mark my rite of passage as an anthropologist, they also illustrate recent shifts in the ethnographic equation or relationship between anthropologists and Native America.

When I first visited the site the future MPMRC was being coordinated from a collection of trailers linked together in a dirt lot near the construction site but beyond the guard kiosk for the reservation proper. Original administration for the museum project was headed by the museum liaison team: Theresa Hayward Bell, tribal member and sister to the tribal chairman, Skip Hayward; archaeologist

Kevin McBride, who has worked in and around Mashantucket since 1983; and anthropologist Jack Campisi. Perhaps better known for his work with the Mashpee, Campisi began working at Mashantucket in 1978 (see Campisi 1991).

I first approached the MPMRC in 1994 through Campisi with a proposal for a collaborative photo project involving tribal members. I met McBride through my repeated visits to the reservation, and he was supportive of my work and my projected future research. I hoped to eventually work with the museum's education department to create a collaborative photodocumentary project with tribal members (see Bodinger de Uriarte 2001; this article is evidence of a collaborative project but not of a collaborative project with tribal members).

In the initial phases of fieldwork I was accepted as a volunteer intern and turned loose to research American aboriginal dog "types" for the creation of facsimiles for the museum's walk-through precontact village. I was later hired to write three grant proposals for the Mashantucket Pequot Tribal Nation. The first was for the National Park Service's Historic Preservation Fund Grants to Indian Tribes, Alaskan Natives, and Native Hawaiian Organizations. Titled "Indiantown: Survey and Inventory of a Transitional Community," it proposed a program of archaeological investigations and ethnohistorical research at a late-eighteenth-century community on the Mashantucket Pequot Reservation. Indiantown inhabitants were influenced by Christian Indian missionary movements and used adoptions and adaptations of Euro-American-style farmhouses and farming techniques. The second proposal was also for the National Park Service. Titled "The Fort at Mashantucket: Second Phase," it sought funding to initiate a new phase of archaeological and historical research at the Fort at Mashantucket site with the purpose of assessing foodways and food production technologies and domestic, spatial, and social organization. The fort had been discovered in 1992; it reflected European design (it was square with corner bastions) and was evidence of the Pequot-English alliance during King Philip's (Metacom's) War (1675–76). The third proposal, entitled "Assessing NAGPRA-Related Inventories: Toward a New Methodology," looked to expand the base of relevant information for public inventory searches for objects and remains relevant to NAGPRA through researching primary documents to expand the information contained in public museum inventories.

These proposals offer a quick thumbnail sketch of the research projects important to the tribal nation: those combining a thorough grounding in archaeological and ethnohistorical method and dedicated to firmly establishing both the history of place and the role of ongoing cultural adaptation. Each of the proposals illustrates different Mashantucket Pequot historical interactions with existing dominant cultural, spiritual, and governmental structures, and each shows particular Mashantucket Pequot adaptations to those structures. The research projects illustrate a strong attribute of the Mashantucket Pequot Nation, the appropriation of elements from dominant discourses, like archaeology and ethnohistory, to meet Mashantucket Pequot ends.

I was soon hired to start writing panel text for the museum's opening gallery exhibition, The Mashantucket Pequot Tribal Nation, which was designed to introduce the contemporary reservation, its industries, and its community services. I also shot a number of photographs for DDI, including inset photos for panel texts and wall-size panoramas. The work exposed me to a number of different hierarchies at Mashantucket, including the tribal government, the museum's administration, and the independent exhibition design team. My overlapping responsibilities provided ideal vantage points for my fieldwork.

The politics of a tribal or any relatively small community are often tension filled. Potential sources of conflict often describe or overlap political and familial structures, especially where they intersect with other hierarchies. The overlaps can be uncomfortable, and the politics of ethnic identity, demarcation between "traditionals" and "progressives," and participation in the tribal political structure can create a system of power that is difficult for an outsider to navigate. The MPMRC's internal political structure was no exception. In addition, as the body of the elected tribal council changed over the course of the museum project, support for the project as a budget line item was often difficult to secure, and approval for the yearly budget was often delayed until well past the beginning of the fiscal year. The effects of budget-approval delays were felt everywhere, from the ability to hire permanent personnel to securing museum objects and narratives necessary for exhibition.

As an anthropologist my position was marked. Native America has provided subjects for anthropologists and their antecedents since European colonial contact. Often hand in hand with the forces of territorial expansion and relocation, anthropology's project of representing "others" has created a legacy of suspicion and unease. In contemporary Native America relationships between anthropologists and Native communities are often the subject of scrutiny and entered into with skeptical apprehension. My Mashantucket experience was flavored by this tradition as I attempted to navigate conflicting expectations and responsibilities, not the least of which focused on my academic discipline.

Nevertheless, the ambitious plans for a MPMRC intrigued me: what shape would such a project take? As I learned more about the resources and information being brought to bear on the museum I was determined to understand more about (1) the design of the exhibitions, (2) the mix of dominant historical and anthropological discourses and methods with counterhistorical or oppositional narratives, and (3) the interface between the museum's architecture and the surround of the reservation. I was also increasingly committed to working on the museum project. I was fortunate enough to do this and to be introduced to a number of different people and perspectives at work in Mashantucket. When my work there was finished I accepted a position as curator of the nearby Connecticut River Museum.

Yankee Fieldwork: Alternate and Dominant Histories

The Connecticut River Museum (CRM) is in the riverside town of Essex, about thirty miles from Mashantucket; it provides a more dominant "Yankee" perspective on local history. Like many well-preserved small towns in New England, Essex foregrounds its connections and contributions to New England history as a source of community identity and tourist attraction. Essex has a small harbor and active yacht clubs; the majority of the population are white Euro-Americans.

Although the CRM's mission includes "the collection, preservation and interpretation of materials related to human history in the Connecticut River Valley," the museum presents a primarily Yankee, Colonial, and maritime historical narrative. A small case contains the entire Native presence in the permanent exhibition, displaying a few trade beads and a variety of stone points. The accompanying text identifies the artifacts by archaeological period and gives a quick overview of contact and the Pequot War. The closing paragraph reads: "Those of the small remnant native population who had neither relocated nor been assimilated into the European settlements, withdrew to the shadows, inhabiting small, inconspicuous back-country sites, living as best they could."

The exhibition's wholesale erasure of Natives in the Connecticut River valley following the Pequot War reflects a dominant discourse in New England history. All effects of Native presence are transferred to the past, a historicized connection supporting a larger common narrative of disappearance. The CRM is but one node in a greater, linked exhibition narrative that the MPMRC counters. The CRM exhibitions participate in the same narrative of Colonial history as do many nearby historic places, including Mystic Seaport in Connecticut and Plimouth Plantation in Massachusetts. These living history sites are part of a localized history and tourist attraction network. As in the MPMRC, the CRM's *affect*—what Roland Barthes identifies as the power to move the viewer, to create a deeply felt response—also depends on its location. The museum is housed in a National Register historic site in a well-preserved Colonial town, inhabiting a tourist-oriented and imagined understanding of New England and its history.

Perspectives for Analysis

This ethnographic project links an analysis of representation in public spaces with concepts of cultural and ethnic identity as self-representational practices by examining the different methods and poetics of museum and casino representation at Mashantucket. Critical theoretical approaches include imagining the nation, ideas of national and ethnic identification, and the uses of the past in the creation of community. These three perspectives depend on Eric Hobsbawm's (Hobsbawm and Ranger 1983) concept of the invention of tradition. Invented traditions serve three associated purposes: (1) to establish or symbolize social cohesion or group membership (identity); (2) to establish or legitimize institutions or authority relations (community); and (3) to socialize or inculcate beliefs, values, or conventions of behavior (tradition). The invention of tradition is critical for the formation and maintenance of the nation-state and for what Raymond Williams (1977) terms the ratification of a present order.

This paradigm has provided a significant contemporary direction for anthropological inquiry that challenges the concept of tradition as unbroken continuity by focusing on the constructed aspects of the idea of continuity itself as part of contemporary cultural practice. A critical engagement with tradition, what Williams calls "the most evident expression of the dominant and hegemonic pressures and limits" (1977:115), guides an understanding of self-representational efforts that participate in or oppose hegemonic representational orders.

Public Mashantucket Pequot and Indian identities are a central element in the practices of the reservation community and its industries. Understanding the history of this identification is critical to understanding its manifestations in the casino and the museum. As in all Native American tribes, current understandings of "tribes" and "tribal nations" as unique political entities are the products of a long processual relationship with colonial powers. Like that of many Native peoples whose first experiences with Europeans were largely through the fur trade,

30   Chapter 1

the Pequots' need for a political organization recognizable to Europeans was not initially paramount.

Historically, the Pequots understood themselves by their place of origin, kinship ties, trade relationships, and shared language. Their communities existed as fairly broad entities with multiple points of contact and relationships with other nearby peoples for trade, political alliance, or simple sociability. The need for the kind of political organization that could be understood by Europeans grew as the bases for relationships with them changed from the fur trade to colonization. This marked a shift from understanding the frontier as a space for social and cultural relationships to one of legal relationships between governments. Increasing demands for land and resources mandated treaty relationships, the ability for one person to speak for a group to make binding agreements.

Identity formation depends on creating and maintaining boundaries. "Pequot" and, later, "Mashantucket Pequot" are permeable and mutable social and political constructs that developed over time and in direct relationship to dominant U.S. social and political structures. The representational efforts at Mashantucket make palpable the tension between Mashantucket Pequot reckonings of identity and those of the federal government or the popular imaginary.

Siting Mashantucket

Mashantucket presents an ethnographic dilemma—it is difficult to *site* Mashantucket, to contain it as a discrete and bounded place (geographically, thematically, ideologically, politically, culturally, or socially; see Dorst 1989). Divining what comprises the community of Mashantucket, what mix of the reservation residents, the tribal nation members, and the vast transient population of casino and museum patrons, is a complex and multidirectional exercise. The Mashantucket visitor experience overlies and overlaps other independent and contingent communities and identities, beginning with the initial highway billboards and including the state historical markers on the main roads into Mashantucket. At the level of surrounding community Foxwoods can be experienced as an increase in traffic, a corresponding accelerated erosion of highways, ever-present shuttle and charter buses, or a permanent homestead in everyday discourse.

Understanding the postmodern site as indeterminate helps explain some of the ethnographic difficulty in fully explicating the multiple site of Mashantucket. Much of this difficulty must also be understood as part of the dilemma that currently faces anthropology. Not only is the containability of a site, particularly one in the ethnographer's homeland, difficult to transcribe, but the resistances employed by the "ethnographees" have become more powerful.

Some of this is the common sense of contemporary ethnographic work carried out in the United States. Advanced consumer capitalism—or the postmodern effects of flattened boundaries and depthless and infinitely reproduced images—and the processes of self-inscription and self-identification have effectively blurred both cultural distinctions and a firm belief in niche sites. Ongoing practices of cultural self-texting or text generation—perhaps most pervasive in public Mashantucket brochure text, architecture, and exhibition or interior design—helps to create an environment of jostling perspectives. All have voices to be heard, and all display extensive and complex overlapping and intertexting.

My study appreciates the difficulty in understanding the ethnographic dilemmas of "the site" and recognizes that they face the entire practice of anthropology. As Dorst suggests, "postmodernity consists largely in the processes of self-inscription, indigenous self-documentation and endlessly reflexive simulation. Theorists of ethnographic representation have for some time now acknowledged that all cultures generate texts about themselves (taking 'text' in an expanded sense), but postmodernity virtually consists of this activity" (1989:2).

The self-referential processes of places in-filled with historical significance stretch between the landscape as historic canvas and the creation and establishment of museums as intensified markers of this same historicity. Mashantucket realizes

32   Chapter 1

its borders as a contingent geopolitical unit, a sovereign tribal nation with its own complex government-to-government relationships with the state of Connecticut and the federal government. Mashantucket occupies a powerful location as host to the single most successful "Indian casino" in the United States. At the same time, the processes of reassembling a reservation community from the descendents of the original Mashantucket Pequot Reservation tribal members yielded an ethnically and racially diverse community core, and Mashantucket entered the map of contested ethnicity and racial and national designation as a white-hot spot of contestation. Here the diversity of the community presents a point of challenge to "Indian" identity in the popular imaginary.

Given the above and the multiple pressures and limits of the bounded and uncontained elements of the communities at Mashantucket, the site is profoundly multiple. I work from Mashantucket textual and visual artifacts, adding my own notes, observations, descriptions, and photographs. The photographs offer a parallel journey made with a methodological difference. This strategy acknowledges that the narrative technologies at Mashantucket are constantly in a state of becoming and that no representation is the ultimate word on the subject. Photography is used as a means of exploring the public spaces and framing different subject positions at Mashantucket. The photographs are immersive and mimetic of the looking-centered experiences in the casino and the museum. These "souvenir" artifacts will be woven through the text that follows, providing different sites for exegesis, observation, and multiple reflexivities.

The "Indian" as Hegemonic Locus

The designation "Indian" is part of a hegemonic descriptive order. It occupies popular discourse at a deep, commonsensical level and participates in legal, ethnic, racial, and cultural mechanisms of representation. As part of this order, "Indian" is also a powerfully exclusionary category. Following Roy Harvey Pearce, Robert

Berkhofer succinctly states: "The Indian was judged by what Whites were not" (1978:28; see also Strong 1999; Harmon 1998). The term "Indian" reflects an ongoing relationship between Europeans, Euro-Americans, and Native peoples, one necessarily increasing in intensity throughout history and subjected to the pressures and limits of trade, colonization, warfare, legislation, relocation, and revitalization. However, while "the increasing association of Indians and non-Indian threatened to reduce the difference between them, it also focused attention on these differences" (Harmon 1998:72). Indian museums and casinos are powerful performative spaces for the poetics of these differences. They are also the tangible results and ratification of the politics of identity.

While "the Indian" plays a major role in Foxwoods design and thematics, this same popular notion is challenged at crucial points and in part by the very scale of the complex. As a thematic site Foxwoods experiences its own pressures and limits in self-representation and in engagement with popular notions of Indianness. While the "traditional" is often mobilized to ratify an existing order, here such an order both parallels and collides with efforts interested in establishing a *new* order. Through their involvement in Indian gaming the Mashantucket Pequots come into conflict with an existing *representational* order. Clearly, their success is won and measured through an active participation in hegemonic structures of business and politics; the productive spaces at Mashantucket resist simple categorization as counterhegemonic. However, Mashantucket projects of self-representation and industry reflect what Ross Chambers (1991) identifies as oppositional responses to existing hegemonic orders.

Mashantucket self-representation mobilizes local, national, and pan-Indian dialogues on the meaning of tradition and how it is recruited as confirmation (or contestation) of contemporary projects. The pivotal point is the practice of tradition as a *ratification* of the present. Raymond Williams asserts: "What [tradition] offers in practice is a sense of *predisposed continuity*" (1977:116). The measure of this continuity is a keystone for a museumized history of a reservation—a historic people in a historicized and located place. Discourses of tradition and continuity also prove important in the understanding and representation of a racialized identity, one that conflates natural and cultural spheres of classification. At the same time, a museum offers a ratification sometimes appreciated as only another interpretive level for existing understandings. As MPMRC director Theresa Bell stated following the confirmation of historical information by an archaeological dig: "We don't need an archeological site to learn a lot of this. . . . Outside people have to have proof to change the history books" (quoted in Dobrzynski 1997:B4).

Understanding tradition as a selective version of the past, as part of sustaining hegemonic order in the present, is both a powerful and a vulnerable practice. One element of the tension at the MPMRC is that the narrative representing the Mashantucket Pequots in the past and the present is the project of a "domestic dependent" *tribal* nation. Tribal nations have enjoyed a long-standing and unclear, yet proprietary, relationship with the federal government.[6] Limited by historical practice and legal decision, tribal sovereignty is important as a site of contemporary struggle. While the concept of sovereignty has suffered different advances and restrictions over time, it is a crucial resource for Native resistance and self-determination.

The MPMRC is a national project at one remove from the larger (U.S.) national project of similar museums operating under the auspices of the dominant culture. The 2004 opening of the National Museum of the American Indian (NMAI) forever changed the practice of representing Native America to a majority non-Native audience, especially how this practice was felt in a central, national (and Smithsonian) venue. The NMAI replaced long-contested exhibitions of Indians in the National Museum of Natural History. Both the museum and casino at Mashantucket walk a line between presenting a particularized narrative of Mashantucket Pequot national identity and participating in and speaking to a larger national museum discourse involving the portrayal of American Indians in non-Native-owned and -operated museums in the United States.

Richard Handler and Jocelyn Linnekin suggest that "there is no essential, bounded tradition; tradition is a model of the past and is inseparable from the interpretation of tradition in the present" (1984:26). We must be careful, however, in assessing the role of tradition as *resource*. Tradition is a tangible *force*, shaped by and responsive to historical and contemporary pressures and limits. As Marx asserted: "The tradition of all the dead generations weighs like a nightmare on the brains of the living" (1978 [1852]:594).

The power of tradition as a selective practice lies in making active connections and disregarding those elements that do not support created theses and foundational narratives. As Williams points out, "it is significant that much of the most accessible and influential work of the counter-hegemony is historical: the recovery of discarded areas, or the redress of selective and reductive interpretations" (1977:116). The MPMRC is an engaging site because its selections matter. Simply put, the Mashantucket Pequots have the resources available to create and support a state-of-the-art museum and research center devoted to presenting a Native American perspective that redresses reductive popular interpretations of local and U.S. history. The representation of a national past is critical to perpetuating and legitimizing the hegemony of the nation-state and the members of groups and classes—of state and "civil" society—that control it. As Benedict Anderson states, "nations loom out of an immemorial past and . . . glide into a limitless future" (1983:12–13). Dominant histories seek to smooth over dissension and alternative readings, to build a gliding linear descriptive narrative, a historical progression that always culminates in the present as unavoidable outcome. Anna Maria Alonso observes that "historical description, 'what really happened,' is not the result of self-evidences which we gather and string together but instead, the product of a complex interpretive process which, like any practice, is inflected by broader social projects, by relations of domination which seep into the private sphere" (1988:37).

Educational and interpretive structures are integral elements of consensus building, and museums are particular manifestations of both state and civil structures of

36   Chapter 1

knowledge. Museums, in their narrativized mobilization of history and tradition, are often a focus of social contestation; the designations and the attendant meanings of the past define both the stakes of the present as well as the terms in which it is understood. State and civil structures of knowledge are intimately involved with structures of political and social power. As Pierre Bourdieu recognizes, "a theory of knowledge is necessarily a dimension of political theory because the specifically symbolic power to impose the principles of a construction of reality—in particular, social reality—is a major dimension of political power" (1977:165). Hegemony's "common sense" is the naturalized arbitrariness of any given established order that embraces, directs, and enforces a field of common assumptions, or what Bourdieu defines as "what goes without saying because it comes without saying" (1977:167). Hegemony is an evolving and dynamic process that defines cultural practices through ongoing enactments. Ways of knowing, of making "common sense," are asserted and transformed, reflecting a dominant group's desire for control and the exercise of power without the exercise of coercive force.

Vignette 1: Indians in the Attic

The curator's office at the CRM was on the third floor. Noninsulated and partially unfinished, this floor also housed the museum's collection, records, and bits and pieces of exhibition hardware. There were no partitions on this floor, and the elevator opened onto an uninterrupted but loosely organized mass of augers, ship models, sextants, quadrants, flat files, stuffed animals, and maritime hardware. At one end a large window overlooked the river.

During my first month I was taking stock of the third floor's organization and stored materials. In one area I came face-to-face with two life-size transparencies of a man and a woman dressed in elaborate buckskin, framed for backlighting. The images were about six feet tall and three feet wide. Their eyes met the lens straight on, and the finished photograph conveyed the sense that the viewer and the subject were looking at one another. In one of the pictures I recognized the Mashantucket

Pequot Tribal Historic Preservation Program officer with whom I had shared an office on the MPMRC museum project.

Later I was speaking with one of the CRM board members in my office, and I asked about the history of the images. I was told that they had been created as part of the museum's 1997 Before New England exhibition, which explored local history before English colonization, when Dutch traders and Native peoples established a trade relationship based on furs.

When I mentioned that I recognized one of the subjects the board member made a disapproving sound and asked, "Did you see her hands?" I had not noticed them, and the two of us went back to look at the image. The tribal member's hands were held low, clasped in front of her. "At least she could have done something about her fingernails." I looked again. Her nails were striking—long and glossy with bright polish.

I suggested that the woman was, after all, a contemporary citizen of Connecticut and subject to the same fashion opportunities and range of choices as the board member. "That's not the point. The point is that she is supposed to be depicting someone from the 1600s. She could have at least removed the polish." It was an uncomfortable moment when "playing Indian" was made particularly problematic for a tribal member who failed to pass a check for anachronism. This check, in turn, was carried out by a board member for a local history museum that displayed its own intensely selective narrative and perspective as unmarked.

The fingernails offer a moment of arrest, what Walter Benjamin (1969) calls a "shock of recognition." The glossy nails vibrate against this image of the Indian; they are marked. They unsettle this simulacrum and draw all of the evidential parts of the image—the clothing and the identity of the subject—into question, or at least into a heightened sense of apprehension. Was the presence of nail polish any more anachronistic than the figure's gleaming white teeth? The pristine quality of the buckskin? Or the museum's continued narrative of the Native as doomed to "the shadows" of history?

In Native America the practice of self-representation reflects ongoing conflicts

38   Chapter 1

concerning sovereignty, identity politics, access to resources, and the perception of a generalized American Indian figure or icon in the public sphere. Large public spaces for popular intersection between Native and non-Native peoples are important theaters for self-representation. The introduction and dynamic expansion of Indian gaming make Indian casinos one of the largest and most public of these intersections. Here a large segment of non-Native clients or customers comes into mediated contact with an element of Native America. Here, too, popular conceptions of Native Americans may brush uncomfortably against—or be used oppositionally by—contemporary Native practice, industry, and self-representation.

Native-owned museums provide another important Native and non-Native intersection for mediated and intensified contact. Self-representations in Native-owned museums often offer counterhistories and cultural narratives that challenge widely held public notions about Indians. Museums and cultural centers created and controlled by Native Americans, like other museums in the United States, have recently experienced a period of expansion and construction.

Museums and casinos rely on different strategies of visual, narrative, and architectural representation to support and authenticate public claims to national, ethnic, and cultural identities. The process of authentication suggested here often responds to specific identity challenges from outside the reservation or community. Such challenges may be in response to land claims, the pursuit of federal recognition, or the desire to open or operate casinos or other potentially lucrative businesses. The intensity of the authenticity challenge often relates directly to the resources at stake. With this in mind, the counter- or authenticating narrative is most acute in areas where the stakes are felt to be the highest.

While Foxwoods easily enjoys the larger number of yearly visitors, the historical and cultural narratives offered by the MPMRC are more deeply nuanced and saturated. These narratives experience part of their representational power through the theater of their display and through the popular role that museums play as vehicles for narratives of the rarified and the authentic or, in Stephen Greenblatt's (1991) terms, the wondrous and the resonant. The casino's overall thematic projects and affirms its public space as both natural and Native American. More subtle placements of artifacts assert both a general Native American and a specific Mashantucket Pequot identity. The museum and research center derives some of its strength and effect from its bold architecture and the relationship between the building and the reservation surround. But much of the museum's *affect* comes from its role as a museum: a powerful and traditional structure designed to explain and present factual or authentic historical narratives. The very existence of Mashantucket as a site for successful and contemporary industry also supports a different and dynamic set of identity construction and affirmation.

The material consequences of maintaining a recognized Mashantucket Pequot identity are obvious. It is the legal cornerstone for an economy that affects the reservation, the state, and, through active lobbying and example, U.S. policy making concerning Native America. The site requires an analysis that blends an image-oriented economy critique with the grounded analysis of a material economy critique, locating the points of tension and the points of mutual support. The continued ability to participate in the gaming industry is founded on a practical and legal demonstration of claims of historical continuity. Such demonstrations also reflect a sincere desire for the reclaiming of a traditional presence and heritage, both as Pequots at Mashantucket as well as American Indians. The Mashantucket Pequots continue to develop a narrative of cultural continuity and belonging for a reinforced sense of community on the reservation and as a counter to critiques of their cultural legitimacy.

2 Tribal Renaissance

Great and doleful was the bloody sight to the view of young soldiers that had never been in war, to see so many souls lie gasping on the ground, so thick, in some places, that you could hardly pass along. . . . Sometimes the Scripture declareth that women and children must perish with their parents. Sometimes the case alters; but we will not dispute it now. We had sufficient light from the word of God for our proceedings.

—Capt. John Underhill, one leader of the Colonial forces in the 1637 attack on the Mashantucket Pequot village at Mystic (Hauptman 1990:74)

A History of the Mashantucket Pequots: Death and Rebirth

The views from Foxwoods contain elements that resonate historically and geographically; the casino is *located* along axes of history, cultural presence, space, and time. The Great Cedar Swamp and its inclusion in the Foxwoods vista is resonant with historical significance. A band of survivors from the 1637 Pequot War sought refuge in the swamp but were hunted down and killed. Their deaths marked the bloody and brutal end to a bloody and brutal war, carried out by English soldiers, Colonial volunteers from Connecticut and Massachusetts, and their Narragansett and Mohegan allies, culminating a long period of increasing interaction and hostility with a quantum shift in power relations and new restrictions on Native freedoms.

The history of the European colonization and conquest of the "New World" is a complex one. Violence, duplicity, betrayal, and profound misunderstandings of the scale and stakes of colonists' demands mark the Puritan "settling" of New England, what would become a foundational fiction for U.S. historical self-understanding. As Francis Jennings (1975) asserts, the city on the hill's self-definition relied on an image of righteousness under threat from savagery.

The perception of the New World as fertile but unpopulated wilderness, bestowed in "discovery" as a recognition from God, confirmed this righteousness even as the introduction of European pathogens during the fur trade began to decimate Native populations (Salisbury 1982; Todorov 1984; Greenblatt 1992). By the time the means of production had shifted to conquest and settlement, the colonists found many empty settlements with areas already cleared for agriculture. Jennings states: "The so-called settlement of America was a *re*settlement, a reoccupation of a land made waste by the diseases and demoralization introduced by the newcomers" (1975:30).

What disease did not clear the English took, often by violence. The invasion and conquest of America was an exercise and enlargement of power and the beginning of what Edward Spicer refers to as a conquest state: "a political organization with an established territorial boundary that has, by means of military power, incorporated other peoples under the control of the conquering people" (1994:34). Political control necessitated the control of structures of knowledge, ways of knowing and describing, including arrangements of instrumental dichotomies—savage/civilized, dark/white, heathen/God-fearing—that preceded occupation and subjugation and justified its aftermath. History is something produced in the present to reflect and extend discourses of power. History's "other" serves as a category not only of difference but also of enforced and continued marginalization. The above dichotomies, useful in describing colonial conflicts, also frame the limits and shape of contest. Poles of "civilization" and "savagery" accept that shape and effectively remove alternative ways of conceptualizing difference.

42   Chapter 2

Of Englishmen and "Savagery"

At the time of first colonial contact in the beginning of the seventeenth century Pequot territory—for travel, trading, hunting, gathering, and agriculture—included most of the Connecticut River valley, a total area of about two thousand square miles. The Pequots practiced agriculture, lived in villages, and produced and traded wampum (beads made from clam shell) and other products with neighboring groups. Their precontact population is estimated at thirteen thousand (Starna 1990:46). Before the Pequot War of 1637 diseases introduced by the Europeans reduced the Pequot population to approximately three thousand.

The origin stories for the Pequot War are varied and often contradictory (see Jennings 1975; Salisbury 1982, 1990; Hauptman 1990; Cave 1992; Pasquaretta 2003). Between 1634 and 1636 hostilities between the Pequots and Colonial Connecticut and Massachusetts escalated to a state of open violence, attacks, and reprisals. On May 26, 1637, a combined force of English soldiers and colonist volunteers under Capt. John Mason and Capt. John Underhill—with Mohegan, Niantic, and Narragansett allies—attacked a Pequot village at Mystic.[1] The assault was quick, brutal, and decisive, and it delivered the deathblow to Pequot freedom and sovereignty. Estimates of Pequot dead vary from three hundred to seven hundred. Following the massacre at Mystic, Pequot survivors were hunted down and killed, captured and sold into slavery, or given over to the control of other tribal leaders. Soon after the attack at Mystic the Pequot population fell to an estimated 2,000 to 2,500 (McBride 1990:104). The majority of the surviving Pequots found refuge among the Mohegans, a rival Pequot splinter group, led by Uncas, that had become staunch allies of the English, supporting them in the Pequot War and in later wars against other Indians and the French.

The incorporation of Pequot survivors by the Mohegans reflected ties of kinship and social relations. Existing social, cultural, and familial associations rendered Pequot self-identification strategically elastic. As Alexandra Harmon notes, "like other humans, Indians have had multiple loyalties and multiple ways of situating themselves or conceiving of themselves in relation to other people" (2002:254). The relationship between each Pequot survivor and his or her new community is an individual tale of social and cultural structures and contracts (see Strong 1999, 2002). Such self-negotiated identification foregrounds existing tensions in fixing popular notions of an "authentic" Indian identity through adherence to past ways of being.[2] Indianness as Harmon asserts and Mashantucket Pequotness as I would particularize are ongoing creations.

The Colonial victory in 1637 violently disrupted Pequot organization and power, "justified" the appropriation of their lands, and culminated in the erasure of legal Pequot identity. With the 1638 Treaty of Hartford declaration that "the Pequots shall no more be called Pequots, but Narragansetts and Mohegans," the Pequots became North America's first "terminated" tribe, landless and unrecognized.

Thirteen years after the Treaty of Hartford officially disbanded the Pequot Nation a Pequot reservation was created near Noank, Connecticut. Here, under leader Robin Cassacinamon, the Pequots were able to practice self-government and to live within a portion of their original lands. In 1658 the Pequots petitioned to expand the reservation, and in 1665 the General Court of Connecticut granted them the use of three thousand acres at Mashantucket. The Pequots soon quitclaimed the land at Noank for survey and clear title to Mashantucket.

Overseers, first appointed by the colony and later by the state, managed Mashantucket reservation lands and resources.[3] Though the Pequots had reclaimed their name and identity, they occupied a radically different political and property relationship to colonial powers as reservation Indians. They were now contained within a location—geographic, political, and discursive—fixed to a bounded site and held within an "other," dominant structure of power.

The Mashantucket reservation and its population consistently decreased over the following three hundred years. The land base shrank as portions were sold by

44 Chapter 2

overseers or lost to encroachment. In 1855 Connecticut sold off all but 204 acres of the reservation.[4] By 1972 there were only two remaining resident Mashantucket Pequots: Elizabeth George Plouffe and her half-sister, Martha Langevin Ellal. When Plouffe passed away in 1973, her grandson Skip Hayward took up full-time residency at Mashantucket and set out to repopulate the reservation by encouraging the return of active and potential tribal members. The tribal government was reorganized in 1974, with fifty-five tribal members listed on the rolls. The new tribal council elected Hayward as chair at its first annual meeting in 1975; he was consistently reelected to the position until 1998.

In researching and defining tribal membership Hayward and the council adopted blood quantum as a requirement, a concept of American Indian identification introduced with the General Allotment Act of 1877.[5] The federal government considers one-sixteenth the minimum blood quantum necessary to make a legitimate claim of tribal belonging; tribes set their own limits. In the beginning the Mashantucket Pequots set theirs at one-sixteenth.[6] The tribal council recognized members able to prove descent from the tribal rolls recorded in the 1900–1910 census.[7] The council found, as it contacted potential tribal members, that many lived elsewhere and sometimes primarily identified with other tribes or ethnicities.

Tribal members were granted two-acre house lots on the reservation, and the Mashantucket Pequots tried a number of different enterprises to achieve community financial independence, including maple syrup manufacturing, hog farming, and cutting and selling cordwood. These efforts were initially funded by a mixture of small state, federal, and local grants; none proved successful in providing the community with a secure financial base. Hayward also began to research possible legal action for the return of reservation land and for the federal recognition of the tribe. In 1976, with the help of Native Americans Rights Fund attorney Thomas Tureen, the Mashantucket Pequots filed suit against Connecticut for recovery of improperly sold tribal land.

Tureen had recently won the first case successfully using the Indian Trade and

Intercourse Acts (1790–1834) on behalf of eastern tribes.[8] The 1834 act regulated Indian land transactions and established that tribal lands could not be sold without the express consent of Congress. Appointed overseers and tax assessments had whittled away many tribal lands, particularly in the Northeast. Tribes in the "thirteen original colonies" had entered into treaty relationships with Colonial governments predating the United States (and thus federal recognition), and courts often ruled that these tribes existed outside the jurisdiction of certain legal protections. In *Joint Tribal Council of the Passamaquoddy Tribe v. Morton* Tureen pursued the question, Was there a federal trust relationship between these tribes and the government?[9] The claimants sued for restoration of their traditional hunting grounds, an area that encompassed 60 percent of the state of Maine (Scully 1995). In 1980 the Maine Indians settled for $81.5 million, most of which was used to purchase land.[10]

For Mashantucket Tureen followed a successful strategy from the Maine land-recovery cases; the pressure of resolving new doubt on existing deeds and titles had contributed to the case's settlement. In 1983 the Mashantucket Pequot Indian Claims Settlement Act combined the Pequots' federal recognition with the settlement of the 1976 suit and awarded the tribe $900,000.[11]

Claim, Settlement, and Indian Gaming

The question remained, What would the tribe do to ensure their future self-sufficiency? Hayward and the council used the settlement money to buy land and a small restaurant and to make housing improvements on the reservation. They also looked into other ways to generate sustainable economic development. In the early 1980s Hayward traveled to Florida to meet with Seminole chief James Billie. In 1983 Billie had successfully defended high-stakes bingo games on Seminole land in *Seminole Tribe of Florida v. Butterworth*.

Hayward returned from Florida to open a high-stakes bingo operation at

Mashantucket. The bingo hall, named Foxwoods, opened in 1986. Following its quick success (it grossed an estimated $6 million in the first year) and the passage of the IGRA in 1988, plans were made to extend the operation to include casino-style gambling. The casino was completed in 1990, but court battles with the state delayed its opening until February 1992. As per the 1987 *Cabazon* decision, since the state of Connecticut held a yearly "Casino Night" fund-raiser offering all kinds of gaming except slot machines, the state could not restrict the Pequots from operating the same games.

In 1993 the Mashantucket Pequot Gaming Enterprise, the casino corporate entity of the Mashantucket Pequot Tribal Nation, negotiated a deal with Connecticut that secured the exclusive right to operate slot machines in the state. In exchange for the monopoly the tribal nation agreed to give the state 25 percent of the slots' annual net win, or a minimum of $100 million per year. The state compact faced public opposition and open challenge from public and private figures, including Atlantic City casino developer Donald Trump. In 1993, before a special Connecticut legislative subcommittee, Trump said: "'Go up to Connecticut, and you look at the Mashantucket Pequots. . . . They don't look like Indians to me. They don't look like Indians to Indians'" (Lightman 1993:A1). While mainly a strategy to stop nearby competition, Trump's critique was partly based on the popular perception of race as integral to cultural integrity and to the authenticity of the Mashantucket Pequot claims to "Indianness."

In the same exchange Trump added business insights to his analysis of phenotype and insisted that Indians would not be able to defend themselves against organized crime: "'It will be the biggest scandal ever,' Trump warned, 'the biggest since Al Capone. . . . An Indian chief is going to tell Joey Killer to please get off his reservation? It's unbelievable to me'" (Lightman 1993:A1).

Recent efforts to both encourage and regulate the Indian gaming industry provide a parallel to and possible consequence of earlier efforts to bring "the Indian" into the "intelligent selfishness" of capitalism and citizenship. According to Merrill E. Gates, president of Amherst College and the Lake Mohonk Conference of the Friends of the Indian, "to bring him out of savagery and into citizenship we must make the Indian more intelligently selfish before we can make him selfishly intelligent. We need to *awaken in him wants*. . . . Discontent with the teepee and the starving rations of the Indian camp in winter is needed to get the Indian out of the blanket and into trousers—and trousers with a pocket in them, and *a pocket that aches to be filled with dollars*!" (1896, quoted in Berkhofer 1978:173).

Indian gaming has become the fundamental economic development initiative for Indian nations in the United States. And gaming wealth can provide the means to truly experience self-determination and sovereignty. Foxwoods provides the most remarkable example of the potential success of Indian gaming. Located within approximately three hours' driving distance of over 22 million people, the casino grossed almost one fifth of the 1996 total Indian gaming gross revenue in the United States ($5.39 billion).[12] Nearly ten years later total tribal governmental gaming revenues had climbed to $18.5 billion, or 23 percent of the total national gaming industry (Foxwoods and the nearby Mohegan Sun account for approximately 20 percent of this figure [Chen and Le Duff 2001:A1]). Indian gaming provides approximately four hundred thousand jobs nationally, 75 percent of which are held by non-Indians (National Indian Gaming Association 2004).

The phenomenal growth in Indian gaming must be contextualized as part of a national explosion in the industry. The most recent wave of the gambling business in this country began with the legalization of gambling in the state of Nevada in 1931. In 1977 legal gambling was extended to Atlantic City, and by July 1998 some form of gambling was legal in forty-eight states. Comprehensive figures for 2000 put the gross annual wager—the amount wagered on all forms of regulated gambling in the United States—at $823.6 billion, with gross revenues of $61.2 billion.

Obviously, Indian gaming plays a part in the national industry, but it can also be understood as an oppositional industry, in Ross Chambers's sense, a use of survival tactics that do not challenge existing structures of power but make use of

48   Chapter 2

their opportunities and circumstances for different purposes. Here opposition plays a delicate balance with established power to challenge in subtle and sometimes substantial ways without becoming a fixed point of struggle.

Describing the Mashantucket Pequots as tactical oppositionalists may at first seem facetious, but their participation in Indian gaming depends on accepting the concept of "domestic dependent nation" and the legitimacy of the federal government to oversee and control many aspects of their tribal nation and identity. Many Mashantucket Pequot aspirations, and the means for achieving them, are not significantly different from those in the existing hegemonic order. And the appropriation of dominant discourses at Mashantucket is a potent practice. Foxwoods manager Michael Brown described it during a 1994 interview with *60 Minutes* reporter Steve Kroft for a segment eventually titled "Wampum Wonderland":

Kroft:	You have a very small number of Native Americans with maybe 1/16th Indian blood . . .
Mr. Brown:	Mm-hmm.
Kroft:	. . . who, through good fortune and good legal advice and good business sense . . .
Mr. Brown:	Mm-hmm.
Kroft:	. . . and the hiring of the right people, have lucked into a multi-billion-dollar business.
Mr. Brown:	God bless America. That's the American way.

But tactical considerations provide only one part of the Mashantucket Pequot picture. Mashantucket Pequot cultural practices include a combination of economic power and the reassembly of community as well as the assertion of a tribal identity as active and vital. "Community" at Mashantucket is a contested field supporting public images presented to Mashantucket, local, pan-Indian, and national communities.

Identity: Politics and Poetics

Eve Darian-Smith suggests that "casino operations offer, at this moment in history, the only reasonable opportunity for Native Americans to achieve any semblance of respect and equity in our dominant society" (2004:96). Much of the profits from Foxwoods have been spent building community services, including a new fire and medical complex, a community center, a childcare facility, and a significant investment in the higher education of tribal members. The Mashantucket Pequots also diversify their holdings to include a variety of businesses and real estate—their landholdings increased from 180 acres in 1979 to over 5,000 acres in 2005.

But the Mashantucket Pequots not only assert themselves in terms of economic capital, they are also expanding an expressive ability in terms of symbolic capital. They host Schemitzun, the Festival of Green Corn, a pan-Indian dance competition with the largest prize purse in the United States. Mashantucket Pequots made significant financial contributions to the construction of the National Museum of the American Indian ($10 million) and to the Democratic Party. They are busy researching and expanding their cultural repertoire by adapting forms of language, dance, and music, drawing from the expressive cultures of other tribes as well as their own, and the MPMRC is a significant resource on things Indian and things Pequot.

The 1983 act granting federal recognition was the key to reaching this point. The Mashantucket Pequots eventually parlayed this status into the world's most successful casino-based reservation economy. But an authentic legal Indian identity has not been enough to stave off protests over the authenticity of the Mashantucket Pequot cultural identity, located mostly in popular discourse and based on ambiguous concepts of Indianness and race. Trump's arguments are similar to others concerning Indian authenticity and the gambling industry. On the one hand, the Pequots are judged "inauthentic" Indians by their appearance, their dress, and their participation in "nontraditional" industries. They don't match a popular cul-

50   Chapter 2

tural and nostalgic image centered on maintaining difference, on maintaining a sense of the "other." As Berkhofer asserts, "the very attraction of the Indian to the White imagination rests upon the *contrast* that lies at the core of the idea. Thus the debate over 'realism' [or authenticity] will always be framed in terms of White values and needs, White ideologies and creative uses" (1978:68, emphasis mine).

On the other hand, if the Mashantucket Pequots really are *authentic* Indians, this same contrast must render them unable to cope with contemporary problems like murderous gangsters and capital accumulation. And their wealth is a primary reason why their enterprise and identity come under fire. The image of the "rich Indian" is a means to challenge the authenticity of Native Americans involved in Indian gaming. Katherine Spilde (1999) suggests that the rich Indian image is used as a way to undermine tribal sovereignty by insisting either that gaming tribes no longer need the rights guaranteed by sovereignty or that being "rich" negates claims to authentic Indian identity—"real" Indians are poor.

In 2000 Connecticut journalist and lawyer Jeff Benedict published his book *Without Reservation: The Making of America's Most Powerful Indian Tribe and Foxwoods, the World's Largest Casino,* in which he attempts to establish that Mashantucket Pequot claims to tribal identity are fraudulent; he finishes by calling for the revocation of federal recognition. Benedict was a candidate for the U.S. Congress in 2002; he is president of the Connecticut Alliance against Casino Expansion. In a follow-up piece to "Wampum Wonderland" Steve Kroft interviewed Benedict in 2000:

Mr. Benedict:	It's fraudulent. I mean, frankly, to go to the Congress of the United States and to portray yourself as something that you're not and to get benefits, dollars, as a result of it—status—is fraudulent.
Kroft:	I think you would have to admit also that if Skip Hayward were up there growing vegetables, nobody would care.

Mr. Benedict:	Right now?
Kroft:	Yeah.
Mr. Benedict:	I would agree with that. I think what makes this an issue, though, is that he's not up there growing vegetables. He's up there bringing in a billion dollars a year.

Benedict and Trump are not the only ones to voice concerns over the authenticity of Mashantucket Pequot cultural identity. In the face of growing financial power, some surrounding townspeople are also angry that the Pequots will not stay within a limited and marginalized sphere, sliding irrevocably toward a "noble" absence. Following the tribe's purchase of the 1,214-acre Lake of Isles Boy Scout camp in 1993, four hundred local townspeople met in North Stonington, near the reservation (Overton 1993:B4). The Pequots were interested in building a theme park on the camp site. (The tribe has since built a nine hundred–acre golf resort there instead.)

The meeting was called to voice opposition to further expansion of the reservation. The townspeople's anger was not against an asserted Mashantucket Pequot identity per se but at the concomitant shift in power and the ability to claim public attention. This opposition was voiced in a number of ways, including describing the conflict in racial terms ("for all intents and purposes, the Mashantuckets are either white or black" and thus not Indian) or in cultural terms (Overton 1993:B4). As Hugh Crow, a resident of nearby Ledyard, put it at the meeting: "'There really is no culture. The Mashantucket culture was lost long ago. This cultural stuff, this struggle to retrace their roots, it's all a smokescreen. The tribe is no endangered species—they are already long dead'" (Overton 1993:B4).

The use of static and generalized concepts of Indians as a yardstick for cultural authenticity is not limited to popular critique. Anthropologist James Clifton (1990) also cites cultural adaptation—and land and federal recognition suits—as indicators of "identity dissolutions," discounting the legal bases and battles over land and sovereignty. Here cultural "invention" and cultural "authenticity" represent poles

52   Chapter 2

in a dialectic of the factual: a move that brings Indian identity closer to "invention" moves it farther from "authenticity."

Berkhofer notes that the identity "Indian" permitted the union of "character and culture . . . in one summary judgment" (1978:25). The conflation of individual tribes, peoples, and cultures into a larger abstract term served to departicularize peoples being conquered and displaced. "Indian" also provided a discursive space, an open category of otherness assessed against a popular and increasingly vague notion of what an Indian might be. "Indian" became a term of normalization indicating marked and unmarked categories determined by non-Native majorities. The designation "Indian" is a conferred identification, defined from without, through legislation and popular imagination. Most significantly, "Indian" as a general term became fixed in time, arranging a "true" Indian identity against a white background and identifying changes in traditional cultural practices as ruptures in essentialized identity constructs. Cultural identity became a generalizing and static concept, and change, adaptation or adoption, and invention became markers of inauthenticity. Locked in structures of time and power, "Indian" operates as both evaluation and identification. Mashantucket radically displaces this equation with economic and political power and in self-conscious uses of "Indian" imagery and cultural invention or construction.

Much of the discussion concerning cultural identity still centers on popular and critical understandings of authenticity as static and essential. And academic debates over the authenticity of cultural traditions recognized as dynamic or constructed can endanger practical microstruggles over sovereignty and self-determination. Linnekin correctly cautions against the (complete) scholarly deconstruction of authenticity, stating that authenticity "remains nonetheless entrenched in popular thought and is an emotional, political issue for indigenous peoples, particularly for those who are engaged in a struggle for sovereignty" (1991:446).

The construction of tradition and its fundamental ties to community and identity is "good to think," but it also has its own potential for misuse and misdirection. As Linnekin also observes, "what many anthropologists view as an advance in cultural theory can be read popularly as 'destructive' of native claims to cultural distinctiveness" (1991:447). But cultural invention and borrowing are integral and traditional elements of indigenous peoples' cultural practice. Indeed, invention is one proof of continuity, a means of merging dynamic forces of change with particular, and adaptive, cultural practices.

The construction-of-tradition paradigm is a useful tool to assess hegemonic constructions of Indianness, identity, tradition, and authenticity, to critique them, and to recognize their own constructive practice. Constructivist theories of identity attempt to understand the processes by which articulations of culture acquire authenticity, but understanding the "constructedness" of cultural forms is only a beginning. How is it that constructions are felt, naturalized, and put to work? Answering this question calls for a shift away from seeking cultural survivals and toward examining the ongoing dynamics of culture, the forms in which they are represented and understood, and how they change. Paradoxically, essentialist arguments have real, pragmatic value: "'Indian blood'—and especially its more differentiated, tribe-specific varieties—is one forceful hegemonic discourse within and against which indigenous identity is defined" (Strong and Van Winkle 1993:555).

At Mashantucket this intersection of the "authentic" merits further exploration. On the one hand, an ability to live up to nostalgic or colonialist expectations calibrates Indian authenticity. On the other, Indian participation in "modern" projects guarantees a determination of inauthenticity. This intersection involves two particular stances in regard to time, place, and the uses of the past. The first reflects an effort to firmly place Indians within an anthropological present that, as frozen or fixed, is constantly *past* (see Fabian 1983). The second focuses on an ability to achieve phenomenal success in the landscape of contemporary American business.

In an interesting reversal of historic colonial encounters between Native peoples and European settlers, discourses of development both out of control and

54   Chapter 2

"without permission" have also been mobilized to critique the Mashantucket Pequots. The 1994 *60 Minutes* transcript offers the following illustration:

(Footage of residents of communities surrounding the reservation)

Unidentified Woman #1:	They can increase the commercial development without any control—no environmental control, no land-use controls, no public-safety controls, none of that. No tax—no tax bite at all. Any businessman would like to develop under those circumstances.
Kroft:	Do they have a lot of political power?
Unidentified Woman #2:	Immense.
Unidentified Woman #3:	Money is power. Money is power.
Kroft:	We talked to the tribal chairman the other day, and he said, "Our people have gotten the short end of the stick for 300 years. This is justice."
Woman #2:	Well, they're taking in, like I said, last year, a half a billion dollars, and there's 300 members. Now is this justice?
Woman #1:	We have a big city that's been plopped down next to us. A city of 40,000 in the course of a year has been put right there at—at our boundary.
Kroft:	How big do you think it's going to get?
Woman #1:	I don't know. Ask—ask the tribal chairman.
Woman #3:	They won't tell us.
Woman #2:	And, you know . . .
Woman #3:	They say there is no plan. (Kroft 1994)

Townspeople refer to injustice expressed in tribal nation dollars. If Mashantucket Pequot enterprises were considerably less lucrative, such expressions of public outrage seem unlikely. To talk about the practices of construction at Mashantucket, in all of its venues, requires a discussion of what is at stake and the terms in which the arguments are raised. Paul Pasquaretta affirms that "it has been by an assertion of land-based tribal sovereignty that Native peoples have claimed rights of self-determination. High-stakes gambling is just one of these rights" (2003:162). The Mashantucket Pequots use their sovereignty as a powerful locus of their ongoing "invention": autonomous self-determination and self-identification. They skillfully use hegemonic concepts of nation or state in the pursuit of specific and strategically Mashantucket Pequot ends.

Here identity is a process of self-definition, a recognition that the dynamics of tradition are in a constant process of formation. Gerald Vizenor (1994) calls this practice "survivance," the ability to survive by adapting and adopting ways and means of dealing with a powerful colonizing force by seeking out and inhabiting contradictions in the dominant system. These contradictions open spaces for an oppositional continuation and transformation of dynamic cultural presence. Survivance not only retains cultural practices but also makes the issues of resistance and adaptation integral elements of culture.

At Mashantucket the construction of community, identity, and tradition succeeds precisely because it parallels terms of the overarching structure and takes advantage of their contradictions. Such constructions offer the most powerful means to arrange arguments of contingent independence.[13] This analysis is not limited to a contemporary moment. The more than three hundred federally recognized American Indian tribes and tribal nations are, in large part, the invention of eighteenth- and nineteenth-century federal American Indian laws and treaties. Prior to the eighteenth century, tribal designations were used in treaties and agreements between Native peoples and colonial or European powers. By examining specific tribal identities and continuities as constructed, popular ideas of cultural continuity begin to

56   Chapter 2

erode. During the formation of reservations the forced relocations and sometimes blending of different tribal groups often created the possibility for a particular tribal group's cultural continuity to be measured from a particular reservation's formation. Rather than being a question of *yes* or *no*, construction then becomes a question of *when*, *how*, and *to what extent*. My interest is not in how constructed or renewed traditions reflect or transform authentic and unbroken historical continuities. It is in how construction fosters a contemporary sense of community and identity: how the construction of tradition can be an ongoing affirmation of the dynamic practices of community and identity. Constructionist theories push process into the foreground, recognizing it as an authentic and integral part of culture.

Phenotype: The Mashantucket Pequots and "Black Indians"

Many of the popular challenges to the cultural authenticity of the Mashantucket Pequots are framed in terms of race. "'We've been called every name you can think of,' says Joey Carter, a Black Pequot tribal member and head of public relations for the group. But what I tell them is, 'You can call us anything you want, but when you call us, call us at the bank'" (Chappell 1995:50). Like many Indians, the Mashantucket Pequots intermarried with other populations, including African Americans, Latin Americans, and Anglo Americans, over the course of history. Race in the United States is popularly understood through a reading of signs, a decoding of physical characteristics and appearances to reveal a certain categorical belonging. This phenotypical understanding is joined to an idea of "blood"—race is not only observable, it is biological. The racial category most often invoked to counter a Mashantucket Pequot *Indian* identity is African American, or black (although Skip Hayward's bona fides have been challenged for self-designating as white in a 1969 marriage license application [Kroft 2000; Benedict 2000]). This categorization serves either as an affirmation of a mixed racial identity or as an attack on Indian identity at Mashantucket. In truth, racial and cultural categories at Mashantucket are (at least) two separate genres of identification.

"Black Indians Hit Jackpot in Casino Bonanza," proclaims the title of a 1995 *Ebony* magazine article on the Mashantucket Pequots, referring to tribal members as the "black Indians" of Connecticut and successfully confounding an authenticity figured through racial difference by combining two divergent racial and ethnic markers, "Indian" and "black," within one identity (Chappell 1995). The category "black Indian" is not original to Mashantucket; black Indians have long been a part of American Indian, African American, and U.S. history. Rather than representing a discontinuity between the categories of "black" and "Indian," the Mashantucket Pequots, as black Indians, display the characteristics of an "other" continuity.

The categories of black and Indian identity as reckoned by blood quantum have been explored by Jack Forbes, who problematizes the concept that one drop of "black blood" is enough to render a person "black" (black as a biological category), whereas "Indian" represents a cultural and historical category, one that must remain unchanged in order to be considered authentic (1990:23). Donald Trump has referred to the Mashantucket Pequots as "Michael Jordan Indians," attempting to shift popular perceptions of racial identity ("blackness" contaminates or consumes Indianness) and thereby delegitimate Mashantucket Pequot claims to Indian authenticity (Chappell 1995:46). As tribal member Gary Carter explains, "Most of it is racial. There are people who believe that dark-skinned people shouldn't be making money, and they'll do anything they can to try to stop us" (quoted in Chappell 1995:46).

Indian racial and ethnic identifications—both self-designated and assigned by others—are complex, and the boundaries between such popular markers as white, black, and Indian have, over time, proved permeable.[14] Race is but one of the many facets of a Mashantucket Pequot "Indian" identification, and many Mashantucket Pequots reframe the racial question in terms of family or relatedness. Tribal member John Perry states it this way: "If you look at the Pequot today you are going to see light-skinned ones, you are going to see dark-skinned ones. Some are going to look white, some black, but we are all related" (Goffe 1999:77).

Domestic (In)dependents

Authenticating Indian identity provokes multiple questions. Is Indian identity biological or cultural, essential or constructed? How is it configured and verified? What does federal recognition actually recognize, and how has it become a primary means of establishing cultural validity? Is it as tied to the colonial project as the mechanics of blood reckoning? Should treaties between the United States and separate indigenous nations be decided by heredity—a biological conception of nationality—or by cultural coherence and continuity—a sovereignty that depends on ideological and cultural belongings?

Annette Jaimes (1996) rejects blood quantum and calls federal authentication a direct challenge to tribal sovereignty, a practice that transforms the sovereignty of Indian peoples into a formulation of bloodlines and biological heritage and the continuation of a positivist method of discerning cultural difference. This argument holds that such authenticity-establishing structures continue a colonized peoples' relationship to a dominant federal government, that Native Americans thus perpetuate their object position within a colonial discourse, and that blood reckoning counters the spirit of treaties between individual tribes and the United States.

These arguments must be tempered with a realization of the unique position of Indian nations as "domestic dependent" entities, a conditional measure of independence that depends on the recognition and jurisdiction of the federal government. Counterarguing colonial hegemony, however, may be most effective through an oppositional use of dominant discursive elements, including legal identity and popular culture, to rearticulate and take advantage of potentially weak structural links. Here, pursuing recognition is a kind of strategic essentialism—the utilization of elements from multiple possible identifications to gain advantage within a dominant system of figuring identity (Spivak 1990). Federal recognition allows Indian peoples specific access to federal monies and programs. This reckoning system provides possible economic stability and cultural continuation, and recognition is one very important key to engaging in Indian gaming. Indian law reflects and influences popular cultural conceptions of identity and "otherness." While choosing to struggle within the legal parameters of an occupying colonial force may seem a willing incorporation within a dominant discourse, options for struggle outside of these parameters are limited. Joanne Nagel asserts that "political mobilization based on African American (not African) or Indian (not Cherokee or Ojibwa/ Annishnabe or Seminole) identity reflects the dominant discourse and realpolitik of race in America. Nevertheless, the reality is that the United States is the arena in which these debates and challenges occur and in which these battles must be won" (1996:70–71).

While this statement calls for the recognition of Indians as a pantribal ethnic identity, tribal sovereignty and the ability to participate in Indian gaming depend on individual tribal reckoning. Ethnic and cultural identifications at a pan-Indian level must also incorporate nationalisms imagined at a tribal level, no matter how proscribed or domestically dependent they may be.

How can these processes of identification, between a specific tribal membership and identity and a pantribal ethnic Indian identity, be reconciled? Underlying this question is another concerning these two perspectives of identity and how they reflect conflicts between identity by choice and identity by assignment. The first emphasizes "survival"—an unbroken continuance of traditional forms unaffected by contact with other cultural forces. This reflects an ideology that supports a legal configuration of precedence and continuation. This notion of culture as something discrete and able to be fully contained within geographic and ethnographic boundaries has lost credibility in contemporary anthropology. The second perspective posits identity as a process of dynamic self-definition, recognizing, as does Vizenor's "survivance," that change in the face of challenge is its own kind of continuous cultural (and traditional) practice. Change resists a grand argument of continuity as fixed, raising the possibility that the idea of continuity itself deserves

60   Chapter 2

a more thorough analysis. Where the perspectives meet is a continuum, a fluid and energetic assertion and use of identity.

Indian reservation communities, whose boundaries mark their difference from surrounding state and federal governments, dramatically foreground the concepts of imagined communities, constructed traditions, and created identities. Foxwoods and the MPMRC, as integral parts of a nation-building effort, provide legitimate symbolic capital for narratives of historical and essential continuity. American Indian nations draw many tenets of an "imagined nation" paradigm into sharp relief, and the historic transformation of Native peoples into "Indian nations" also implicates the translation of Indian land into a European sense of property (see, e.g., Cheyfitz 1991; Jennings 1975; Todorov 1984). As domestic dependent nations, Indian nations are unable to enter into treaties or alliances with other national powers or to sell lands to other nations. They are subject to certain federal and state jurisdictions and, in many situations, unable to decide national membership for themselves without meeting federal criteria. The cross-identities of Indian nations make them unique: they are figured as ethnic minorities with access to particular federal programs, as treated nations with obligations and privileges described by such treaties, and as an imagined confederation of belonging not limited to membership in reservations or even specific tribes.

Active engagement with this reckoning, based on past cultural and material constructions, allows the Mashantucket Pequots to participate in the Indian gaming industry. Their success affords them the ability not just to construct tradition, community, and identity but to do so on a remarkable scale. While the casino complex is an economic generator for the community's projects, the museum and research center powerfully articulates particular Mashantucket Pequot and general Indian identity through registers of history, material culture, and experiential displays.

Communities, like nations, prefer to imagine themselves as Benedict Anderson suggests—as timeless and limitless. The mechanics of this imagination, what John and Jean Comaroff call the "tangible practices" (1992:44) of identity, recognizes tradition as a deliberately selective and connecting process that offers historical and cultural ratification of a contemporary order. Tradition, a project of the present enacted by an active use of the past, legitimates contemporary practices by representing them as unbroken continuities both distant and time honored.

On a micro- and practical level, the Mashantucket Pequots' self-construction includes the incorporation and adaptation of different traditional cultural performances, such as dances and songs for powwows. But the Mashantucket community also has an ongoing project to establish traditions that carry forward new practices, such as Indian gaming. The Mashantucket Pequots provide a powerful example in the public perception of Indian gaming shifting from anomaly to active practice in much of Native America.

The construction-of-tradition paradigm enables an investigation of contemporary practices in order to critique and define ongoing cultural processes. Mashantucket Pequot identity must be realized in the same light. A large number of tribal members have moved to the reservation, establishing a new community and a new sense of belonging that will, in turn, support a common and particular Mashantucket Pequot identity. The Mashantucket Pequots are not closed-community survivals but a group busy defining just what their cultural and reservation perimeters embrace. Culture and tradition construction and the discursive processes used in these projects provide the reciprocal perspective necessary for further analysis of contingent authenticating practices, both those within Mashantucket and those with Mashantucket as their critical focus. The American Indian subject—a formative representational project not limited to anthropology but extended through such domains as state and federal government, photography, art, and literature—is integral in the imagination and construction of "Mashantucket Pequotness."

The concept of authenticity is an unfixed authenticating device, one in which multiple users draw from similar wells of knowledge resources. The point of theorizing cultural construction is not to reveal how different cultural practices become hegemonic, seemingly natural and immutable. The performance of "Indianness," as an ongoing constructed practice, has an important political edge: reworking commonsensical performances of identity, community, and tradition—those that can be located in the white imaginary or "the white man's Indian"—and reinvesting them with particular, relocated power. The ability to rework and reinvest carries its own performative message: that such practice can move out of the margins and into a powerful center connected with other significant forms of reckoning and placing. The economic and political power of the Mashantucket Pequot attests to such effective practice.

3 "The Wonder of It All"

Vignette 1: First Encounter

May 1995, Mashantucket Pequot Reservation: Having finished informal meetings with tribal members and assorted museum and library personnel, I decide to take a long walk through the casino complex to find the small museum there. I pass through the main entrance at the top of a long, arching driveway. (This original main glamorous entrance has been consumed by the new Rainmaker Casino, and the completion of the Grand Pequot Tower in late 1997 provided a new opulent entrance [fig. 3.1].) Once inside, I find myself in an enormous atrium, complete with a twenty-foot waterfall spilling over rocks into a large fountain. Directly ahead lies the cocktail bar and lounge, to the left is a mixed-gaming room. To the right is a room filled with slot machines and the thick noise of jackpot bells and payoffs. In the center of this room, above the level of the machines, rests a new car—the grand prize for one of the cumulative slots. Foxwoods, like many contemporary casinos, offers a debit and points-gathering card that tracks patron play and betting habits. Many of the slots players keep these "Wampum Cards" on brightly colored and tightly coiled leashes, often attached to their clothing with alligator clips for safekeeping. Looking into this first slots room, I can see a number of people connected to the machines, their card tethers like tiny umbilical cords. Outside this room is a small glass-fronted case filled with southwestern Indian baskets and pottery, each with an identifying card and an estimated value. A nearby wall, between the case and the souvenir and information booth, holds a framed collection of portraits of the Mashantucket Pequot tribal council.

Figure 3.1 The Grand Pequot Tower. (Photograph provided by the Mashantucket Pequot Tribal Nation)

I head for the bar, then cut through it to reach an atrium beyond. This atrium is at the intersection of a passageway leading to downstairs tour bus drop-offs, another leading back to the hotel, a third gaming room, a collection of electronic rides and arcades collectively called Cinetropolis, and the passageway from the main entrance. At the center of the intersection stands an enormous fountain. Made of simulated rock, it is surrounded by four large false trees, complete with branches that hug the ceiling and extend over the fountain's main pool. A heavily planted platform built of stone rises from the center of the fountain. On its flat top is the gigantic statue *The Rainmaker*, an Indian on one knee holding a cocked bow fitted with an arrow pointing heavenward; he turns almost imperceptibly on his platform (fig. 3.2). Above *The Rainmaker* the roof comes to a four-sided, peaked glass skylight, and the light from outside plays on this milky, polyurethane figure. Gaming chips, change, a few waterlogged bills—all tossed in "for luck"—fill the bottom of the fountain's pool. Five minutes before the hour automated blackout curtains slide up to cover the skylight, and *The Rainmaker* comes to a temporary halt. Fog billows out from beneath the central platform, and hidden lights play across the huge figure. Against the skylight's blackout curtains are projected a small assortment of generic "Native" pictographs: a spiral, a crooked arrow, a buffalo, an eagle. Accompanied by the sound of a hawk's screech, a narrative begins through nearby speakers:

> Long ago before the Ancient Ones, the land still stood under a heavy blanket of snow several miles thick. As the climate gradually warmed, the giant freeze began to melt; for a thousand years great rivers flowed, eroding, forming and rearranging the earth's landscape.

> Gradually, a summer began to take place. Trees from warmer climates began to edge northward. The first were spruce, fir, birch and the great oak.

> Game such as caribou, bison, mastodon, elk, giant beaver and the woolly mammoth were the first explorers of this land. They were soon followed by the giant game hunters. Later, nomads in search of food first came to this area as seasonal hunters, retreating southward as the harsh winters came.

> The climate became warmer. This warming, along with the use of fire and animal skins for protection, encouraged these first people to stay and eventually settle this land.

> These people believed that the spirits controlled their destiny. A displeased spirit could cause drought, thunder, and even death. When pleased, these spir-

Figure 3.2 *The Rainmaker*, located in the casino's main pedestrian concourse. (Photograph provided by the Mashantucket Pequot Tribal Nation)

its could bring sun, rain, and bounties of food and game. Soon man came to believe he must honor, respect, and pay homage to the power of these spirit gods, for they, not man, controlled destiny. (Holder 1994)

A red laser bolt shoots out of the end of the arrow and catches the swirling mist and fog playing against the ceiling. The show ends with a thunderclap, marking the beginning of a "thunderstorm." Water falls from the ceiling near the figure and pours from the branches overhanging the fountain to reach a crescendo of water and thunder. Then the lights come up, the blackout curtains slide back into their recesses, and the rain stops.

The Rainmaker is based on the bronze *The Sacred Rain Arrow* by sculptor Alan Houser (1914–94), who was a member of the Fort Sill Chiricahua/Warm Springs Apache Tribe. One of the original castings stands in the Russell Senate Building's Indian Affairs room dedicated to the Senate Committee on Indian Affairs.[1] John Holder, tribal member and former draftsman with Electric Boat, designed *The Rainmaker* and wrote its accompanying story (he is also its narrator). He was charged with the task of creating a spectacular sculpture that would parallel the fantastic thematic constructions of Las Vegas casinos. *The Rainmaker* is in Rainmaker Square, "a place that was separate from the gaming and where people could go in and experience a fun thing," said Holder (from the Mashantucket Pequot oral history project).

A number of different ideas were originally floated for filling this public space, including elves, a glass castle, and a Native American storyteller. Skip Hayward mentioned he had seen the statue by Houser and had been impressed by it. Holder and then–Foxwoods CEO Al Luciani decided to take *The Sacred Rain Arrow* a few steps further by making it twelve feet tall and translucent and by changing the original Apache figure to one featuring Eastern Woodlands clothing and artifacts. It was Holder's idea to create an indoor thunderstorm. "Ours being a Native American casino, I wanted to have a Native American theme through an awing experience,"

68   Chapter 3

he said. Holder worked painstakingly on *The Rainmaker*. He took bark molds from area trees, had tribal archaeologist Kevin McBride verify designs for the breech-cloth and moccasins, and kept refining the figure's muscular definition. The finished sculpture weighs 4,500 pounds. Mystic River, the Mashantucket Pequots' drum, created four songs to accompany the different stages of the thunderstorm.[2]

Since its installation *The Rainmaker* has proved a popular site for taking photographs. As it begins to cycle through its hourly display the atrium fills with a flutter of camera flashes, increasing as the figure builds to its display climax. Photographs of the figure, of the fountain, of the atrium. Photographs of the family: Mom, Dad, enormous polyurethane Indian man with bow and arrow. *The Rainmaker* serves as an extensively trafficked symbol for the casino. The statue is the reservation's best-known emblem and its most popular piece of public material culture. It appears on postcards, menus, mouse pads, coffee mugs, and jackets. In countless articles and stories *The Rainmaker* serves as introductory icon: eerily lit, wet and dripping in its own private rainstorm.

Throughout the five-minute show casino visitors come and go, some stopping to watch or to toss offerings into the fountain. The nearby cart vendors carry on their business. One is selling T-shirts from last year's Schemitzun, or Festival of Green Corn, and a small monitor plays a videotape from the event. The next vendor hawks sweatshirts and souvenirs for the upcoming Special Olympics in Hartford, which is being partially sponsored by the tribe.

Stretching past a section of Victorian facades and on toward the futuristic arcade, Cinetropolis, the concourse's enormous windows overlook the nearby hills and forests, with some of the land already mapped out for future development by the reservation's architects. The surrounding trees and the supporting rocks of the fountain and statue share nothing with the gingerbread of the nearby concourse storefronts, but *The Rainmaker*'s narrative provides a prehistoric introduction for what is to come.

Embedded within this foregrounded moment are many of the issues that arise at Mashantucket. One important element at Foxwoods is the blurring of spectacular, Las Vegas–style visual displays with the sober, didactic placards of the display-cased artifacts near the casino's main entrance. Another is the way in which popular discourses and stereotypes of Indians are incorporated within an enormously successful economic enterprise fully owned and operated by Indian people. Obviously, my "instant recognition" of the figure in the fountain as "Indian" participates in the popular imagining of the American Indian male: highly stylized, bare chested and well muscled, dressed in breechcloth and moccasins, mythical in proportion, and brandishing a bow and arrow. But the figure's location at an intersection between gambling rooms, surrounded by a pool of money and a clockwork rainstorm, with the Connecticut landscape made clear through the glass walls of the building, is a central part of the vast endeavor of the Mashantucket Pequots. It reflects certain goals at Foxwoods (and, I would argue, at many Indian casinos): how to use popular essentialized or naturalized representations of Indians from dominant historical narratives in conjunction with self-representations and contemporary views of Native peoples very much at home with modern projects like real estate development, donations to national charities, and the resort and gaming industry.

The Rainmaker display offers an epiphanic moment that problematizes an untroubled understanding of Indian identity configuration at Mashantucket. It employs advanced modern technologies to evoke the primordial: the "Indian," oozing fog and dripping moisture, kneels within a specially constructed fountain that emphasizes the natural. The spoken narrative introduces a cleared history in the highly public space of Foxwoods, a history that begins with the end of the Ice Age. From this initial configuration *The Rainmaker* narrative suggests an unbroken continuum from post–Ice Age hunters to an emerging present and an undetermined future, firmly located at Mashantucket. The Ice Age narrative creates a frozen tabula rasa where the foreground is redrawn and history in-filled. That unseen beings or forces, not "man," control destiny provides a perfect aside for casino patrons.

70   Chapter 3

The Casino as Cultural Allegory: Saturation and Separation

The performance of cultural representation—understood as an "on-the-ground," day-to-day event, a museum exhibition, or any other activity played out in public space—draws from contingent structures of history, ethnographic understanding, and narrative. At Foxwoods these structures overlap and blur. *The Rainmaker* draws its narrative from ethnographic and historical research, folded together to make a presentation in keeping with the overriding thematics of the casino—the figure and its thunderstorm. Representations are by nature based in the past and in an appreciation and application of history (understood here as a discursive site without privilege). Ethnographic representations are often intensified textual depictions of cultural sites and practices written to evoke a compelling "other." As in any shift from lived experience to written text, with an opening and closing supported by boundaries both temporal and narrative, ethnographic texts are limited in their ability to create persuasive and contained descriptions of experience in the world. Part of this transition from experience to text is the loss of dynamic time—the process of representation tears practice and discourse from the flow of time (Bourdieu 1984). Clifford (1986) proposes that ethnographic texts are allegorical in form and content: they describe "the real" while simultaneously practicing values-influenced interpretation. Casinos can also be understood as allegories, as sites of intensified representation creating compelling narratives of exotic and bounded cultural space. In generating this significant space casinos seek to evoke a significant "other." At Foxwoods this environment and compelling story are also used to make moral and values-influenced interpretation part of its political project: to relocate the Mashantucket Pequots in the history and "place" of New England and the United States.

As a site in the state and national landscape at the beginning of the twenty-first century Foxwoods reflects a deep engagement with Las Vegas and Atlantic City casino design thematics, particularly those stressing a connection to fantastic history or a saturated sense of the exotic and marvelous. Over the history of its establishment and expansion Foxwoods, like Las Vegas and Atlantic City casinos, has shifted toward a more complete thematic enclosure of space, effectively severing connections to the place and time of *location*.

As in Las Vegas, enclosed space and time support a sense of the fantastic, placing one in a sea of referents to an imagined Imperial Rome (Caesars Palace) or Arthurian England (Excalibur), for example, while also removing referents to the outside, erasing a recognition of "real" time. The control of temporal and spatial referents is critical in the casino's self-representation as gambling hall and entertainment and as a creation of mythic history. As Benjamin asserted for the Paris arcades, a phantasmagoric shift in the casino—where practical value recedes while representational value advances—is part of the experience. Here the fantastic "history" presented in the casino is crystallized as commodity, a site where production and consumption relations meet. For Foxwoods history itself—what might be called an assemblage and sequencing of narrative elements with an eye on the present—is implicated as a similar phantasmagoric shift.

Benjamin recognized history as a jumbled pile of wreckage whose vanishing point is the present. Rather than being a chain of events, the past is "one single catastrophe which relentlessly piles wreckage upon wreckage. . . . That which we call progress is this storm" (Benjamin cited in Buck-Morss 1991:95). Arrangements of information, images, concepts, and objects composed from the debris offer configurations of the present, salvaged from the past. Narratives created from these elements produce *a* history that serves a particular purpose in the present. The wreckage generated by progress indicates the materiality of destruction, which marks time as an array of fragments.

If history as a narrative is an imagined progression toward the modern with a linear advance from the past, the casino and its discrete, contained constructions are this historical configuration writ small. Theming depends on the creation, manipulation, control, and tight organization of central narratives (Waldrep 1999). In this instance the casino's thematics represent a structured (if spectacular) history. Containing this history depends on three things. First, there must be control of the narrative's container. At Foxwoods this includes architecture, interior design, traffic patterns, and ways in and out. Key interior sites, such as *The Rainmaker*, reinforce the casino's thematic. Second, tension must be maintained between the included and the excluded. A critical element for all casino design, this includes distinctions between high rollers and smaller fish, players and spectators at the table games, and the demarcation between gaming space and "family" space. Las Vegas further complicates these demarcations: casino interiors play to an included crowd, while the exteriors work to seduce passersby. Third, visitors must realize the limits of the experience. Casino thematics request a certain suspension of disbelief or at least a willingness to participate in the projected story. While virtually no one would mistake the waterfalls, raining trees, and plantings at Foxwoods for true "nature," they do provide elements of the "natural" as part of themed experience.

In Las Vegas casinos designed as family destination resorts began to take center stage near the end of the twentieth century, and their thematics extended out to the sidewalk: the Mirage's erupting volcano, the gaping maw of the MGM lion-as-entrance with amusement park–style rides just inside, and the hourly pirate battles in front of Treasure Island. Neon signs once sufficed as the key exterior attractions for casinos. More recently, however, casinos approach Disneylands, trying to keep a generation raised on amusement parks and special effects interested in their own created environments. This is partly a recognition of demographics, opening the casino visitor experience to more of an immersion in a represented theme, a kind of interactive diorama. It also reflects a keen marketing assessment of aging baby boomers, complete with significant disposable income and children with their own entertainment demands. But it is also a shift in the strategy of seduction. The spectacle on the sidewalk carries the show from the inside to the outside, it previews the pleasures within while realizing itself as another type of sign—experiential, tactile, and spectacular—referential to the interior dream landscape while indicating its own exterior separation. The show on the sidewalk ends on the sidewalk; the theme leads you inside.

During the 1990s Las Vegas casinos became more and more monstrous in size, as if attempting to compress and synthesize the attractions and territory of an amusement park within a casino's more modest footprint. The Luxor, Mandalay Bay, Treasure Island, Excalibur—each of these "supercasinos" represents a reach to or a grounding in a mythic past or present, a connection made fabulous by an intense overlay of mythohistoric themes. The connection to an imagined past has been scripted, performed, and made obvious. Toward the middle of the 1990s, however, this mythic referent changed, and casino foci shifted to include New York New York, Bellagio, the Venetian, and Paris Las Vegas. The mythic continues, but the grounding of the narratives ties directly to other existing and *located* sites. The global landmark reference point is miniaturized—compressed and intensified through forced-perspective juxtapositioning—to achieve a reduction that saturates the remainder.

In many ways this miniaturization and accompanying saturation parallel the formation and evolution of the American Indian domestic dependent nation-states realized as reservations. Such reservations serve as compression centers, as geographically located sites where Native populations were placed within new boundaries less permeable and more limited than their traditional areas of free travel. Over the history of federal and Native American relations the majority of these original reservation sites have been significantly reduced, both drawing the interior remaining populations closer while continuing a government-to-government relationship from a diminishing geopolitical site. Mashantucket is but one example of this kind of reductive but intensifying evolution.

At Foxwoods this compression participates in the near mythic qualities of celebrated and imagined locations, extending them by drawing them through a Las Vegas–influenced lens, anchoring the authenticity of their specific origins while releasing their themes to active roles in the myth economy of fabulation. The casino's sense of the fantastic reflects a mediated space created from a configuration of representational narrative elements—the contained, scripted, thematic experience that represents the modern casino. The modern theme casino provocatively blends the fantastic and the seductive not only in the obvious narrative of an exoticized and imagined history but also in the narrative of chance, the risk taken that defeats the odds to gain (fantastic) material wealth. This imagined wealth provides another transition point from the text of the casino to that of the exterior: "real" time and space. This relationship supports the notion that a nonmediated and transparent text of the everyday, of history and progress, exists beyond the casino doors. Immersion in the intensified casino environment not only points out the constructedness of this interior fantastic narrative but also either questions or enforces that of the "nonmediated" and "transparent" text of the exterior everyday narrative as well.

Foxwoods Resort Casino: From "Gaming in Its Natural State" to "The Wonder of It All"

The negotiation of a federally recognized tribal identity can be seen as a step toward the control and exercise of a group's own performative identity politics. It is also clear that an integral part of many casino presentations is the formation and extension of an elaborate mythic theme: densely layered and textured interiors and exteriors that reflect particular narratives. Foxwoods displays elements of complex thematics. It differs from its Las Vegas or Atlantic City counterparts in its isolation from neighboring casinos or cities and its incorporation of space, time, and history connected to the location of the reservation itself. From the opening of the original bingo hall in 1986 to the casino's first phase in 1992, Foxwoods participated in the challenges of changing casino design strategies, in some ways following Las Vegas and in some ways not.[3] The Foxwoods casino complex emphasizes the "American Indian" in general and the Mashantucket Pequots in particular as thematic locations for extended narratives of the exotic, and its placement at Mashantucket further emphasizes these themes. This original direction has itself shifted since the beginning of gaming at the reservation.

Built as an expansion on the original bingo hall, the first casino emphasized a connection to the land at Mashantucket. The main gaming room had floor-to-ceiling windows overlooking the Great Cedar Swamp—a site important to a particular Mashantucket Pequot creation story: the arrival of persecuted Pequot War survivors at Mashantucket. Here localized legend, or an exoticized specific historical rendition of Pequot origins at Mashantucket, became part of the casino's public space and visitor experience.

Things "generally" or "popularly" Indian were worked through other public registers, including employee costumes and uniforms, interior design motifs, the purchase and placement of large-scale sculpture, and small, cased collections of "Indian artifacts." Some of these elements reflect the Mashantucket Pequots' own processes for coming to grips with an extended separation from a tribal experience and the absence of a significant amount of material artifacts. In many ways popular understandings of Indians are used as resources for both tribal members and the visiting public, and "Mashantucket Pequotness" is a site under active reconstruction and rediscovery. While this process is perhaps better understood as part of the museum's project, Foxwoods was the first large-scale Mashantucket Pequot venue for public self-representation.

As Foxwoods became the defining standard for Indian casinos the emphases of its constructions changed. Like contemporary casinos in Las Vegas Foxwoods includes itself and its immediate surroundings in its collection of referents, and the exoticized narrative of "the Indian" has shifted as Indian casinos have changed from anomaly to established industry. In many ways Foxwoods presents a compression of the time line and history for casino development in Las Vegas, from active interplay with its site and its sense of location to an emphasis on a more dislocated or globalized sense of luxury. Each stage has reflected different agendas and influences, and the casino complex shows elements of its profit-making agenda and its

76   Chapter 3

political agenda in its use of public space as a place for self-representation. Still, the Mashantucket Pequot casino occupies a unique position at the juncture between inside and outside, between a fantastic mythic narrative of a themed casino and the equally mythic narrative of history. In part this stems from its singular positioning within the landscape. Isolated in the Connecticut forest, Foxwoods refers back not to surrounding casinos but to its reservation site, a complex blend of ethnic, political, traditional, and historical narratives. Also, as a *place* it evidences some of the twists and turns that are part of the Mashantucket Pequots' project of major and modern development.

Representations at Mashantucket work in an active intersection of "Indianness." The invocation of general "things Indian" works in a tenuous balance with those aimed in opposition to similar hegemonic notions, like the scope of the enterprise, on a grand level or the framed photographs of the tribal council showing a mix of phenotype and dress, including buckskin and business suits. In part this opposition works to destabilize the popular imaginary. The challenging and incorporating of refigured or reordered elements of cultural texts of "Indian," "Pequot," "modern," and "traditional" continues throughout the casino complex and related structures. The tension between the two, between stabilizing and destabilizing hegemonic notions and representations of Indianness and Mashantucket Pequotness, echoes the tactical moves within legal and ethnic discourses that brought the Mashantucket Pequots to their current status as a tribal entity and an economic force.

The Mashantucket Pequots use legal definitions of tribal identity and inclusion to revitalize a once much-diminished community. Challenges to this identity often use popular, monolithic notions of Indians to counter Pequot identity claims as being discordant with static views of Indianness (see also LaCroix 1999). But as Jane Sequoya notes: "The problem indicated by questions of who and how is an Indian is that the material conditions of being Indian have changed over time, while the images of Indianness have not" (1993:455).

The current population of Pequots in Mashantucket represents a disparate and diasporic group. To reestablish or newly establish traditions they have conducted research into their past, employing archaeologists, anthropologists, and historians. They have also incorporated different rituals, traditions, and representations of "Indianness" borrowed from other tribes. This sampling and retextualization of other representations finds itself played out in cultural performances (like Schemitzun or the museum) and in the themes that run through the casino itself.

Navigating Foxwoods

It is hard to figure out the Foxwoods layout during a first visit. Different areas were built in different phases, then were melded together through the use of common materials and colors, and are now united by the low sounds of omnipresent background noise. There is the sound of people walking—the hush of rubber soles on bright tiles and low-pile carpet—along with the smell of restaurant foods and the thick reek of cigarette smoke that air scrubbing never quite eliminates. The pedestrian avenues stretch out in a number of directions, meandering through retail areas and lounges, past frozen yogurt and T-shirt carts.

The original grand entrance was recently enveloped by the addition of a Hard Rock Cafe and a casino room expansion. The Grand Pequot Tower now harbors the complex's grand entrance. A second entrance downstairs is devoted to big tour buses ferrying in players from all over New England and the Northeast. From here passengers soon find themselves on an escalator that ends at Foxwoods' large food court: to the left are the main entrances to the bingo hall; to the right windows look out onto the parking lot below and the Great Cedar Hotel directly across.

78   Chapter 3

Vignette 2: Tacking across History—Yankees in the Concourse

The main concourse (fig. 3.3) begins at *The Rainmaker*, near Foxwoods' original grand entrance. Like the entrance, the concourse has gone through a number of changes since it first opened. It once featured a trio of animatronic figures, and the following reflects my introduction to this space.

Friday, late afternoon—too soon for a full after-work crowd, but the complex still hosts thousands: early arrivals for the weekend, groups of retirees, tour groups, groups of seniors, people with more flexible schedules. The main concourse is well filled with pedestrians, and the glass walls amplify the shuffle and slap of shoes, the bubble of conversation, the sounds of retail, and the not-too-distant bells and cash spills of the slot machines. Here also are the mixed sounds of children on family outings: the concourse is a "family friendly" space.

Some people sit and eat ice cream cones, watching other people progress down the walkway. Older women with thin hair teased into dyed clouds with pale mottled domes showing through. Men with their remaining hair plastered tightly over bare scalps. Sensible shoes. Bright sweaters. One person in a sweatshirt featuring a picture of a hand-lettered cardboard sign: "Will Bingo for Food." A man sits on a bench, his belly on his lap like a gift. A number of employees make their way to the parking lots at the end of the day shift or simply get away from the gaming rooms for a moment before heading home. Cocktail waitresses in small tight skirts, heavy makeup, too many bright teeth, and single dyed-feather headbands. Their jobs are considered the best in the casino—they keep their own tips (the rest are pooled), and the drinks they serve are free.

One of the more arresting examples of thematic construction in the casino can be found in the wide, main pedestrian concourse. The concourse is constructed on two levels. Running down one side is a wall of glass, in some places over two stories high, overlooking the second-growth forests and rock formations of the reservation. The ceiling of the concourse features a subtle light show with a projected sky loop-

Figure 3.3 The concourse. The two-story Victorian façade is on the right. Windows to the left, behind the retail displays, look onto Mashantucket and help illuminate the space. (Photograph by the author)

ing from sunrise to sunset and back again. Opposite the glass wall is a collection of two-story facades decorated with gingerbread, widow's walks, bow windows, and verandas. The lower level allows access to one of the casinos, a travel agency, visitor services, and Indian Nations (a store that sells jewelry and other merchandise made by Native Americans). Above this level are second-story windows, finished with glass, glowing lamps behind draperies, small balconies, and three separate speaking animatronic "Yankee" figures: a whaling captain, a tavern proprietress, and a clergyman who also seems to be a schoolteacher. There are a few sound effects: a ship's bell, the sounds of an interior crowd, the ringing of a hammer

80   Chapter 3

mixing with the canned music and the distant sound of slot machines. Each of the figures plays a role that occasionally interacts with the others through anecdote, question, or admonition—opportunities for a quip or a mini "informative" narrative. The figures and facades comprise a walk-through historical amusement-representation evoking a past and placeless town that combines elements of nearby Norwich and Mystic.[4] A nod is made to Yankee ingenuity, industry, and progress through a spatial and temporal transition from whaling days to industrial mills. These changes are further emphasized by changes in facades as the visitor navigates the concourse from *The Rainmaker* to Cinetropolis.

The concourse is filled with a thick mixture of sounds, all bouncing back from glass and hard tile. After a few moments of concentrated listening, during which you filter out background noises to fix your attention on the figures' speech, you learn that they are Captain John Barnes, Abby Wilson, and Father Tom: a triad of industry, entertainment, and church combined to offer a selective rendition of New England community, an animatronic gathering in which there is no mention whatsoever of Indians.

The captain stands on a balcony over the Mashantucket Travel Agency, surrounded by heaped nets, fishing rods, a hanging yellow slicker, and a lobster pot. Wearing a peacoat, he moves through a series of slow and limited gestures, a stiff Tai Chi loosely tied to his narrative, nodding his head every now and then, jerking his arm back and forth. The captain's voice mixes with the sound of the nearby *Rainmaker* fountain, the burble of the crowds, and the shuffle of feet: "Look sharp. A whaler's no place for dreamers. . . . I'm Captain John Barnes. I hope you've been looking out for whales. Every man must take his turn watching out. . . . You haven't seen any yearling whale today, have you? We killed it this morning but it swam under. . . . If you find it, we'll share it, but the irons come back to me."

A second-story window swings open wide, allowing a female figure to lean forward and address the crowd. She glides up to the window, stops, leans, speaks. She is Abby Wilson, the tavern keeper of Wilson's Tavern: "Hey, John. Will ye be coming by the tavern this evening?"

"You know I wouldn't come ashore without raising a glass with ye," responds Captain John.

Father Tom sits in a rocking chair on the largest balcony, overlooking the escalators from the lower hotel level, every now and then standing to gesticulate. He has gray hair and wears a black cassock. On his right is a table with a writing slate propped on its surface next to a telescope on a tripod. On his left is a globe on a stand. A barometer, a chronometer, and a thermometer are mounted on a nearby wall. The double doors behind him are open. Father Tom speaks about tending his flock or the wages of sin. His observations are often followed by a tart rejoinder from Abby: "Last week, Father Tom gave a sermon on virtue. He asked all the virgins in the congregation to stand. Not a woman stood. The third time he asked, a woman with a babe in arms stood. 'Young woman,' he said, 'why are you standing?' 'Well, you can't expect a six-month-old child to stand by herself!'"

Captain John's narrative weaves together anecdotes about whaling and facts about spermaceti whales, whalers, and whale oil. Like the captain, Abby addresses the passing throngs of tourists and gamblers, and most do not seem to notice her at all: "Been a working girl all my life. Hey, John, why don't you come by tonight? I'll keep your stool warm for ya. . . . I've been proprietor for over fifteen years. Well, it's long hours and low pay, but what do you want, egg in your beer? . . . We serve sailors drinks here." Abby talks of the laborers at the local mill—hired one day, fired the next. Muggy heat and clanking machinery, mill workers "drenched in sweat and covered with dust." She states that the sea is a better place: "Ah, but these people are good folk. Walking home from the mill, playing checkers with the family. . . . Wake up, Father Tom—looks like you've got some customers."

"Young woman, I am not engaged in commerce. I deal in men's souls." Father Tom talks of Judgment Day, "when the earth will tremble," against the ambient noise of the casino's gaming rooms and shuffling foot traffic: "Pride goeth before a fall. . . . There's no such thing as a self-made man. . . . Forbear ardent spirits and tobacco. . . . Remember, cleanliness is next to godliness."

"Hey, Father Tom, half of your congregation's down at my place," says Abby.

"Were I younger, I would teach you proper reverence." Father Tom speaks of the power of the Good Book, the value of a strict moral code, and the importance of keeping clean. Abby extols the virtue of enjoying oneself while one can and back talks Father Tom's homilies and minisermons. She asks Captain John to send his sailors by her place for some spirits before they head out to sea. Although there is not a representative character of a mill worker, each of the figures mentions the new industry of the mills and how difficult, dangerous, and dirty the work is there.

The animatronic technology is like that pioneered at Disneyland. The white figures' faces are nearly blank, smooth, with a slight indication of cheekbones, nose, and mouth. Father Tom's face is more finished and more terrifying than either Abby's or Captain John's—shiny plastic with a distinct nose. Projected onto these masks to animate them are the images of moving faces. Perhaps the effect is more successful viewed head-on. From the floor below they are deeply spooky, and it is hard to figure out that they have projected facial features at all. On first sight they present a faceless trio, going through their jerky dances, opening windows, rising from chairs, gesturing toward an imagined sea, while their voices loop on and on.

This collection of figures is the only place in Foxwoods, except its small museum, where "whiteness" is a part of the casino's thematic use of history. In the casino's museum whites are featured in pictures as English soldiers and Colonial volunteers or as the disembodied voice of power intoning, from the Treaty of Hartford, the first tribal termination in U.S. history. In the concourse the Yankees offer a kind of "living" historical representation and speak a set of interlocking narratives. The figures serve to intertwine three chosen perspectives from dominant "white" history while providing an amusement for the passing crowds.

Dressed in period clothing, the figures are surrounded by facsimile artifacts and tools that support the roles they have as representatives of people, professions, and, through their singularity, whiteness. They are surrounded by a casino that uses generalized Indianness as a theme and Mashantucket Pequotness as an anchor to the land near a museum and research complex complete with artifacts from on-reservation digs and a re-created village with its own representative figures.

The Yankees in the concourse marked some of the clear distinctions being made between the use of history as casino thematic and the use of history as vehicle for a revised "museum understanding" of the past. The Foxwoods concourse also marked itself as part of the larger Ye Olde New England Colonial history machine by referring to the discourses of New England progress and industry that guide narratives for nearby places like Mystic Seaport or the Connecticut River Museum.

The concourse Yankees were marginal figures in this history, the voices of historicized experience replete with stale jokes and awkward gestures. Their narrative processes were only a segment of this area of active multiple constructions. The entire Mashantucket industry, its development and surrounding projects, continually reminds one that the location of power in this equation differs radically from many other constructions of Indians and whites, including those in amusement parks and casinos, the old-timey themes of living histories and Colonial re-creations, and the elaborate public spaces of malls and resorts. This is a Mashantucket Pequot casino and a Mashantucket Pequot industry. The Mashantucket Pequots exercise their own interpretations and articulations of different multiple identities—historic, ethnic, and cultural—through the structures and narratives of the casino. Their legal identity has gained them financial power and enabled these constructions to be presented through the same elaborately high-tech methods as those offered within institutions reflecting dominant discourses.

Foxwoods Resort Casino is neither a counterhegemonic nor completely hegemonic structure. Constructed in a series of building phases, Foxwoods necessarily reflects changes in architects, designers, and Indian gaming. While many design elements mobilized throughout the casino work in opposition to a sense of "generalized Indianness," there are others that affirm this same sense. The Mashantucket Pequots, like many of the designers and architects they employ, work from some

84 Chapter 3

generalized concepts themselves. As in the past and throughout Native America, the Mashantucket Pequots practice a certain amount of cultural borrowing. And the rebuilding of a tribal and cultural presence is a difficult process, especially in a community built from dispersed and disparate individuals and families. Importantly, Foxwoods is a business that is constructed to appeal to a large clientele of mostly non-Native occasional and professional gamblers. The "Indian as Exotic" theme that runs through the casino delivers a certain, perhaps expected, narrative to its countless visitors.

If we accept that no casino is complete without a theme, a representation of a mythic past or luxury and wealth, then how does Foxwoods contradict or support this? At first gloss, the "Indian" theme of the Mashantucket Pequots' casino seems little different from exotic themes at other casinos. For example, *The Rainmaker* goes through its hourly paces, a persistent reminder of some sort of represented Indian-ness. And yet there are significant differences.

Foxwoods uses generalized and specific American Indian representations as thematic elements to tie itself to the land in two important ways. First, it participates in a popular imagination of a generalized "American Indian" ideology. For example, during Foxwoods' final construction phases the trade magazine *ConnStruction* dedicated three issues to the casino. Articles discussed the casino's unique design and the demands of its accelerated construction. Many made statements about how the construction project exemplified American Indian beliefs and practices. In one article Stewart Sebastian, tribal member and director of the Mashantucket Sand & Gravel Co., described his decision to crush gravel from on-site rock as an actualization of the "American Indian practice of using all of the parts of an animal they have trapped so as not to squander one of nature's gifts" ("An Eagle's Eye" 1994). The mobilization of such tropes over economy or Yankee pragmatism, for example, offers one illustration of the use of generalized American Indian ideology as a positioning discourse.

Second, "the land" is used as a material recognition of the Mashantucket

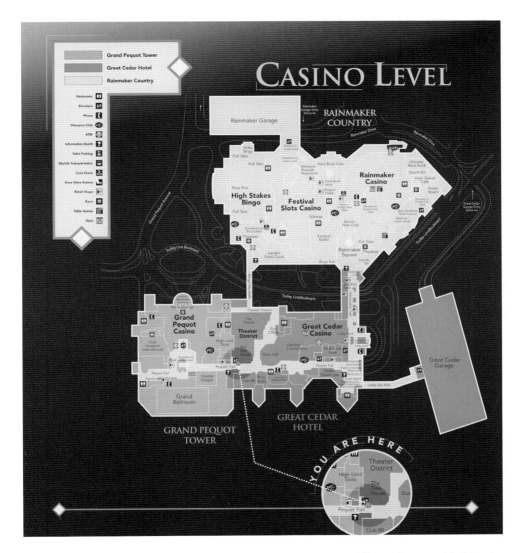

Figure 3.4 The casino level of the Foxwoods Resort Casino. (Illustration provided by the Mashantucket Pequot Tribal Nation)

86   Chapter 3

Pequot reservation, with nature as part of a timeless continuity between the tribe and the environmental surround. "Gaming in Its Natural State" was an early Foxwoods slogan, and views of the reservation landscape were an important part of the casino's gaming rooms.

This actualized connection to *place* is used to construct a mythic history that refers not to ancient Rome or Egypt but to the geographic surround. In later phases of construction and expansion the windows were removed from the gaming rooms. The glass pedestrian arcade now offers the visitor the broad scenic vista of Foxwoods' "natural state."

The gaming-room windows incorporated the reservation into the casino's design, framing both a picture and a reinforcement of "the natural," significant in both Indian and Mashantucket Pequot discourses. That the reservation is framed is only part of the picture; what is not framed is equally important. In Freemont Street casinos in Las Vegas, for example, windows and glass doors are part of the wall facing the street, itself a roofless arcade of casinos and businesses. Looking out, one sees other casinos, other players, an electric environment presenting other possibilities for action that do not challenge the basic interactive structure, gambler to gambling room. The referents offered are more self-referring mirrors than reminders of other realities. No sweeping vistas break this short sight, no uncontrolled acknowledgment of space and time. Including the natural as part of the Foxwoods thematic includes time.

The casino recontextualizes elements from the discourses of Indians, nature, and the Mashantucket Pequots from within the context of the reservation. Working these through with representations of luxury and the exotic, both "Indian" and "natural," the casino's theme combines these narrative elements in a number of ways. First is its relatively remote placement on the landscape. Visitors to the reservation and casino travel two-lane highways through villages, farmlands, and woods. The road to Foxwoods is marked with signs for the casino and the Mashantucket Pequot Tribal Nation, indicating the distinct transition from the surrounding New England countryside through the reservation boundaries.

Figure 3.5
In an earlier phase of the casino the gaming rooms featured walls of glass that looked out onto the Great Cedar Swamp. (Photograph provided by the Mashantucket Pequot Tribal Nation)

Once inside the casino the natural is a repeated element in the material design. Other design elements include the carpets' fallen-leaf motif, the plant and flower designs of the stained glass windows, the repeated use of water and fountains, and the building itself, which features abundant indoor plantings, windows, sky-lighted arcades, and soaring atriums. Woven through these physical constructions are "Indian" and Pequot elements: repeated geometric patterns representing basket and weaving designs and the "Pequot colors" of mauve and green, black and white. John Everett, a principal designer for New England Design, which worked on the interiors for Foxwoods, offers the following about design decisions:

88 Chapter 3

The Native American motifs came from a number of sources. The Pequots had compiled a great deal of information on their tribal history and a number of local historians, art historians, anthropologists and archeologists also provided research and information. In certain cases information was drawn from a more general idea of regional Native American cultures. Finally the use of natural materials, native wildlife, and natural light were very important to the tribe. (Personal correspondence, 2002)

For the 1996 redesign of the bingo hall the head of New England Design, Kevin Tubridy, stated that copper was incorporated into the hall's floor tile patterns to reflect a "Native American medicine wheel motif"; the designers used copper because "it is the only metal found among pre-Europeans . . . [and it] has very strong medicinal value" (Weaver 1994:44). Similar statements can be found throughout texts created around the construction project, as tribal members, designers, construction engineers, and architects mobilized imagined and popular notions of Indianness as part of the Foxwoods theme. Countering these statements against historical discourse, which might include mention of other significant precontact metals or the medicinal value of copper when used as a floor tile element, only serves to underline differences in the positioning of factual and cultural elements within these narratives. Tubridy further stated that his firm was interested in "obtaining a mix of both tribal designs and pure design. 'You don't want to get so symbolic and so serious that you get a museum format'" (Weaver 1994:44). Highlighting the tension between "tribal" and "pure" design is not to suggest that there is some discoverable "real" representation lurking beneath these constructed facades. Historical discourse is only one possible arrangement of the imagined past, of what Fredric Jameson refers to as the "absent cause." This absent and generative narrative engine allows particular depictions of the past, what Kathleen Stewart calls "allegorical re-presentation[s] of absent presence itself" (1996:58). Read ideologically, as Jameson's "narrativization in the political unconscious" (1984:35), the arrangement and deployment of these casino interpretive and representational texts implicate the parallel Mashantucket Pequot projects of rebuilding and extending their own cultural narratives and tribal identity. Foxwoods is a particular (multi)textual realization of (historical) narrative(s). The casino's representation of an exotic "theme," its position in the landscapes of both the reservation and "the natural," and its material function as a capital-generating industry for the Mashantucket Pequot Tribal Nation reflect different positionings of its ideological intents and functions.

Susan Stewart recognizes narrative as seductive and that this seduction depends on a feeling of recognition that she calls nostalgia: a sense of longing that animates a narrative structure by creating a desire for completion, a desire to fill the gap between signified and signifier. Nostalgia lives in the space created by this desire for a smoothed juncture at the overlap of memory and recognition. Efforts to achieve this smoothing reconfigure (by decontextualizing and then recontextualizing) different elements of narrative (different evocations, segments, images, and feelings that imply other states of being by referencing an imagined real, historical or fantastic). The tension between a configured narrative and its indexical reference to a material real drives the themed history that is the casino.

Representations at Foxwoods are deliberate. They are designed to evoke an exotic, weaving together more obvious elements of dream imagery with quotations from "traditional" histories and depictions. The casino affirms a seductive longing, a nostalgia located in the gap between historical object(s)—actual things, represented narratives, markers of the past—and the narratives built around them, encasing and extending them. This seduction plays with memory, with object descriptions and representations that spark a flash of recognition. Recognition here is a narrative of the past that lights on that which seems to fit the space of memory, an imagined rendition of the past.

Ethnographic texts are allegorical in form and content, stories that make moral, ideological, and cosmological statements, and ethnographic practice is implicated

90   Chapter 3

through its use of texts as vehicles for ideological expression (Clifford 1986:98).[5] The casino and the museum serve as allegories for the Mashantucket Pequot project of reestablishing the tribe and a tribal culture. The casino does so with a number of different allegorical overlays, including (1) resurrection, the reestablishment of a tribal entity after near total political and historical erasure; (2) an Algeresque rags-to-riches narrative for the tribal nation and its members; (3) the American Dream of capitalist opportunity and triumph; and (4) the risk taken that succeeds (a high-stakes bingo hall in the middle of the Connecticut woods that becomes the world's largest casino).[6] As Susan Stewart suggests, "allegory draws special attention to the narrative character of cultural representations, to the stories built into the representational process itself" (1993:100). The *Oxford English Dictionary* defines allegory as the "description of a subject under the guise of some other subject of aptly suggestive resemblance . . . an extended or continued metaphor."[7] Importantly, the casino can be read as an allegory for culture—an extended metaphor of cultural practices and boundaries semicontained in a permeable shell. Foxwoods thematics present a saturated space of multiple meanings and fantastic narratives, while Foxwoods practice and what it provides have a far-reaching effect on the terrain of Native America.

The construction of fantastic and historical narratives for use in intensified representations of a particular way of life—one with its own methods of seduction, its own plays within memory and desire—parallels the workings of culture, an active site where meaning is immanent and performed, a lived, shifting, and contested ground. It defies outline and encapsulation. Like the casino and its thematic, culture seeps and transgresses boundaries, influencing and giving body to its own narrative(s). The casino, by overlapping narratives from exoticized and multiple pasts with a project of reestablishing a history for the reservation, offers a site where these concurrent and similar motives can be read in relation to one another. The seduction to suspend disbelief, or at least a willingness to allow the narrative to play, lives within the desire to create a discrete representation of history and time, an intensified exotic "other" in a narrative strategy compelling the reader to extend credibility and participate in an experience of imagination.

The casino-created miniworld narratives construct an "other" time, separate and distinct from yet indicative and supportive of "real" time. Seductive strategies describe but also validate comparisons made between constructed and "real" time. With its blurring of traditional casino tropes (time, space, inside-outside distinctions, and the world made miniature) and its transgression into other indicated narratives (nature, Indianness, the surrounding landscape) Foxwoods draws the "real" into question. The signified oscillates between exotic theme and surrounding site, and the suspension of disbelief assumed and given as one enters this intensified site of representation doubles back on itself.

Foxwoods as Authenticating Register

Building Mashantucket Pequot and Indian identity and extending and intensifying the casino's exotic narrative are parallel and overlapping projects, and issues of authenticity play out within an intoxicating evocative seduction of signs. Desire, realized as both an element of the discourse of chance and wealth and an element of a nostalgic discourse (blending an idealized past with a representation in the present), drives and perpetuates a circulation of intensified representation. But nostalgia as a cultural practice "depends on where the speaker stands in the landscape" (Stewart 1993:100). Nostalgias at work in the casino reflect those of hegemony and resistance, middle and working class, mass culture, and "the local." They respond to richly immersive representations that animate the casino and provide strategies for navigating its surfaces.

The casino and the reservation are postmodern exemplars displaying the effects of cultural explosion. Here commodity capitalism forcefully pervades all expressions of cultural identity. Industry, commodity, and capital intertwine with identity articulation and affirmation, blending categories of asserted cultural presence and exoticized commodification. The reservation and casino form a simulacrum of cultural presence as formal entity replaces substantive entity. On this level, discussions of the "authenticity" of Mashantucket Pequot claims become assessments of

92   Chapter 3

the displacing strategies of signification and commodification. As simulacra, both the Mashantucket Pequots and the casino displace particular senses of the "real" through a rich surface interplay of signs.

Asserting that a displaced sense of the real negates the existence of the real or authentic, however, would lose sight of the recognition that simulacra do not indicate the authenticity of their particular locus and offer little use as means for verifying or uncovering the real beneath the representation. Jean Baudrillard acknowledged Disneyland thematics as "a deterrence machine set up in order to rejuvenate in reverse the fiction of the real" (1994:172). With the theme park as a fiction the corresponding assertion follows: that which is not the theme park is "real."

At Foxwoods not only is the counterindicated real (or authentic), but as such, it resists further investigation as a simulacrum in its own right. If investigated, it is to seek latencies and the different manifestations of discovery that do not question its underlying reality. In this regard the casino counterindicates the realities of the community and the process of identity construction and affirmation within the federal structure of the United States. It reaffirms the reality of federal Indian law and its identity categories, which conflate discourses of nature and culture. If we isolate "intensified representation" as belonging only to the seductive mythic thematic world of the casino, we understand only a segment of Mashantucket.

For Baudrillard seduction is the enchantment of the sign, the outward appearances of represented forms that evoke an "other" and create a space for desire, a desire manifested as the engine of production. Seduction is created through a play and circulation of signs, negating the idea of deep or hidden meaning, moving away from an analysis of instrumentalism and toward consideration as an instantaneous operation that is always its own end: "There is no active or passive in seduction, no subject or object, or even interior or exterior: it plays on both sides of the border with no border separating the sides" (Baudrillard 1994:160). Seduction and desire are realized as the extents of their own motivation and exchange.

The overflowing boundaries of Mashantucket Pequot constructions in and around Foxwoods evidence this borderlessness. The intensified representations challenge static images of Indianness and conceptions of ethnic and biological identity and reintroduce time and history in the construction of themed casino narratives. They also continue certain hegemonic discourses: Indians as exotic "others," ethnic identity as a legislatable entity, and a casino design that reflects current trends in mall and amusement park public structures. In recognizing the multiple possible readings of Mashantucket, what Foxwoods makes clear is that any such attempt is but one of many.

The explosive growth of the gaming industry, based in part on the strong U.S. economy of the late 1990s, fueled the latest wave of casino design. Here all bets seem to be sure bets, and stories of instant millionaires proliferate in the media. These conditions indicate two possible directions for casino development at the beginning of the twenty-first century. One is to a completely exotic and self-contained world that extends its boundaries outside its own physical plant or the extended "large sign" effects of its building(s). This direction includes places where suspended disbelief also incorporates another world, with its own mythologies and history outside of the known, resplendent with its own artifacts and archaeologies.[8] The second direction relies on the oversaturation of the known, made thick with glossy excess and compression (e.g., New York New York, Paris Las Vegas, or the Luxor). These are places that make the known or the knowable exotic, that reference an actual sociopolitically, historically, and geographically *located* place and make it strange through dramatic temporal and spatial transposition, performance, and translation.

Foxwoods walks the line between these two genres, referencing both historical and commonly imagined ideas about Native America. While its reason for being is necessarily caught up in its location and the knowable quantities of its history and tribal members, the Mashantucket reservation that surrounds Foxwoods remains largely unknown, figured through the talk of the local townspeople's I-remember-

94   Chapter 3

when narratives, through speculation on the expansion of the reservation and future possible losses of non-Native-owned land, and in the tribal nation's museum exhibitions.

Vignette 3: Farther down the Concourse Time Line

The Victorian facades end, and the concourse turns ninety degrees to enter the Cinetropolis area. The turn is marked by a bronze of Alan Houser's *The Sacred Rain Arrow* in the center of the tiled hallway. Across from the sculpture is the entrance to the Mashantucket Pequot museum information center. The room, carved from the wide intersection that also leads to a main parking garage, is walled with glass and has faux tree trunks at the corners as if to hold up the ceiling. The center features a small exhibit of artifacts, a brief history of the tribal nation, and a life-size Indian figure as well as lots of information about the MPMRC. The information center has replaced the small museum on the casino's lower level (fig. 3.6).

As a corollary to the Yankee history of the concourse, this earlier museum, a pilot project for Design Division, Inc., offered material support to *The Rainmaker* narrative and incorporated a number of the themes and ideas central to the later MPMRC. The basement museum was off the beaten track, below a waterfall and close to an alternative entrance to the smoke-free slots room. It offered a few objects of "traditional" Mashantucket Pequot material culture encased in glass-topped vitrines, text-panel narratives, a section of wooden palisade, a small wigwam, and a rack full of the tribe's monthly newspaper. Visitors confronted a large photograph of past tribal member Elizabeth George Plouffe, whom Skip Hayward credits with the initiation of the reservation repopulation effort in the 1970s. A wooden plaque reads: "Hold on to Your Land."

The small museum was moved to the concourse and changed; it is now in a highly trafficked area. The room kept some of its earlier exhibition elements, including a multimedia display entitled "The Massacre at Mystic Fort." A recorded

Figure 3.6 An exhibit in the casino's first museum. The text panel shows Capt. John Underhill's portrayal of the attack on the Pequot village in 1637. (Photograph provided by the Mashantucket Pequot Tribal Nation)

narrator covers the 1637 massacre and its immediate aftermath, from April 1937 to the Treaty of Hartford, signed September 21, 1638. Other voices include those of Captain Underhill, unidentified Pequots shouting the warning of attack, and an unidentified male "authority" reading from the Treaty of Hartford. There are engravings of Captain Underhill, a dog, maps, a Pequot fort, the Underhill rendering of the massacre site, and a portrait of John Winthrop (the Colony of Massachusetts's deputy governor and a leading instigator of the war). The display ends with pictures of a map showing the postwar Pequot diaspora and an image of the Treaty of Hartford fading out while the narrator's voice intones: "The English conclude their war of genocide and arrogantly declare the Pequots extinct. Nevertheless, the Pequot tribe continues to survive and endure."

The small exhibition narratives continue where *The Rainmaker* leaves off, moving from an unspecified period in a near timeless past and a mention of pre–"Ancient Ones" progenitors, to a selection of artifacts locating the Pequots in a history oppositional to dominant narratives of Colonial New England. The museum's casino location confirms the suggested endurance of the "Pequot tribe," while the "face-to-face" meeting with Elizabeth George Plouffe prepares the visitor for an introduction to the more contemporary history of the Mashantucket Pequots. This history includes the return-to-the-reservation movement that led to the establishment of community and the construction of Foxwoods. The casino's museum also provides an entry point to the larger effort of the tribal nation's museum and research center while tangibly illustrating the mixing and contaminating experiences of casino and museum, of distraction and the possibility of contemplation.

Outside the room the concourse moves past brick-fronted facsimiles of early-twentieth-century office and store facades: a print shop, a newspaper office, a dance studio. Across the "street" a wall of monitors displays the multiple exotic images of music videos. The monitors are next to an old-timey theater entrance, complete with Art Deco–style neon and chrome. Cinetropolis, billed in the 1998 Foxwoods Resort Casino brochure as "the city of specialty theatres," includes a large-format, large-screen film theater and motion-simulation and virtual-reality "rides." During the last leg of its journey to the Grand Pequot Tower the concourse is marked by a strategic representational shift. While earlier stages of construction and design emphasized a connection to the natural and the reservation, the Cinetropolis area emphasizes an idealized experience of an early-twentieth-century urban setting (fig. 3.7). The MPMRC information center now included in this passage provides another element linking the place of Mashantucket to its representational enterprises. The passage to the Grand Pequot Tower, in contrast, emphasizes a dislocat-

Figure 3.7 Cinetropolis. (Photograph by the author)

ed referent: the sense of rich luxury—or the recognition that luxury now presents its own emphasized (and transnational) location.

A wide, carpeted hallway leads away from Cinetropolis. On the left is the Golden Dragon, one of the higher-end Foxwoods restaurants. Opposite, a set of large display cases contains mannequins advertising clothing available for purchase in Foxwoods shops. In the first case a couple wears expensive resort togs; in the second, expensive buckskin regalia. Both are equally inaccessible and raise similar questions about price, practicality, and the line between fashion and costume.

At the end of the concourse the Grand Pequot Tower lobby—complete with

98   Chapter 3

rich decorative materials, thick carpet, and abstract glass sculptures—dislocates its patrons, emphasizing a sense of the luxurious over place as its own particular and marvelous "siting" of the Foxwoods slogan: "The Wonder of It All." At the same moment this sense of dislocation relies on a discriminating realization of global resources, and press releases for the lobby refer to its "exotic wood veneers from South Africa," marble floors, and "Turkish crystals."[9]

The pedestrian concourse is not only a space of directed transit or window-shopping. It also leads from the food courts to the luxury tower, a combination of highway and vestibule, a traveling and interstitial space gained only as part of the process of getting elsewhere. Once entered, it presents its own particular environment and offers different spaces of located perspective, a moving point of entry as well as a space of its own. The concourse provides an all-encompassing and porous space, a gap in the closed environments of gaming, entertainment, eating, and buying, which may be why it seems the primary destination for family outings. It serves as theater for the visitor experience of Mashantucket-as-background and a reminder of the wooded roads traveled to get to the reservation.

Vignette 4: Gaming Space

Excluding the high-roller enclaves, Foxwoods has five main casinos (see figure 3.4), and slots dominate the overwhelming majority of these spaces. In a place that focuses close attention on design details in pedestrian and full-access areas, what are the atmospherics of the casinos? The rooms are cavernous, and the lighting is dim. Across the carpeted floor stretch rows and rows of machines, each with its own dedicated chair firmly bolted down. A careful number are chairless for wheelchair access; there is no place to sit if you are not playing.

There are slots at every betting level, from two cents to five hundred dollars. The spaces are resonant with lights, bells, and assorted electronic noises. In some of these rooms, like the Great Cedar Casino, a few large openings look out on the concourse. In the Grand Pequot Tower casino windows look outside onto the grand entrance, and a large round hole looks down into the hotel lobby beneath a massive domed skylight. The spaces mix inside and outside, but the referents shift. As Foxwoods works through different phases of additions or reconstructions, it surrenders theme to sheer use of space. While the 1998 tower addition shifted the theme from "other" to opulence, subsequent constructions focus on packing the gaming spaces tighter.

Outside, the parking lot is middling full: a late afternoon crowd. People walking through the gaming spaces seem driven, clutching promotional Wampum Club fanny packs featuring the Foxwoods logo and rattling plastic cups filled with coins. Elsewhere, large people eat large ice cream cones. People with wheelchairs, walkers, oxygen tubes. Families. Last midnight's toddlers flipping through board books while Mom and Dad took turns in the casino. As Foxwoods expands, it turns over more and more space to slot machines, its biggest moneymaker. The Hard Rock Cafe and an expansion of the Rainmaker Casino swallowed the original grand entrance and porte cochere. Mixed gaming space is in the minority, and serious high-stakes table games are in the twenty-fifth-floor Club Newport International and Stargazer casinos.

> Super Blazing 777; Texas Tina; Hexbreaker; Carnival of Mystery; Double Diamond; Lucky Larry's Lobster; Pompeii; Turkey Shoot; Wheel of Fortune; Betty Boop; Creature of the Black Lagoon; Red, White, & Blue; Enchanted Unicorn; Slotto; Star Wars; Money to Burn; Sherwood Treasures; Monopoly; Snap Shot; Phone Tag; In the Money; Money Bars; Black & White Double Jackpot; Easel Money; Wild Cherry; Bonus Frenzy; Rapid Double Jackpot; Double Lucky 7s; Triple Diamond; Red Carpet; Wild Game; Perfect 7.

In 2000 Foxwoods had more than 4,500 slot machines; by 2005 it had more than 7,400. Most of the slots rooms smell of smoke, the high ceilings—punctuated by the black bubble housings of surveillance cameras—don't seem high enough.

Cocktail servers, security personnel, and change-makers, their carts just fitting through the aisles, regularly cruise the rooms. Everywhere the beckoning sound of the spill. Flashing lights. Racks and racks and racks of machines, each with different names, different figures and graphics, different sounds and colors. Each locked into the same odds, the same rate of payout, each curled around its own open secret: the house, ultimately, always wins.

People from tour buses, on vacation, on the way home; with families, solo, in groups; with betting systems, lucky charms, lucky hats, lucky shoes, lucky shirts. Sharp cracking their coin rolls to pour clinking change into waiting cups. People eating like aquarium fish in glass-fronted restaurants. The rolling trundle of supply carts and maintenance carts and the soft purr of electric three-wheeled scooter chairs. People looking lost or found or elusive or completely open, people dressed up and people dressed down. Children wandering about—they know something's going on that they don't completely get, and they gamely try to participate in the atmosphere or surf the current.

Although their names differ, the actual casinos (gaming rooms) appear like many others. The more exotic elements crystallize in the names of the machines themselves—the thematics have been distilled to individual glowing and mechanical boxes potentially crammed with money. The more powerful thematic theaters are now generalized, outside of the gaming spaces, in the concourse and the open spaces of the shops and lobbies. The Houser sculptures scattered through Foxwoods present one of the few common elements, the Victorian facades, the use of faux trees as architectural components for the new museum information center. But the rest keeps getting modified, swallowed, re-presented, or erased. As the casino continues it surrenders certain narratives, primarily historical connection and Native thematics, as it pursues others: a relentless flattening of affect to achieve a self-referential mall-like mix.

On Location: The Effects of Emplacement

Mashantucket both depends on and defies its surround. The *location* of Mashantucket offers an immersion into a densely populated intersection of complementary and competing discourses and representations, including those of site, history, cultural identity, mythic thematic, and legal category. The density of possible readings and understandings complicates Mashantucket Pequotness and Indianness by revealing them as registers contingent on and responsive to change. Foxwoods presents public articulations of identities mapped against popular and specific understandings of multiple histories.

Foxwoods serves as an inspirational model and prominent example for all Indian casinos. The Mashantucket Pequots have welcomed other tribal leaders and business people interested in establishing their own gaming enterprises, and Foxwoods has served as a resource for training, information, and, in some cases, monetary assistance for establishing other Indian gaming concerns.[10]

The financial success and accompanying high profile of the Mashantucket Pequots come at a significant price. This emerging Indian nation has become a lightning rod for a number of turbulent issues in the larger Indian community, the political economy of the region, and the United States. Anglo-Americans—and other Indian tribal peoples as well—challenge the legitimacy of the Mashantucket Pequots' self-identification as an American Indian tribal nation on issues ranging from cultural practices to phenotypical appearance and blood-quantum reckoning. Paradoxically, these often-pejorative constructions also provide the Mashantucket Pequots and other Native Americans with the means of asserting claims to sovereignty, claims to dominion over lands, and national identity. These claims make accessible resources not available to other marginalized and subjugated groups in the United States. In a larger context, therefore, Mashantucket Pequot attempts at self-definition and autonomy must be understood as often antagonistic—but always related—processes of contestation between local definitions and discourses of self and the dominant narratives of racial essences and cultural stereotypes that pervade the historical encounters between a majority "America" and this America's Indian "other." This must necessarily include the curious role of the Native American in U.S. history, both as tragically erased opponent and as integral figure in the imagination of an "American" history. Examining the politics and poetics of the casino complex and the MPMRC proves crucial to achieving an understanding of the dynamics of local community formation as well as the entangled and continually transforming histories of the United States and Indian nations in the making.

4 "Discover a Nation in Your Own Backyard"

The slender spire of the MPMRC's observation tower reveals itself just over the shoulder of Foxwoods' buildings and the nearby woods as one approaches the Mashantucket Reservation (fig. 4.1).[1] The rest of the 316,000-square-foot structure is nestled low, blending into the surrounding forest and swampland. The building is "designed to interact with its surrounding environment and maintain the ecological integrity of the area . . . to emphasize and complement the permanent exhibits and their relationship to the landscape."[2] Two of its five stories are underground, and the building's construction was designed to preserve as many of the site's trees as possible. The surrounding landscape is harsh, a postglacial moraine strewn with rocks and boulders. Difficult as cropland and without access to waterways, Mashantucket is a typical reservation location. Although its history includes different periods of limited agriculture, the poor, remote land is mostly not worth the effort to farm.

One outcome of the land's quality, however, is that the reservation offers an intact and extensive archaeological record. The Archaeological District of the reservation was designated a National Historic Landmark in 1992. The Mashantucket Pequots have protected and researched their culture and past through historical and archaeological investigation since 1985; archaeologists, historians, and college students have done the majority of this research. Exceptions to this pattern included the Fort at Mashantucket Project, which focused on producing an inventory from a seventeenth-century Pequot fortified site, and a project on Indiantown, the late-eighteenth-century agrarian reservation community influenced by the Brotherton movement and Mohegan minister Samson Occum (see chapter 1).

Figure 4.1 The Mashantucket Pequot Museum and Research Center observation tower. (Photograph by the author)

The fort project was designed to train tribal members in archaeological and ethnohistorical research methods and as docents. Plans once included incorporating a walk-through tour of the fort site as part of the overall MPMRC exhibition plan. The Indiantown project was also designed to train interested tribal members, and final plans for the site included paths with signage for public, docent-led tours. At the time of my research two tribal alumni of recent archaeological projects were using their acquired knowledge in working for the tribal nation: Gail Graham was the Mashantucket tribal historic preservation officer, and Michael Goodwin worked in the tribe's Cultural Resources Center.[3]

The Museum: Site of Negotiation, Space for Contemplation

The constructed ethnicities, identities, and nationalisms that increasingly are critical foci in anthropology and other disciplines depend on representation. Authenticating these facets of identity making often depends on relating a complex narrative augmented by images, objects, or locations that convey or represent resonant structures of meaning for consumption by a public audience. At Mashantucket, photographs of neighbors and ancestors, objects of ritual or heritage, and the land itself stand as evidence of a sustained relationship with a located identity. These registers do not work by only looking backward, positioning objects of the past within narratives of tradition located in the present. Museums work at a complicated intersection of poetics and communication, meaning and message.

The continuity suggested by *The Rainmaker* narrative is traced large in the MPMRC. The museum visitor starts with an introductory gallery featuring the present-day reservation community and its enterprises, then travels back through time to begin again, with the Ice Age providing the thematic tabula rasa. Use of archaeological theories, data, and materials provides one way to bind the museum to its own historic site, to *locate* it and invest it with a "sense of place" (Basso 1996). This includes an exhibition featuring an archaeological core sample presented in front of a wall of glass that looks out on the site of its collection. One then travels to Pequot pre- and postcontact events, including periods of trade, disease, and colonial massacre, and on to the many historical stages of reservation life. This latter part of the journey is made along floor-to-ceiling glass walls overlooking the wooded reservation, with a re-created eighteenth-century farmstead in the near distance. The visitor finishes in a room displaying oversize black-and-white photo-portraits of current tribal members and filled with a soundwash of oral histories.

The museum and research center is an important site for the tribal nation and community, and it is a productive site for examining issues of articulated and displayed cultural identity. It provides a community resource for tribal history and identity affirmation and holds an extensive archive of historical documents, objects, and photographs. The library offers story and reading programs in conjunction with the tribe's Child Development Center. And the MPMRC offers an opportunity for job training and future career possibilities for Mashantucket Pequots. It also provides examples of museum administration, decision-making processes, and design strategy. The Mashantucket Pequots are wealthy enough to enact any exhibition strategy they choose, and many of the people in decision-making positions at Mashantucket did not have specialized experience. As in most museums, upper-level decisions were influenced by politics and power. Unlike most museums, funding was an influential but not controlling element. The research center is an important resource for building a scholarly profile for research on and narratives about the Mashantucket Pequots.

Museums are significant as traditional spaces for exhibiting narratives of the past, and the MPMRC occupies a dynamic intersection of identity and community building. Its ownership and its placement reflect a connection to a naturalized historical presence. Foxwoods also incorporates historical and cultural displays embedded in a spectacular entertainment space that generates enormous capital. Not only are the casino and the museum connected by ownership and economy, but they also articulate diverse elements from discourses of history, nature, tradition,

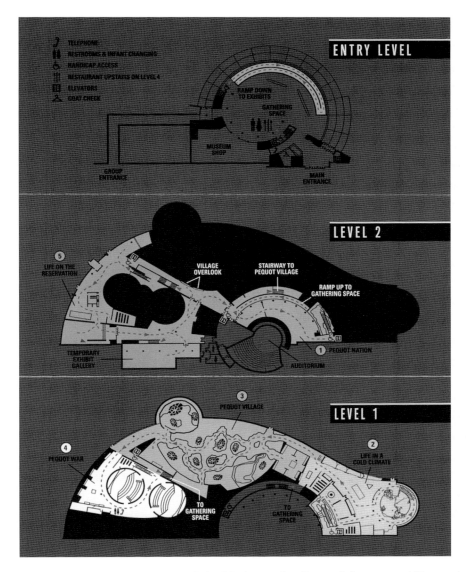

Figure 4.2 The public spaces of the Mashantucket Pequot Museum and Research Center. (Illustration provided by the Mashantucket Pequot Museum and Research Center)

108　Chapter 4

and community. The two structures are counterindicative and countersupporting industries devoted to generating both material and symbolic capital.

That the structures exist at all, especially as such state-of-the-art facilities, is nothing short of phenomenal. Both use displayed and intensified narratives of Indianness, a specific Mashantucket Pequot attachment to and placement in the landscape, and configurations of history specific to the projects at the reservation. Their financial success and growing development serve as powerful self-supporting narratives. Further, the museum's location on the reservation, both as a point within an Indian nation and as a counterpoint to the expanding casino and resort complex, is fundamental to its projected narrative of Mashantucket Pequot identity. Representation necessarily changes the dynamics of the past by relocating them within an ongoing present and an active community.

Mashantucket as Exhibition Site

The museum's undertaking—to tell the history of the Mashantucket Pequots—matches its impressive size. It begins in the Gathering Space, an immense public space on the entry level. This massive glass atrium's double semicircular design (fig. 4.3) was inspired by John Underhill's seventeenth-century etching of the 1637 attack on the Pequot fortified village at Mystic (fig. 4.4). Its deep blue terrazzo floor, inlaid with bits of seashell, is meant to recall the Pequots' habitation of Noank on the Long Island Sound and their traditional manufacture and use of wampum.[4] In the near distance, through the atrium's glass walls, the Grand Pequot Tower can be seen through the nearby trees.

A long, curving ramp descends to the first gallery. The ramp's walls are glass and covered with life-size and semiopaque pictures of local trees. The outside view of the reservation is slowly eclipsed as visitors become immersed in the building. The first exhibition, The Mashantucket Pequot Tribal Nation, tells the story of the reservation community's rebirth, and it begins with a large group photograph of

Figure 4.3 A side view of the Gathering Space exterior. The observation tower is in the background. (Photograph provided by the Mashantucket Pequot Museum and Research Center)

tribal members on the reservation (fig. 4.5). They are gathered in front of Elizabeth George Plouffe's former home, also known as "the homestead."

The gallery displays life-size contemporary artifacts, including Mashantucket EMT uniforms, a slot machine from Foxwoods, and a Pequot war club on loan from the National Museum of the American Indian.[5] The gallery is an important interstitial space in the overall exhibition design; it initiates the transition from a contemporary to a historicized place in part through the "museumization" of particular artifacts and their inclusion in the museum's representational displays and narratives.

110   Chapter 4

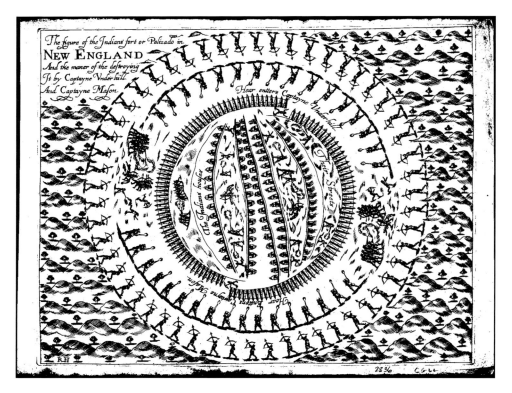

Figure 4.4 Capt. John Underhill's portrayal of the attack on the Pequot Fort at Mystic in 1637. (Photograph provided by the Mashantucket Pequot Museum and Research Center)

Vignette 1: Symbolic Capital, Museumization, White Gloves

Preliminary decisions made while designing the exhibit The Mashantucket Pequot Tribal Nation involved choosing artifacts. The Mashantucket Pequot museum is not an object-centered institution, but the choice of artifacts determined supplementary text, case and text panel design, and strategies for gallery narrative and

Figure 4.5 The entrance to the Mashantucket Pequot Tribal Nation gallery. (Photo by the author)

traffic. At meetings convened to make these decisions the museum collections manager wheeled in a cart filled with archival boxes. At one meeting the boxes were filled with EMT uniforms; emergency medical technicians and firefighters were some of the first Mashantucket community service workers. The collections manager donned clean white cotton gloves, then opened a box to peel back layers of acid-free archival tissue, exposing a uniform beneath, carefully tagged with an acid-free label filled out in pencil. That the cotton-polyester uniform had likely been delivered to the museum trailers fresh from being handled by dry cleaners as recently as the week before made no difference in how it was handled. It had entered the gravitational field of the museum organizational system, shifting from everyday object to exceptional artifact, and it was newly entitled to different care and deference.

All of the artifacts from this gallery enjoyed the same handling, including pizza boxes, T-shirts, restaurant menus, and softball uniforms. This is standard museum practice: the creation of archival storage schemes and detailed record systems, culling objects from everyday (past or present) circulation to incorporate them in the museum's project. Once entered into the system the object is arrested, and the emphases of its life as public object change as its use value goes through radical transformation. It changes currency and, like a photograph or a quotation, is fixed as a representative icon.

Partly, this is a phase in a contextualizing process. The object—in this instance the uniform—is decontextualized or removed from its role as an artifact that functions independently from the museum. The uniform signified many things while it was being worn, including sovereignty, safety, and the capital necessary to support the tribe's specialized emergency medical services. The uniform is then recontextualized, changing its pool of signifiers to those appropriate for a museum setting, significantly, the "national" museum of the Mashantucket Pequots. Abandoning its pragmatic use as a uniform, the object gains symbolic capital and gravitational weight, reflecting its new exhibitionary orbit. As a representative element presented under glass it shifts from the everyday to a position saturated with significance. The uniform now performs a particular period of Mashantucket history and in turn indicates the museum itself as a further measure of that history. The museum serves as a chamber to authenticate the introduction of the uniform as an artifact, and the uniform's presentation counterauthenticates the chamber that presents it. While one of the museum's primary purposes is to perform and explicate its representations, one powerful unspoken narrative is the existence of the theater itself, the grand structure that is the MPMRC.

Museums are time machines and performative spaces; objects entering a museum's signifying field are frozen in time. At the same moment, the museum's master narrative confirms both the backward glance at history and the modernity of its own project, the distancing and explication of history as foundational narrative. The correspondence between the historicity of the objects and the narratives and the modernity and contemporary technological representational strategies being employed is not accidental. One main role of museums is to confirm the respective perspective of visitor and museum subject, the viewer and the viewed. Museums involved with creating counterhistorical narratives take advantage of tension within this space of confirmation while recognizing that the window for changing existing structures of knowledge is limited.

The museum and exhibitions at Mashantucket serve as counterexample to current critical discussions focused on traditional museums as participating in colonial and colonizing power. The Mashantucket museum is one of a growing number of Native museums in the United States created and operated by Native peoples. It straddles the roles of national, anthropological, and natural history museums and strives to be part of the regional community of tourist-centered historic sites by also promoting itself as part of historic and historicized New England.

Big and Small

The Mashantucket visitor experience includes inversions of subject position and of interior and exterior space. Transitions in scale and accompanying shifts in perspective and role influence the experience of the museum's exhibitions. The opening gallery's largest object is a three-dimensional scale model of the entire reservation under plexiglass, surrounded by a waist-high border of small photographs and panel texts (fig. 4.6). Each photo and text corresponds to a particular point on the map. For example, pressing a button near the Public Safety Building text lights up a small structure on the model. An interactive, miniaturized model is a fairly

Figure 4.6 The model of the reservation in the Mashantucket Pequot Tribal Nation Gallery. (Photo by the author)

standard museum device. Moving from text to text, the pushing finger navigates different sites, matching text or photograph with an imagined correspondence in a miniaturized landscape.

The gallery juxtaposes miniaturized reservation with life-size artifacts, creating a sense of the grand from the mundane. And the model reverses the relationship between the visitor and Mashantucket, one that was reinscribed in the Gathering Space as the visitors were under glass, surrounded by the reservation. The confirmation of "life-size," underscored by the arrangement of the exhibitions and their information, returns the visitor to a "normal" relationship with the presented world. Miniatures gain power through the representation and containment of their subjects. While the power relations between museum visitor and miniaturized reservation are metonymic to relations outside its case, they are further complicated at Mashantucket. The role of the museum visitor—overwhelmingly non–Mashantucket Pequot and non-Native—includes witnessing a historical narrative substantially different from and often counter or even antagonistic to standard tropes of New England history. And scale—miniature, life-size, and larger-than-life—plays a critical role in this storytelling effort. The MPMRC moves visitors between these subject positions, at once supporting their distance from and control of their experience and subtly subverting it.

Like the reservation model, the museum also reduces, miniaturizing and rendering a complex cultural and historical narrative within its building and exhibition cases. From the observation tower to the mini-Mashantucket under glass, a complex relationship of scale establishes the visitor as its central, affected point. The museum also uses the reservation exterior, seen through its windows, as an active element in its exhibition narratives. The visitor occupies a shifting location, moving between *now* and *then*, between object and subject. This dislocation plays with the time framed by the museum and the time of the tribal nation's history, its renaissance, and the visitor's afternoon spent in the Connecticut woodlands.

Navigating the Mashantucket Pequot Tribal Nation: Poetics, Politics, Time, and Space

Objects deployed in the gallery extend the tension of the museum's display strategies: tribal police and firefighters' uniforms, mounted trout from the reservation's stocked lake (part of its water-reclamation plan), artifacts from Schemitzun, a Dream Catcher slot machine. Contemporary Pequot (and Indian) ways of being are recognized and re-presented within a place that acknowledges the modernity of the tribal nation while simultaneously raising subtle questions on the processes

116   Chapter 4

Figure 4.7 The Mashantucket Pequot Tribal Nation gallery. (Photo by the author)

of display. Museums invest exhibit objects with a resonance that exceeds their material presence: a museum poetics. Intensified narratives of history and tradition are expected in a museum like the MPMRC. Museums, especially those devoted to history and anthropology, are designed to represent and draw from the past and, through the display of objects and the extension of supporting narratives, to connect them with the present.

Walter Benjamin identifies objects as meaning-laden materialized indices located at axes of history and myth, of reality and consciousness. For Benjamin, material history stresses position and retelling as a state of waking (awareness) or dreaming (subconscious). The difference between the two relies on the recognition of historical flows represented in objects and narratives; objects are material crystallizations of historical dynamics. Presented within spaces that call particular attention to the activity of display, museum objects resonate with their own intensified sense of meaning. As these objects are projected farther back in time this resonance increases, echoing larger as the chamber built around it grows, opening backward to embrace history and the past.

This concept of resonance also works for more contemporary objects. The Dream Catcher slot machine that accompanies the Foxwoods panel text, for example, is a deeply resonant exhibition object (fig. 4.8). In its simplest gloss the machine metonymically indicates Foxwoods. It also illustrates that national gambling machine manufacturers are embracing the lucrative and expanding Indian gaming market. The slot machine as object carries the potential for a number of readings and realizations, not the least of which is the recognition of a relationship between the casino and the museum.

The museum administration was not always comfortable with making this relationship obvious. The connection between the two—one a capital-generating business with a lot of public attention, one a museum project almost completely funded by that capital—was deemphasized in preopening museum publications and interviews. Since its opening efforts have been made to attract visitors from Foxwoods to the museum through materials made available inside the casino or by directing potential visitors from the casino's small museum information center.

The museum would benefit from increased patronage and membership not only to increase its impact as a museum but also to supply an independent funding base for operation. The audience bases for the two enterprises may be too mutually distinct to provide much crossover visitation. Prior to the 1998 opening the museum projected five hundred thousand yearly visitors. Actual yearly visitation numbers for the museum and research center are slightly more than half that.[6] The casino—with an average of over forty thousand visitors per day—gets more visitors in a week than the museum does in a year.[7]

118 Chapter 4

Figure 4.8 The Dream Catcher. (Photo by the author)

The inclusion of a Foxwoods panel and gaming artifact opened a museum-casino connection in the interior public viewing space of the gallery. The exhibition panel text reads as follows:

Foxwoods: The Gaming Enterprise

How does a community provide for itself and its members, and how does it create opportunity for growth? For the Mashantucket Pequot Tribal Nation, the advent of reservation-based gaming in the United States supplied a way to provide for the hopes and dreams of its people, and to build a dynamic community at Mashantucket.

The Indian Gaming Rights Act (IGRA) was signed on October 17, 1988. It allows the operation of specific gaming enterprises on the reservations of federally recognized Indian tribes, and the Act's passage began a new era in tribal industries. For the Mashantucket Pequots, gaming granted a way to generate significant income, income to be used to build housing, a community center, a child development center, and facilities for police, fire, and rescue. Gaming proceeds are also used to provide health and education benefits, and for diversifying business.

The first gaming structure built on the reservation was the high-stakes bingo hall, in 1986. Its success was nothing short of phenomenal, and the proceeds were used for community development as well as to improve and expand the facility. The casino complex—including gaming rooms, restaurants, and shops—has continued to grow over the years. Currently, Foxwoods is a world-famous destination resort and world-class facility that employs over 12,000 people.

The placement of the Dream Catcher acknowledges the museum-casino link (even if the panel text is devoted to discussing community development and employment over profits), though no mention of the museum is made. The slot machine and text also acknowledge the national and now normalized scope of Indian gaming. The economic power and large clientele of Indian gaming in the United States is indicated by the machine's popularized "Indian" motif.

The slot machine is a concretized intersection of the axes of history and myth materialized in object details, and it provides complex nuance to ideas of display and exhibition. The narratives supporting its viewing are open: the machine enters into an intensified space and is, in effect, released. The meaning-making experience that such an object generates is not under the control of its exhibition, supporting literature, or display environment. The object contains the potential for its own rereading, for the generation of its own Benjaminian "shock of recognition," which actualizes its display and carries the potential to shift it outside the confines of its own representational discourse. That this object, like the EMT uniform, could be found in day-to-day use at Mashantucket also contributes to an active intersection of knowledge production as the visitor brings another set of information to the object's recognition(s).

Museum narratives are displayed through and alongside material artifacts. The construction of an authoritative oppositional or dominant narrative and the recognition of the gaps inherent in any representational project highlight one area for dynamic slippage: an opening of interstitial interpretive spaces between the volume of galleries, the shape of their objects, and the telling of their stories. Museums are potentially dangerous and open spaces; in exhibiting and curating they open a traffic in knowledge construction that potentially exceeds the limits of exhibition.

Museum poetics parallel the poetic function of language and image, which exceeds formal boundaries to create meaning through escaping structure. The museum at Mashantucket participates in many discourses, including ethnic identity, natural belonging, nationality, cultural continuity, colonial and current histories of Indian and Euro-American relations, and none of them are exclusive. These narratives suggest others, blending elements dependent on readings and actualizations of the museum's texts. Museums like the Mashantucket Pequots' carry the additional weight of their underlying narratives' historicity. It is constructed in part to contextualize the Mashantucket Pequots within New England and Connecticut history, to naturalize a connection to the land, and to firmly place the Pequots within national discourses of Indians and Indianness. These discourses necessarily draw on feelings of nostalgia through re-creations of the past and presentations of historic artifacts. The display of potentially nostalgic objects marks the past as a site for longing and museums as sites for the performance of such longing. Museums are generators and theaters of nostalgic desire.

The museum and the casino use a poetics of location, "the land," in the museum's narratives. Its use, ownership, and access are material configurings of this poetics. This material tie to Mashantucket is narrativized and supported through the museum's texts and in the ownership and location of the MPMRC and Foxwoods. It is a performance of meaning carried out through formal relationships orbiting the central issue of land, uniting the stories of the museum with those carried on in the practice of everyday life. In one sense, landownership enters as a defensive positioning, an expressive form where relationships and politics are negotiated, enacted, and contested. This position parallels reservation landownership, issues of extrareservation annexation, and the formation of new corporations—the Mashantucket Pequots are currently extending their economic and land base through property purchases and the acquisition or creation of other industries. Different enactments for intensified representations and narratives are located here, as is a poetics speaking through form realized as space: as casino, as museum, as archaeological site, and, deeper in the exhibition halls, as walk-through diorama.

Certain relationships or intersections emphasizing history, ownership, identity, tradition, nature, and independence are located in these spaces. Imagining the displays and exhibitions of the museum as actualized intersections where objects and sites can be read through different axes provides another parallel process. The buildings themselves become as much intensified sites for teasing out different potential readings as the exhibition objects do.

Roman Jakobson (1960) describes poetics as a production of meaning differentiated from the referential through form and style. In a representational system it is what is at play—through performance, intonation, and cadence—in creating the nuances of meaning while relying on its formal referential properties. In other words, poetics signals a shift that carries communicative performance beyond referential signification. Gaston Bachelard (1969) takes poetics a step further to define poetic language as an "emergence from language," as something that *exceeds* the language of signification. Following Bachelard, poetics, or the escape or formation of meaning depends on exceeding or overspilling referential structure.

122   Chapter 4

The end result is uncontrollable. The museum works through offering narrativized objects and passages through controlled space to present a series of impressions focusing on the continuity and ingenuity of the Mashantucket Pequots as a peopled identity, portrayed as continuous, powerful, and adaptive in its ability to overcome hardship and challenge. Identity explored through the museum displays is relational, necessarily located in the tension generated by the structure, not mapped by it. The poetics of the museum reaches through its structure—its galleries, exhibitions, and photographs. It generates meaning by using the narratives and exhibitions to create an experiential force. This is partly structure dependent and dialogic, where meaning is made in the spaces between speaking voices, between the museum's different spheres of representation. The museum's display strategy cannot be limited to either its collection of objects or the plots of its directed narratives. The museum itself enters into this exchange as an intensifying structure, a space that confers specific weight to the dialogues and representations active under its roof.

The MPMRC recognizes and activates some of this exchange and tension in the design of the panel texts that accompany different exhibitions. The overall exhibition scheme employs a "how-do-we-know-this" thread of inquiry made plain, allowing for a critical engagement with the museum's elements. Such panel texts combine examples of archaeological and historical research and the use of Mashantucket Pequot and parallel ethnographic data with narratives of how some display objects were created from descriptions found in primary texts.

The museum opens more relational perspectives than it closes by juxtaposing gallery design with exhibit design. This strategy—to leave connective narrative open—allows the museum to assemble displays that actively overlap elements of voice and image while engaging ideas of historical significance. By picturing tribal business and community enterprises, the opening gallery offers a glimpse into the workings of the Mashantucket Reservation. The glimpse expands the visitor's first notice of the Grand Pequot Tower or MPMRC observation tower from the road as monumental, with a decentering of static or traditional images of Indian tribal members, and transitions the depiction of such Indians from an imagined past into a contemporary moment.

One of the more disjunctive uses of scale and visitor perspective can be found at the end of the exhibit The Mashantucket Pequot Tribal Nation. Here an escalator descends through a simulated glacial crevasse, complete with dripping glacial water, the sounds of ice creaking, and an accompanying drop in ambient temperature, to arrive at level 1's first gallery, A World of Ice (fig. 4.9).

Turning into the gallery, a visitor is confronted by a large model of the earth enclosed by a circular railing. Mapped on this globe are the continents, studded with lights representing masses of retreating glacial ice. The globe is mounted in a depression in the floor so that the visitor's eye easily scans the Northern Hemisphere and the Arctic Circle. Here the world is made small, offered for the visitor's comprehensive grasp. The shrunken earth grants a particular visitor perspective while it cements a certain narrative of the passage of time and history. It also naturalizes a connection to the land through glacial histories and agrarian communities.

The gallery walls have large photographs of contemporary glaciers and different examples of postglacial terrain, most of which are labeled as being taken at the reservation. One display shows the thickness of the glacial ice in Connecticut during the Ice Age. A large slab of "ice," its rough edges to the gallery, offers an illustration: tucked into the "glacier's" base to provide scale is a miniature model of the MPMRC.

The glacial descent marks a dramatic break from the contemporary referential qualities of the first gallery—here time is accentuated and removed, embraced and defied. Its passage is accentuated by this shift backward into an active past. What lies outside the museum is erased through fantastic descent, ready to be re-presented and recontextualized within a series of intersecting displays and models.

Playing with effects of time and space, narratives of natural and social connections to the land and the historical processes, the museum is a resonant and

Figure 4.9
The escalator into the glacial crevasse. (Photo by the author)

intensified space of experience. The glacier gallery's entrance breaks the imagined continuity of a present tense. This thread develops through the museum, placing the Pequots and their ancestors firmly *here* in Mashantucket, the location self-consciously occupied by the museum. Successive displays and narratives center on processes of contact, conflict, subjugation, and final occupation. The basis for this history has been subtly shifted through A World of Ice. By beginning history with the end of the Ice Age, European colonists and later Euro-Americans are firmly placed outside of the narrative of continuity, for later introduction. The glacier room appropriates the dominant anthropological narrative of the Paleolithic and incorporates it into Pequot foundational history.

As a possible balance to the Ice Age the next gallery, Arrival of the People, features a selection of commissioned Native art illustrating different creation stories. It successfully appropriates the form of an art museum by displaying commissioned art and that of an ethnohistorical museum and by placing these objects and their alternative histories following an Ice Age narrative. The different origin stories for the precontact population of North America offer different ways of reckoning the past, ways of knowing that are outside traditional Western epistemologies yet are, as Alice Nash asserts, "more sophisticated than mere wishful thinking" (2001:2).

The museum design juxtaposes the fantastic with its location as a site for colonial and Native history. By maintaining a tension between the fantastic and the materially grounded, the museum's opening exhibitions blur their division. In opening the building outward to include the reservation surround, the museum's master narrative extends an inclusion to the exterior and opens the question of inclusion itself, indicating the reservation with its casino complex and community services. This is reindicated by its use of photographs with tribal members and the reservation as subjects.

Through such devices the museum maintains a dynamic space between its representations and the reservation, between its exhibitions, the embracing landscape, and nearby archaeological digs. Exhibition objects and displays overlap, allowing for cracks and fissures in the museum experience by referring to both its production of meaning and its location. The museum is a methodical device asserting history and identity to work their narratives through the museum's *form*. Mashantucket economic development contributes potent supporting narratives for the museum and casino experiences, and the museum's reservation location fits into the fundamental identity narrative of the MPMRC.

Structures of meaning both hold arranged objects and impart the significance of their collection. Such arrangements depend on intertextual understandings: experience, memories, and informed perspectives. Communication cannot be contained within the form of the communicative act, just as the museum's import cannot be contained within its structure. The museum figures into the reservation landscape, embedded in industry and community, straddling a space between information presented as educational resource and information presented as spectacle.

The museum and research center is but one permeable allegory container holding narratives of history, identity, and location that run through all the structures of the reservation. Each structural node can be realized as its own enterprise for telling stories and conveying meaning. Due to the perceived traditional role of museums, they carry different weight: more than containers for poetic and allegorical exhibitions, they are also poetic generators. Equally important is the collection of objects within the container and the shape and weight of the container itself.

Museums are theatrical spaces, signifiers that transform what they present. Here the poetics of a museum describes how it presents, transforms, and imprints the objects of its exhibition. But the museum is also a poetics, a narrative shift, a tactical intensifying space, a structure of meaning with its own potential for excess and escape. The politics of such a structure are exercised through the shifts and decentering strategies of its display spaces and narratives and through the ownership of the means of display, of the intensified narrative production itself.

The poetics of the museum can be imagined as the way it transforms "things" and its emphasis on dialogic, open-ended displays. Poetics is an anticipated element of performative strategy, an exercise of technique and skill self-consciously rendered, that leaves an open-ended structure in which the viewer lives experience and makes meaning. The dialogues of the museum—text, artifact, exhibition design, architecture, and location—can be imagined as a collection of monologues, directed outward, seeking to engage a listener, a participant.

But this participation takes place within a particular space. In imagining the MPMRC as form, the museum becomes a resonant space of allegorical meaning.

In imagining the museum as a poetics, it becomes the intensifying chamber that necessarily transforms its subjects through the exhibition, an echo chamber of representations heightened by clear thematic distinctions between display and observance, between the visiting subject and the visited object. To imagine the museum and research center as a politics includes both the ownership and the shape of its representative spaces, objects, and discourses in an appreciation of the structure and its import.

The MPMRC, as tourist destination, plays an important role in what Barbara Kirshenblatt-Gimblett (1998) calls a "production of heritage" project, with the reservation its focal point. Like the invention of tradition, the production of heritage understands tradition as a dynamic force configured and used in the present. Heritage is a located industry, a conceptual shift, and a commodity participating in a particular sphere of tourist commerce, with an emphasis placed on *location* and *experience*.

The challenges facing the MPMRC are multiple and deeply enmeshed. It is the national museum for the Mashantucket Pequot Tribal Nation, and it is a site in the same network as Foxwoods and other destination attractions in Connecticut. As the Mashantucket Pequots' museum it has what Kirshenblatt-Gimblett calls "a responsibility that has repercussions beyond the journey within its walls" (1998:139): to actively imagine and define the Mashantucket Pequot Tribal Nation. This is especially true as the museum increasingly becomes a tourist destination, like Foxwoods, where the visitor experiences shifts between the surround of the museum and the museum's display environments.

The MPMRC and the "Department of the Interior"

Imagining the museum is not only a theoretical exercise. Display pragmatics exert their own influences on representational practice. Working in the trailer offices of the MPMRC project, I overheard a conversation between two staff members concerning how to maintain the museum's future walk-through and life-size Pequot Village exhibition. One was describing a conversation he'd had that morning with a colleague at another museum where small-scale open dioramas had been part of its exhibitions in the 1970s. That museum had finally gone to completely sealed dioramas; the maintenance made necessary by the open dioramas was too demanding. Cleaning wasn't an option; the horizontal surfaces were the only ones that could be vacuumed, and cleaning crews used low-pressure air hoses to blow the dust off instead.

The museum staff members were discussing maintenance in terms of the approved budget for the upcoming fiscal year; specialized exhibit maintenance costs had been written out of the most recent council-approved MPMRC operating budget.[8] It had been suggested that the Foxwoods custodial services (whose carts are emblazoned "Department of the Interior") would be in charge of keeping the museum and the walk-through village clean. (Here the staff members exchanged horrified ideas about spray cleaning fluids and buckets with mops, not to mention the "souvenirs" that might walk out of the building.) The above conversation followed another about different methods for making the village wigwams pest-free. The wigwams had been constructed over the summer and were standing in a field next to the parking lot to weather before winter. The staff members discussed the comparative merits of fumigation and isolation or disassembly, freezing, and reassembly.

Museums in general, and anthropology and natural history museums in particular, navigate an often-contradictory path concerning the inclusion of "the real" in exhibitions. The Pequot Village includes real bark and cedar wigwams and real pieces of material culture, either ancient or recently made. Nevertheless, the exhibition must be made impervious to other "real" processes of contamination—infestation, exhibition degradation by foot traffic, and potential pilfering. The "contradictory path" moves between creating the suspension of disbelief necessary for visitor experience and controlling the elements of the display for a variety of reasons, including longevity of the materials and the experience that the materials support. The exhibition is staked against the threats of nature (insects), culture (pilfering), and nature and culture combined (the wear and tear of visitors' visits).

The use of dioramas—a once time-honored museum strategy for representing the "other" and the strange—especially intensifies issues raised here (fig. 4.10). Dioramas are a problematic and objectifying representational practice using mute and suspended tableaus—wherein the "other" stands or sits, or skins an animal, or makes a fire—to stand as emblematic for an entire people. Historically, maintenance and security dictated that such museum dioramas be sealed, usually behind glass, and scaled small.

Arrival of the People

The Pequot Village is one of the museum's highlights. Located at the museum's halfway point, it follows a set of dioramas depicting different Pequot seasonal activities and precedes an exhibition on the wide-scale death of Natives from European-introduced pathogens.

The approach to the village really begins at the bottom of the glacial crevasse escalator. A long journey, it pulls the visitor along a chain of changing time and circumstances, from A World of Ice, past Arrival of the People, to Life in a Cold Climate. This gallery features a walk-around caribou hunt diorama and first introduces the museum's full-scale human figures, dressed in furs and frozen in different tasks of the hunt. The touch-screen interactive stations that circle the diorama introduce the museum's depth of technological expertise and commitment to telling its stories.

The figures become more prominent in the galleries and soon become the focal points of almost every vitrine or open display. Studio EIS, a New York–based company, is responsible for the highly detailed "life-cast" figures, 111 of which were created for the MPMRC by casting tribal members and other Native Ameri-

Figure 4.10 A scene from the Pequot Village. (Photo by the author)

cans in a remarkably "lifelike" material. The final results were often compound, combining body elements from different models to construct a single figure. The life-cast figures in the gallery depicting Pequot lifeways prior to 1637 were made from castings of other Native Americans and support a particular popular sense of the "Indian" phenotype (fig. 4.13). Those in the galleries focusing on the later periods were made using tribal members (Nash 2001:4).

The figures from Life in a Cold Climate introduce the visitor to the magnitude of the exhibition's overall project, while their increasing presence in the galleries' journey through time settles them into the museum's overall narrative.

Figure 4.11 A detail from the caribou hunt diorama. (Photo by the author)

Vignette 2: Life in the Pequot Village

The entrance to the Pequot Village comes as a shift in materials and light. The entry vestibule is finished in dark wood, and a docent's counter sits in front of racks of "Acoustiguides": devices with neck straps that look like a cross between a remote control and a portable telephone.

    The village is in a cavernous room. The high ceiling and supporting crossbeams almost disappear under flat black paint. Small pools of light are cast on different areas of the village. A small "river" runs through it to finish in an estu-

Figure 4.12 A caribou hunter. (Photo by the author)

ary, and the footpath bridges the water. A broadly lit cornfield runs up one side of the gallery near the entrance (fig. 4.14), and a number of domestic structures are presented along the multiple walkways. Many of the bark-covered buildings have openings in their sides, revealing their interiors, made plain for viewing and filled with material detail.

At different points the paths are marked with numbers. The visitor, staking a place near or on a walkway number, keys that number into the Acoustiguide, and a recorded voice unloops a story about what the visitor sees (e.g., a family cooking and eating). Prompts imbedded in the narrative lead the visitor into a deeper and deeper accretion of data. "To go behind the scenes with an expert to learn more

Figure 4.13 Life-cast figures from the four seasons dioramas near the entrance to the village. (Photo by the author)

about hairstyles, press 25+1. To learn about hunting turkey then and now, press 25+2." Following these prompts leads the visitor into deeper levels of subnarratives and contextualizations, assuring that each visitor's experience can be a completely unique navigation of what the gallery offers.

The village is peopled by life-cast Indians forever fixed in midgesture and visitors wandering the pathways with handsets like bulky cellular phones pressed to their ears. It is almost silent except for the shuffle of feet, perhaps some murmuring back and forth as people point out items of interest to their partners, their children, their fellow visitors. In part the village offers an opportunity to "play Indian," to

134   Chapter 4

Figure 4.14 Figures harvesting in the cornfield. (Photo by the author)

inhabit the village and share the same perspective as a village "dweller." The kind of looking that is called for in the village, shifting attention that depends on changes in points of view, is a key characteristic of display environments, spaces that are "simultaneously objects of looking *and* apparatuses of looking" (Dorst 1999:132). The village is open to observation in the same moment that it shapes and directs the observing experience.

Background recordings, which include birdsong and the occasional murmur of Native language (Passamaquoddy, since the Pequot language is no longer known), help to establish the overall aural texture of the village. These noises, partly influ-

Figure 4.15 A scene from the Pequot Village. (Photo by the author)

enced by each visitor's passage through the village, subtly shape visitor experience by producing a unique set or progression of sounds for each walk-through event. As one of the sound designers for the Pequot Village puts it, the museum visitors were imagined as "musicians who played their own music as they moved through the exhibit" (Quin 1999:95).

Tourism and museums intersect in the construction of "heritage," and the museum destination is a site for experiential learning or exposure. Kirshenblatt-Gimblett's concept of *thematization*—the "perfection of [a] restoration as a remedy for the imperfections of history" (1998:8)—offers a way to come to grips with the Pequot Village. It thematizes a precontact living environment, presenting a seam-

Figure 4.16 A cut-away wigwam with a visitor. (Photo by the author)

less walk-through experience of history. Visitor distance is maintained through the use of the Acoustiguides, and the strange disjuncture of fellow visitors navigating the frozen tableau is partially homogenized through the shared practice of using the guides. Each visitor becomes an assertive knowledge consumer, and the tableaus are ingested as the means to constructing knowledge rather than as solely transitional spaces. The walk-through dioramas also effectively and self-consciously authenticate the museum as a museum through anticipated, traditional, and progressive display technologies.

Kirshenblatt-Gimblett states that "exhibitions are fundamentally theatrical, for they are how museums perform the knowledge they create" (1998:138). Two

Figure 4.17 Figures working on the postcontact village palisade. (Photo by the author)

138   Chapter 4

fundamental museum display strategies make up this performance: in-situ displays (re-creations of settings) and in-context displays (displays arranged to meet other conceptual frames of reference). In-situ displays are immersive and environmental, while in-context displays depend on the drama of the artifact. In the MPMRC these two strategies combine throughout the building and its exhibitions, pulling the visitor through immersive sites like the village or indicating the reservation itself, through the museum windows, as a kind of ultimate dramatic artifact.

In performing the knowledge it creates the museum works at the intersection of popular conceptions of Indianness and museum practice. It depends on existing discourses of Indians and exhibition to provide points of contact, recognition, and interaction for its visitors, discourses that parallel popular cultural experiences outside of the reservation, including popular media, theater, and other museums. The overall exhibit design works within what Arjun Appadurai and Carol Breckenridge (1992) call an "interocular field," both within the space of the galleries—moving focus from images to figures, interior to exterior—and in the larger space that embraces experiences outside of the museum (e.g., by an exhibition presenting modern correlatives to ancient tools).

The negotiated nature of viewer experiences in the MPMRC resonates with Bakhtinian notions of the dialogic nature of consciousness and the idea that "reading" museum displays and objects is profoundly intertextual.[9] The audience experience in a museum setting is contaminated by its immediate surroundings—the density of displays and information—as well as by its experiences in the world outside. Museums are social spaces for individuals with differing cultural and personal experiences, places where ideology mixes with matter and sensory experience, not detached venues for quiet contemplation and cogitation. The Mashantucket Pequot museum embodies an evocative nexus between negotiated social interaction and quiet contemplation—in Stephen Greenblatt's (1992) terms, between resonance and wonder. Resonance describes the ability of a museum object or narrative to extend beyond itself into other displays in the museum and beyond, into the world outside. Wonder is kin to Benjamin's concept of contemplation coupled with an arrest, a shock of recognition or awe that stops one in one's tracks (see Buck-Morss 1991; Appadurai 1986; Barthes 1981; Kopytoff 1986).

"Resonance" gains meaning as a function or definition of an object in *context*. Resonance parallels contextualization, where echo's shape is contained within its building. Contextualization is also a form of interpretation, one able to provide answers to questions of provenance, positioned narratives and histories, and the reappropriation of objects or cultural lifeways (performance). Like provenance or panel text, contextualization can be without a clear finishing point. It is but one part of the process, one methodology among others, and it is precisely this being among others that gives it much of its force.

The idea of resonance speaks to the surrounding museum while indicating the need to locate it within other multiple and interrelated structures. This expansion is an integral part of a dialogic framework that keeps these interrelating tensions open and productive. While "resonance" may seem to advocate a kind of "thick" contextualization, it also carries the potential for further or extended understanding, dislocating the end point to a series of unlimited, echoing shocks.

The MPMRC is a signifying space that extends imagined, interconnected registers to play with the museum's formal constraints in a different kind of resonance. It strategically plays with the museum's *formal* properties to "signify on" other museums and itself as a means to create or enhance its message (Gates 1992). Display elements, exhibition designs, and narratives continually fold back on themselves, creating multiple unfixed opportunities for engaging with the density of the exhibitions. Dialogic engagement with the museum avoids presenting a closed or seamless narrative; much of the exhibition design at the MPMRC relies on nods of recognition shared with theme parks, art and natural history museums, dioramas, and mimetic architectural forms.

Museum practices (collection, interpretation, and exhibition), like those of anthropology, have increasingly been the subject of critical analysis, especially for their implications as parts of a colonial project. Alternative museums, Native museums among them, have also gained critical attention (see, e.g., Kreps 2003; Erikson 2002; Weschler 1995; Kirshenblatt-Gimblett 1998; Ames 1992; Karp 1991; Clifford 1991; Houlihan 1991; Stocking 1985).

The process of colonization imposes a previously unfamiliar set of controls on resources, populations, and everyday understandings of time and place. As Johannes Fabian asks: "What would happen to the West if its temporal fortress were suddenly invaded by the Time of its Other?" (1983:35). This question understands museums either as representative formal spaces that owe their organization to a Western sense of time and objects made significant or as fluid and adaptive forms able to reflect different temporal and narrative configurations. James Clifford (1987, 1997) has extensively explored this topic in the differences and definitions between traditional and contemporary, Indian and non-Indian art. He suggests that Native museums depend on a "concrete, nonlinear sense of history—forms of memory and invention, re-collection and emergence, that offer a different temporality for art- and culture-collecting" (Clifford 1987:126). Here is a reassertion of the old within the new and its reversal, an upsetting of linear time with the transposition of another reckoning, another way of authenticating, of figuring and calculating time's passage or its celebration, use, and regard. An activity intimately tied to control, ownership, and object display, "authenticity is reconceived as hybrid, creative activity in a local present-becoming-future" (Clifford 1987:126).

Using any museum as a site for analysis requires a critical stance that takes into account the shape such reconfigurations take and what they support or confound. At the Mashantucket Pequot museum appropriated technologies and knowledges, including museum design and curatorship, anthropology, and archaeology, are a critical part of this reconfiguring strategy. The Pequot Village, realized as a walk-through museum exhibition complete with recorded birdsong and personal audio guides, is a riveting illustration of how these technologies and knowledges are put to work in creating an immersive and engaging site for public consumption.

"Discover a Nation"   141

This reconfiguration relies on the strategic deployment of significant objects, one that depends on nostalgia and desire as powerful motivating factors for interacting with and making sense of saturated representations. The exhibition design at the MPMRC provides a striking example of how these factors are depended on in an imagined visitor's desire for participation or experience. Susan Stewart suggests that "as experience is increasingly mediated and abstracted, the lived relation of the body to the phenomenological world is replaced by a nostalgic myth of contact and presence" (1993:132). The imagined "precontact" state of the village serves as a point of immersive contact for the visitor; while they are mediated by audio guides and signposts, village pathways map the liminal space between contact and imagination, between the ideological and the experiential. Nostalgia as a seductive force attempts to bridge that space.

There are places where such bridging is frustrated, where no amount of nostalgic desire can link the ideological and the experiential, the hoped for and the possible. The Pequot Society gallery is adjacent to the Pequot Village. It explores aspects of Pequot daily social and political life contemporaneous with the village exhibition. In addition to ethnographic materials from the museum's collection, the gallery features a number of videos of different Native artisans making many of the exhibition artifacts on view in the village. At one end of the gallery is an interactive computer station showcasing Algonquian languages, including Micmac, Passamaquoddy, and Ojibwa. A video of a storyteller is combined with text from the story being told. Selecting words from the text on the screen allows the visitor to hear their pronunciation and see the word or word phrase defined in English. Original plans for the station included Pequot as one of the languages.

On the museum's opening day I visited the gallery. As I sat at the station I read the screen menu of languages available for an interactive story. The bottom button, in that ghosted on-screen representation that signifies "unavailable," was an option for Pequot with the notation "coming soon." Unfortunately, the language is no longer spoken, and there is no written record. Later menu offerings in the gallery (seen

142   Chapter 4

on return visits) did not include Pequot as a future possibility. The panel text includes the following statement: "Unfortunately, as Europeans and their languages spread across this continent, many Native languages, including Pequot, faded from use. Today the Mashantucket Pequots regret the loss of their language and would like to see it become part of the community once again." The hopeful inclusion of Pequot as one of the gallery's languages illustrates an uncomfortable moment where nostalgia, desire, and exhibition practice collide; it contains the assertion that the language somehow exists but has not yet been rediscovered or remembered. During my fieldwork there were conflicting reports about the Pequot language and how it might be used in the tribe's Child Development Center. At first the center was going to use a Pequot speaker as part of its curriculum. This plan was later modified to state that a Pequot vocabulary was going to be used as a learning resource. Finally, it was suggested that the center would teach a related Algonquian language, with the recognition that the Pequot language was irretrievably gone.

Nostalgia is put to work to create or bolster narratives of tradition, authenticity, and cultural heritage that may also be linked to significant objects. The multiple projects at Mashantucket harness and direct nostalgic practice, but, as Kathleen Stewart suggests, nostalgia is not a dis-located force: the experience of "nostalgia depends on where the speaker stands in the landscape of the present" (1988:227). As a positioned and positioning strategy, a way to consider powerful feelings invoked by the pasts of objects and stories, it is not a complete answer for how they work. It is a way to understand process not product.

Contexts for interaction with objects—their localized setting and the narratives of use, ownership, and placement that intersect through them—is also key. The MPMRC's location and its active blending of indoors and outdoors reinforces a sense of the "local" through strategic design and placement. James Clifford explored the role of the local in four museums in Canada displaying Indian art and artifact to make distinctions between "dominant" and "Native" institutions. According to Clifford, two exhibited an "aspiration to majority status and aim[ed] at a cosmopolitan audience," and two were better understood as "tribal institutions, aiming at local audiences and enmeshed in local meanings, histories, and traditions" (1997:121).[10] The MPMRC attempts to bridge these two positions—the local and the cosmopolitan—in its scope, its size, and the abundance of its resources. As Clifford also notes, "the local" and "the majority" are terms that may give a false sense of cohesion or uniformity to deeply contested categories. Any consideration of the "local" at Mashantucket must also include neighbors who primarily see themselves as New Englanders and who see Mashantucket Pequot claims to a legitimate cultural identity as highly suspect. The "majority" must also reflect a reckoning of a pan-Indian identity as well as the curious role of the Native American in U.S. history, as a tragically erased opponent and as an integral figure in the imagination of an "American" history (an incorporation of the "other" as both mythic ancestor and sign of degradation) (see Herzfeld 1987; Strong and Van Winkle 1996). Neither a national (majority) museum in Clifford's terms nor precisely a local one, the MPMRC straddles a gap between the categories. The scale of its enterprise pushes it beyond the idea of a local museum, while its location away from urban and federal centers may limit its realization as a (U.S.) national museum. Like the visitor's scale in the trajectory of the museum's exhibitions, the Mashantucket Pequots' project of representing local and national history is imbricated in other local and national projects focused on the past. Navigating through the museum, the visitor comes "face-to-face" with its subject from different and deeply resonant subject positions, including miniaturized, life-size, and larger-than-life.

Life on the Reservation

Distances maintained between the visitor and the life-cast figures in the walk-through Pequot Village exhibition are beguiling. Brochures for the museum talk about "experiencing" a sixteenth-century Pequot village, but the visitor experiences this village much as he or she experiences the reservation surrounding the

144   Chapter 4

museum, at one remove. While the reservation inhabitants are animate, they are invisible; while the village inhabitants are visible, they are inanimate. There is a sense of disjunctive schism, of overlapping intersections of different contemporaneous time periods between the "now" of the village and the other museum exhibitions, the population of museumgoers, and the reservation. The latter is perhaps best understood as an exclusive gated community: beautiful, wooded, and located conveniently near its main source of employment and income.

Part of the museum's project is the reintegration of stories of the past with trajectories of histories perhaps more familiar to its visitors. The Pequot Village offers a narrative of a precontact past, a history before written document or European witness. Later galleries on this floor—Arrival of the Europeans and Death by Disease—explore some of the ramifications of European contact for Native peoples. These galleries are followed by two theaters offering *The Witness*, a short film that dramatizes the events surrounding the Pequot War and the Pequot people's near annihilation. The film echoes fundamental narratives in earlier galleries and in the casino by closing with the linked statements "You must keep the story. You must keep the land."

The journey to the next floor's main gallery brings the visitor into closer contact with more familiar histories (e.g., of the Civil War and New England whaling) and restructures them to include Pequots and their descendents (fig. 4.18). Titled Life on the Reservation, this gallery is peopled with more life-cast figures and tells a history of the Mashantucket Pequot Reservation.

This exhibit hall has one long and curving wall of glass looking onto the reservation's woodlands and Great Cedar Swamp. Life on the Reservation focuses on Pequot history from the beginning of the Mashantucket Reservation to the present day. The gallery is organized in a series of vignettes featuring one or more life-cast figures. The first is of Robin Cassacinamon, the seventeenth-century sachem who first led the Pequots at Mashantucket. Other figures include William Apes, a Pequot Christian minister; Hannah Ocuish, an indentured child servant; Austin George, a Union soldier; and Peter George, a whaler (fig. 4.19).

"Discover a Nation" 145

Figure 4.18 The Pequot Austin George, a Union soldier in the Civil War. (Photo by the author)

A freestanding meetinghouse stands in the gallery; a recording simulating eighteenth-century Mohegan preacher Samson Occum delivering a sermon plays inside. Part of a re-created eighteenth-century farmstead stands nearby. The figures in this gallery present a collection of individual biographical vignettes to tell a different and particularized U.S. history, one that emphasizes Pequot contributions and the different adaptations they made to accommodate a changing world.

Unlike the village, the vignettes offer unique and metonymic tableaus that represent different eras in Pequot history. Rather than an aggregate and immersive experience, this gallery reintroduces the contemplative distance between exhibi-

146   Chapter 4

Figure 4.19 The Pequot Peter George, a whaler, rendering blubber. (Photo by the author)

tion "object" and museum visitor. The traffic pattern is open, allowing for shifting points of perspective.

The exhibition is arranged chronologically, and each figure is part of a scene that tells a corresponding life story. Cassacinamon is part of an exhibition on the beginning of reservation life, the farmstead is part of the story of adaptation and persistence during the eighteenth century, and Apes is part of a narrative of intolerance and changing times during the nineteenth century. The nineteenth and twentieth centuries were marked by Pequots leaving Mashantucket to look for work

Figure 4.20 The Mashpee Meetinghouse. (Photo and photomural by the author)

and to leave behind the difficulties of life on the reservation. Unemployment, meager resources, weak infrastructure, and poor housing made life on the reservation increasingly difficult.

Vignette 3: Through the Looking Glass

The farmstead vignette is part of an exhibition narrative exploring Pequot adoption of Euro-American housing and farming technologies. It begins with a small

Figure 4.21 The farmstead in the gallery. (Photo by the author)

wooden structure that, at first look, appears to be backed against the gallery's glass wall. A second look reveals that the farmhouse bisects the wall of the museum, with the majority of it on the outside of the main building. A simple wooden doorway, accessible from the gallery, provides a way in.

This display is modeled on the history of the Sunsimons, an eighteenth-century Mashantucket family. Inside the one-room house an older female figure is busy with a domestic task and a young girl plays in a loft. The grounds of the museum are visible through the building's small window, and a wooden framed door is in an adjoining wall. Opening it, the visitor can step out of the museum and onto a path that leads through cultivated fields contained by a low dry-stone wall; beyond this is the reservation. The setting is pristine: behind, the gleaming structure of the museum, ahead, tall trees that meet the sky. What is missing in this vista is the enormous Grand Pequot Tower. It hovers, an absent presence just beyond the trees.

On the approach to the museum the casino's tower is more than evident. It looms insistent, supported by satellite parking lots and an ever-present fleet of brightly marked shuttle and tour buses on the highways. The tower is seen one last time from the Gathering Space before the descent into the Pequots' historical narrative. While the reservation presses up against the glass walls and windows of the exhibition halls, the tower disappears.

The farmstead presents a wonderful instant of disjuncture, a powerful moment in one of the Mashantucket Pequot museum's major narrative projects (fig. 4.22). The windows, atriums, and transparent walls indicate the museum's present site, while its interior explores a history of place, actively crossing between past and present. The farmhouse door opens onto an "actual" exterior, rendered historically complete with planted fields and boundaries. The door to the outside represents a strategic shift in framing the visitor's experience. One moves from the gallery, where the farmlands are seen as part of an exhibition-supporting landscape, to finding access to these same fields. Entering the fields, one becomes part of an animate, life-size cast in a diorama turned inside out. The shift also contains a sideways glance, a simulacral moment when the inside opens to the outside to close a circle of experience with the seal of the authentic.

In the museum's precontact village the classic form of the diorama was played with to produce one both full size and walk through, where the visitor experiences an eerie tour as one of a number of figures maneuvering through a community frozen in midgesture. The farmstead also blurs the line between visitor and participant, and the glass of the museum wall becomes its own kind of display frame, encasing visitors as they move through a landscape made historic. Navigating the fields of the farmstead, the visitor becomes the exterior vignette's animation.

The arrested landscape combines with the voyeuristic gaze of the museum visi-

Figure 4.22 An exterior view of the farmstead. (Photo by the author)

tor onto the revealed landscape, both the seemingly controlled farmstead fields and the seemingly uncontrolled surround. The farmstead mediates between inside and outside, contemporary and historic—a disjunctive space between the confirming now of the exterior and an exterior historicized through an exhibition that seeps between the containment of the building and the containment of the reservation. This shift, from inside to outside and back, affects the visitor's processes of contextualization at Mashantucket. As part of the museum's function, display elements and interior spaces are decontextualized through research and presentation, then recontextualized, both within a museum setting and within the embrace of the reservation.

Through the walls of the Mashantucket Pequot museum the reservation is a site for referential processes created or enacted by the visitors. The reservation itself (tribal members' homes, community buildings, and the majority of the land) is not accessible to the general public. This is not to argue that it should be but to state that "the reservation" holds a particularly removed yet compromised relationship with the industries that include it in their referents. These industries are in Mashantucket; the experience of the reservation and of the Mashantucket Pequots by "the outside" is necessarily filtered through the registers of Foxwoods and the museum and research center. Both have multiple stories to tell, and both do so from particular and treasured spaces. Clearly, there is no way to appreciate the MPMRC and Foxwoods without thinking of what they represent to the tribal nation. Nor could they exist without the reservation's physical presence and confines, itself the focal point for the Mashantucket Pequots' land claim and recognition. Engines of tremendous material and cultural capital humming beneath the landscape, the two structures annually cycle through an enormous visiting public.

Looking back, the vision of the museum from the farmstead decenters a truly seamless narrative, but the shift opens a complex and active disjuncture between the museum's historicity and its contemporary reservation site. The farmstead also continues the overall narrative of the exhibit Life on the Reservation. By presenting figures from Mashantucket Pequot history engaged in activities and occupations not usually in the public imaginary concerning things Pequot or things Indian, the exhibition serves as another site for subtle oppositional tactics aimed at unsettling hegemonic notions of Indianness.

Life on the Reservation also leaves at least one key issue untouched: race. Although racial essentialism is one of the means by which Mashantucket Pequot "Indianness" is challenged in the public arena, the museum does not overtly engage the issue of Mashantucket Pequot racial heritage or problematize discourses that link racial phenotype to cultural identity or authenticity. Some of this may be due to interfamily political battles at the administrative and council levels. Much of the

152   Chapter 4

phenotypical variation—the appearance of whiteness, blackness, or Indianness—can be mapped onto distinct family lineages, and political disagreements between family factions sometimes include race as a factor. At Mashantucket the MPMRC was often seen as a Hayward family project, controlled by Skip Hayward and Theresa Hayward Bell. Over the life of the project total projected costs for construction increased, while the deadline for completion experienced a number of delays. For these reasons the museum project was a source for council-level disagreements and tensions. Early plans for the museum did include an exhibition area devoted to engaging race as an aspect of Mashantucket Pequot identity, but the area was removed from the exhibition design.[11] Race, as an issue for the museum's narrative, may have been written out due to a lack of consensus on how to frame the specific exhibition.

Conflict between family factions, a tribal council power structure that shifted in frequent elections, and a tribal council chair whose power eventually waned had material effects at the level of the display environments as well. While council approval for the museum and research center's budget was often delayed, efforts taken to reduce costs to meet council demands for the tribal budget often resulted in changes in the exhibition design. The farmstead is a case in point. All the vignettes in Life on the Reservation were based on carefully researched and documented figures from Pequot history. The farmstead is the only exception. It was originally designed to illustrate a dispersed farmstead (in contrast to the Indiantown era at Mashantucket, a community of small farmsteads), and the Sunsimons became its inhabitants fairly late in the game. As they were not based on document research, the parameters of the vignette were somewhat malleable (and vulnerable to budget decisions). As a result of cost trimming, the intended extended family of Sunsimons now present an anomalous single-child family in the exhibition. As in any museum, funding and administration directly affect the ability to mount exhibitions. It can be difficult to pin down cause and effect between original idea, following design, and final execution. For this reason as well, the exhibitions at the Mashantucket

Pequot museum can be understood as part of a larger oppositional narrative, one that shifts and adapts as the parameters of possibility and support change.

Where to Go and How to Get There

The presence of the museum in the farmstead and the absence of the nearby casino present a complicated moment in the visitor's experience, offering an intense and problematic juxtaposition of the modern with modern-rendered traditional museum narratives that include history, cultural identity, and Indian nationalism. As Eric Hobsbawm (Hobsbawm and Ranger 1983) asserts, the invention of tradition is "highly relevant" to the innovation of the nation—even if the nation in question is Indian and problematically domestic and dependent. The invention of tradition paradigm calls for intensive exploration of the strategic representational deployment of traditional and revitalized practices. The processes of adaptation and change in pursuit of survival are also cultural or traditional constants, where what is measured is not the continuity of a traditional presence as much as that of a traditional practice, that is, ongoing adaptation to enormous and often life-threatening change. The conflict inherent in this understanding, however, is that the continuity of a traditional presence, over practice, is an element in both federal and popular recognition.

The passage out into the farmland also resonates with an appraisal of the constructed and revealed environments of the Mashantucket Pequots as simulacra, as a strategic feint that, by its own dissonance in discovery, supports the authenticity of the narratives *inside* the museum. This recognition acknowledges a vibrating tension made apparent in the overlay of the present (which includes the museum's current narrative of the past) and the future (which includes one direction of Native industry and economic gain). But there is more at work here than a strange disjuncture or the absence of an incorporating text panel in the farmstead's field, gesturing back to the museum or the rest of the contemporary reservation. The

154   Chapter 4

unseen casino and resort is the reason that the 193-million-dollar museum exists at all. Rather than marking a deeply strange moment in the present-day experience of Mashantucket, the absent Grand Pequot Tower may mark a deeply strange moment in the historically assessing industries of museums and anthropology.

This recognition embraces the role of capital not only in Mashantucket's different arenas of representation and identity affirmation but also in museums understood as elements or nodes in a global, representational practice. Anthropology is implicated because of its own attraction to the well-presented story, the engaging "text" in all of its multiple forms, and its part in a global and globalizing practice of representation. At Mashantucket the role of both cultural and economic capital in mounting self-defining representational machines is clearly discernable. What is striking in the museum moment is the bald recognition of the link between capital and the ability to museumize particular subjects and narratives.

Through the efforts of the tribe, the architects, and the exhibit designers, the MPMRC actively plays with its structural *forms* to confound hard distinctions between interior and exterior. The active play between contained representational space and its reservation location is part of what makes the museum so captivating. The MPMRC is a self-referential structure that locates the story of the Mashantucket Pequots as its master narrative, then relates that narrative within a state-of-the-art contemporary building located in Mashantucket—a place rarified by its separateness from the county and state surround. The known or imagined understanding of the casino complex viewed in the near distance (Foxwoods and the Mashantucket Pequots have been extensively featured in news media and promotional campaigns since 1986) further extends the museum experience beyond its immediate and surrounding property.

To understand the MPMRC we need to look beyond the recontextualizing efforts of its exhibitions or the poetics of the museum visit and experience and raise our eyes from the farmstead to beyond the near horizon, to the looming sign of the major Mashantucket Pequots industry. A poetics of the museum provides only one method for entering its vast project. It is the poetics of the reservation and the sensory experience of visiting the museum that transform the *fact* of the site, pulling it through the intensified register of place and meaning. The invention or construction of tradition, like the retelling of history, relies on an interior authentic core of the past, a historical force around which people interact and narratives cluster. History and traditions are stories told in the present by the *means* of the present.

At Mashantucket these means include the museum and the casino as twin registers of historical force and contemporary narrative. The MPMRC, for all of the modernity of its exhibition technologies and the postmodernity of its self-referential construction and narratives, represents a deeply traditional form for storytelling. It embodies a means of explaining the present through a series of connected and mutually indicating historical narratives and naturalizing histories.

Exhibitions are the heart of any museum, its considered and careful representational interaction with its public. Museum exhibitions and exhibition halls are interstitial spaces, rife with narrative gaps and incomplete closures. Through navigating and cross-reading the museum's narratives—a truly multimedia experience—visitors make their understanding. And through such uncontainable and intertextual experiences museums exercise their own poetics: disjunctive spaces that speak through their forms, leaving visitors to make their own sense in the gaps and fissures of environments, displays, and texts. At Mashantucket it is not so much the shape of the museum that is different as the understanding of its surround: a complex intersection of popular imaginary, local history, and current practices of tribal industry. At what point these practices, building on but radically transforming and extending those of the past, enter the canon of tradition remains to be seen.

The Life on the Reservation gallery closes with Bringing the People Home, an exhibition devoted to the first wave of Mashantucket Pequots who returned to the reservation in the mid-1970s. These few tribal members, the beginning of what would prove to be a great renaissance for the tribal nation, first lived in simple trailer homes and campers. Over the course of twenty-five years the reservation

156 Chapter 4

population went from two to over two hundred. The comparatively recent arrival of the majority of the tribe's recognized members (in 1997 the Mashantucket Pequot tribal council dropped the blood-quantum requirement for tribal enrollment; in 2005 there were almost eight hundred members), coupled with the construction and phenomenal success of the tribe's bingo and casino concerns, created a tension-filled cultural arena. Critics and competitors lined up to dispute Mashantucket Pequot claims to tribal and cultural authenticity, regardless of the federal government's official 1983 recognition. And Foxwoods, since its 1992 opening, has been a focal point for national debates on Indian gaming. These debates often locate Indian gaming as unfair competition for mainstream industries, an industry that preys on the consumer or encourages crime, or an "inauthentic" Native American practice. Here the maintenance of traditions and the potential for their loss are often fronted as paramount concerns.

The MPMRC is a charged and deeply subtexted site. A cultural industry in the shadow of an enormous and controversial capital-generating industry, the museum presents narratives of the past, of traditions and history, within a gleaming and modern structure complete with the latest in museum and interactive technologies. Most of this is not unusual. Museums are complex places where stories of nationalism, history, cultural persistence, and appropriation are made interesting or accessible through a variety of different media and spatial design strategies. Computer-based interactives provide a high-tech way to move through exhibits, providing links to short films or other explanatory data. In an age when museum interactivity is most often understood as intercourse with software and hardware, the MPMRC systems are vast and compelling, fabulous with resolution and the promise of information.

Different levels of interaction are woven through the entire Mashantucket Pequot museum experience. Visible from nearly every gallery, the recurring presence of the reservation takes an active part in the museum's intricate dance of representation and incorporation. On the one hand, Mashantucket Pequot history is presented as a discrete, well-researched, and supported narrative. On the other, the museum experience is presented as dynamic and inclusive, calling for individual visitor navigation and self-directed input.

Some of this reflects patterns in modern museums, from the virtual visit that allows you to arrange your own exhibit and tour, to Internet-driven bubble-view experiences offering a 360-degree roller-coaster ride through bricks-and-mortar sites. The modern museum is under siege as a public attraction and is reacting in different ways to perceived changes in audience demographics and expectations. The 1990s witnessed unparalleled museum constructions in both extensive refurbishing and the building of new facilities. At the same time, the museum has never been more unclear as to what its next step should be in terms of representation, interaction with the Internet, or the promise of becoming a popular destination for school and college educational programs. Much of the promise for the future and the attractive hook for funding and support still lie in the perception of the museum as educational resource. While this makes some sense, it also underscores the question of what a museum is—it forces the consideration of the nature of its enterprise. Is it driven by the convictions of its administration and board, the goals of its programming, or the desire and dedication of its staff? This also raises the question, What exactly is meant by educational? Like Stewart's recognition of nostalgia, the vantage point decides or profoundly influences whose educational resource it is and from what perspective.

Bringing the People Home

The last object in Bringing the People Home is a trailer home, furnished as it was when occupied by tribal members (fig. 4.23).

> That was the only way we knew we could do it, was to be able to get a trailer, something that was portable, that you could buy, that you didn't have to build,

Figure 4.23 The trailer home in the gallery. (Photo by the author)

to get a loan for. Something you could pay cash for, an old used trailer to make do . . . because you couldn't build a home. Where was you going to get the money? Where was you going to get a loan? (Voice from the Mashantucket Pequot oral history project)

The trailer is placed against the gallery's ending wall and rests on a large white plinth, its windows and doors open for inspection. The glass wall to its right floods the area with natural light. Like most of the exhibits in this long gallery, the trailer has minimalist force. A text panel in front discusses how tribal members took up residence in Mashantucket and began to work toward self-sufficiency and self-determination.

It was three bedrooms, very, very small. It was hell.

We were all working to get whatever it was that we could get to move back up to the reservation, even if it meant camping, which some of us did do. Some did come back and live in pop-up tents and campers.

I remember boiling the snow on the stove to make water to pour through the hose to unclog the ice from the hose to take a shower.

There wasn't any funding sources for houses. You couldn't get a bank loan because it's on tribal lands. (Voices from the Mashantucket Pequot oral history project)

The exhibit is complemented by the sound of voices. Different pieces of recorded oral histories are played together and are heard most clearly as one focuses on the trailer and its interior. Design Division, Inc., originally suggested the oral history project, and it was started near the beginning of the museum project. Great effort was made to get a wide sample of the reservation population, with an eye on eventually using selections from the collected narratives either as bits of aural representation or as text worked into the exhibition panels. The project's archives are large and were extensively edited for presentation in the museum's texts and recordings.

Pig farming was started, hydroponic gardening, maple sugaring, that sort of thing. Cutting the dead tree falls and selling firewood, those were all things that were done just in order to keep the heat in the houses, just for survival. It wasn't any moneymaking enterprise; it was a survival tactic. (Voice from the Mashantucket Pequot oral history project)

The voices at the trailer are those of tribal members recounting life on the reservation during the 1970s, describing efforts at tribal businesses and the challenges of living in an impoverished community. As an aural artifact, the recordings of the tribal members work at a particular level of distraction. The multiple-voice narrative spins

160   Chapter 4

out in an unspooling linear recounting: a single voice speaks at a time, although the voices change over the course of the narrative.

> One of the first things that we started to do on the reservation was to build a community garden. You know, we weren't thinking about bingo halls, casinos. . . . It was blood, sweat, and tears, . . . grassroots effort to work with the land and create community, a sense of community on the reservation.

> Membership meetings began to grow and—and we began to meet some relatives we hadn't seen for a long time and other relatives we never saw before. (Voices from the Mashantucket Pequot oral history project)

From the recorded voices of tribal members, to the sounds of creaking ice and howling wind in the glacial escalator, to the birdsong and animal calls in the village, background noise verifies the visitor experience in a number of places to more firmly set the exhibitions in time and place. There are also a few sound leaks—the murmur of films in the theaters, the sound of displays on the interactive screens, and the ambient noises of museumgoers and docents negotiating the galleries. Like photographs, texts, and life experiences, the sounds form part of the mix that visitors use to make sense of the museum, part of a multiply located and received representational practice.

Ambient noises are just part of the journey through Life on the Reservation. The long gallery provides a gradual and subtle unsettling of existing stereotypes about Indians in history and in the present. Here Indians are whalers, preachers, farmers, soldiers, and laborers. They change and adapt as their circumstances necessitate. They are the inhabitants of marginal and recognizable dwellings like house trailers. The master narrative of the Mashantucket Pequot museum is a historicizing narrative, and the Mashantucket Pequots' history places them as speaking agents in, rather than subjects of, this story.

5   A Tribal Portrait

> As we look to the past, we admire our ancestors for the hard times and discrimination they endured. We feel fortunate to be reassembled at Mashantucket, on traditional Pequot territory. We believe that our shared history creates a special bond, a common identity, that keeps us strong.
>
> —Text from the introductory panel of the exhibit A Tribal Portrait

Tribal-controlled museums are extremely significant venues where the poetics of self-representation and renewed Indian sovereignty are enacted and performed. Photographs of American Indians are a historically embedded, highly contested genre of identity representation. This chapter focuses on the museum's final gallery to do a close reading of its exhibition–a collection of tribal member portraits. The portraits serve as a museum visitor's "personal" introduction to many contemporary members of the tribal nation. At once evocative and evidential, these large-format images embody a singular moment in the photographic representation and exhibition of "Indianness" and offer a vital site for exploring the use of photography in the museum. The photographs also offer a powerful rebuttal to public challenges to Mashantucket Pequot *Indian* authenticity, organized in terms of racial and ethnic identity. The gallery is the result of a series of choices made about self-representation, and it offers the clearest example of the mobilization of race as a field of assertion.

162   Chapter 5

A Tribal Portrait I

The trailer that closed the last chapter marked the end of the Life on the Reservation gallery as a unified exhibition design. The gallery's vignettes are spare: lone figures stand for periods on the reservation, surrounded by few objects or furnishings. Directional, natural light is a predominant feature of the hall's design; it emphasizes the gallery's clean lines, the absence of encasements for most of the exhibition materials, and the space's volume.

In sharp contrast, the portrait gallery feels dimly lit; here the light from the windows does not seem to carry as far (fig. 5.1). Ceiling-mounted spotlights are trained on a series of black-and-white photoportraits shot with a large-format camera. Their detail is sharp, and many are rendered larger than life-size. The subjects are generally alone, occasionally in pairs or small groupings. Most address the camera, eyes meeting the visitors' through the mediation of lens, viewfinder, and final print. The majority of the portraits hang on the walls, but others are suspended from the ceiling in the middle of the gallery and anchored to the floor in pairs, back to back, their frames guyed top and bottom with slender steel cables. The overall first impression is of entering a different kind of exhibition space, one more influenced by contemporary art or photo gallery conceits. The suspended portraits break up the hall's floor space, providing a variety of possible paths for the visitor to take, winding through a maze of oversized faces and dramatic light.

> A lot of people that come back to the reservation come back sometimes finding out . . . they just found out they was Mashantucket Indian. Sometimes they come back knowing it all along but never practiced it at all. They don't practice their native culture right away. They may not even say that they're Indian at all within the community. But the growth of the community depends on their acceptance of who they are and what the community stands for. . . . So, it's getting the new members that aren't aware of the identity to be aware of the identity so they respect their identity. (Voice from the Mashantucket Pequot oral history project)

A Tribal Portrait 163

Figure 5.1 The final gallery: A Tribal Portrait. (Photo by the author)

Entering the gallery, one hears voices. At first it is hard to tell if they are carrying on a conversation or speaking in parallel. The sounds grow and fade as one approaches or walks away from different portraits. Focusing, the voices are revealed as a single, linear, stitched-together narrative stream of sound. The recordings are the voices of tribal members, and the narratives are from the Mashantucket Pequot oral history project. The tribal members speak, recalling life at Mashantucket and elsewhere before the tribal nation's boom in the 1980s and 1990s.

The reason that I came here . . . is because I believed in what was going on here, and at the time it wasn't "We're going to have a billion-dollar casino."

164   Chapter 5

> That wasn't it. But I believed in what was taking place here, that it would be something unique, because you would have a community made up of a body of people who are also blood relatives.

> We're just a normal community fighting for the rights of our people. We work. We pay taxes. . . . We're just like anybody else. (Voices from the Mashantucket Pequot oral history project)

The voices recall stories of origin, family, tribal identification, and strategies for cultural and pragmatic survival. They embody a space between patterned noise and recognizable speech and call on the same sort of meaning-making process potentially invoked by the first viewing of a photograph, where one begins with initial concentration and a gradual settling into the image, then extends to a recognition based on expectations, memory, and experience. The voices are not explicitly or individually tied to the portraits in the gallery; the two projects, voice and image, were carried out separately and assembled as museum exhibition elements.[1]

> It sounds stupid and it sounds corny, but it is like a dream come true. I am back home. I am on tribal land. My children are here, and my grandchildren are here.

> There's a special feeling that you get from this land, and no matter if you have to put some tar on it or put a building on it, that it's not going to change the vibes that you get from this land and the spirit that's in this land. (Voices from the Mashantucket Pequot oral history project)

The placement of the gallery raises questions about how it relates to the rest of the museum: the shift from the airy wash of daylight in the previous hall and the clear changes in design mark it as a distinctly "other" exhibition space. The gallery makes a shift from the historic to the contemporary at the same moment that the exhibition moves from a grand hall to a smaller, discrete space. The portrait gallery serves as counterpoint to the museum's introductory gallery. The museum opens with a large group photo of tribal members; it closes with individual renderings of some of those same tribal members. From the group image—a color photograph enlarged to pronounced graininess (see figure 4.5)—the representation of tribal members moves to the sharp detail of large-format portraits, mostly studio lit and rendered in black and white.

Up to now, photographs in the MPMRC have provided supplementary, visual documentary images for other representational strategies: they illustrate museum narratives. Text panel photographs in the first gallery match images of buildings to small narratives about business and life at Mashantucket; interactive computer screens around the caribou hunt supply still and moving images augmenting and explaining hunting technologies and histories. Photographs show the features of glacial and postglacial landscapes, and photomurals document the Mashpee Meetinghouse or interpret large-scale death by disease with a portrayal of empty wigwam frames against a low, gray sky. Historic photographs are used in some of the smaller Life on the Reservation exhibitions, but photographs as sole subject for an entire exhibition appear only in the museum's closing gallery (fig. 5.2).

Here also is one of the few places where you hear Mashantucket Pequots speaking. Their recorded voices address the room, articulating their specific thinking about cultural identity, the formation of community, blood and kinship, and the idea of "home" as a particular and returned-to location. In this brief selection of spoken samples tribal members recognize the process of "coming to know" their native culture by learning a Native identity through practice. This understanding explicitly challenges more traditional concepts of acquiring and building "native" cultural identities from birth or from being surrounded by a community of people who share an identity and traditional practices. It also advances the recognition that "coming to know" and affirm a Mashantucket Pequot identity may involve significantly modifying or abandoning previous identifications.

The voices also offer a counternarrative for imagined museum visitors, one

Figure 5.2 Another view of A Tribal Portrait. (Photo by the author)

that recognizes Mashantucket as different or "unique" while, at the same time, defending it as a working and tax-paying community "just like anybody else." The mobilization of similarity and difference problematizes questions of resistance and assimilation within a rarified location and exhibitionary space. Clearly, the Mashantucket Pequots are not "just like anybody else." Here the argument serves as a strategic flattening device, one that seeks to both make connections with a larger public while potentially reducing or redirecting questions of difference. The invoked narrative of "home" as nostalgic location and constructed space contributes to this effort as well.

This is not to say that these narratives are carefully constructed with only a museum-audience reaction in mind. The oral history project preceded the museum and the photoportrait project. But the narratives do offer a way to listen to tribal members as they relate their own reasons and understandings involved in coming or returning to Mashantucket. And the narratives significantly support and extend the image-viewing process demanded by the gallery.

David Neel: Background and Foreground

In 1988 David Neel started a project photographing First Nation chiefs and elders of the Pacific Northwest coast. He also collected interviews from each subject to include with the photographs. The publication of this project in book form in 1992, *Our Chiefs and Elders*, served as his defining project and provides critical background for his selection as the photographer for the MPMRC photoportrait exhibition: "We live in a time of the created image—if you do not create your own, someone will create it for you. The image created for us is one of a people stuck in time, as though we are not part of the twentieth century. As early as the mid-1800s, Native people were viewed as part of the past and were imagined to be a 'vanishing race'" (Neel 1992:14).

Neel's work draws from a number of traditions and influences and contains many of the standard tropes in photoportraiture of the American Indian. In *Our Chiefs and Elders*, however, two things stand out.

First, the portraits are primarily presented in pairs. In one the subject appears in ceremonial regalia or the formal dress of an official role or office. In the other the subject is shown in everyday or casual clothes. The photographs are captioned to provide names, family affiliations, and geographic locations. The book includes interview and conversation excerpts from Neel and the various subjects.

The portraits of Nathan Young illustrate some of the work's prominent features (fig. 5.3). The placement of the subject in the left photograph points clearly to the portrait as a constructed and constraining frame. Chief Young powerfully fills the

Figure 5.3 Chief Nathan Young, from *Our Chiefs and Elders*. (Photos by David Neel)

foreground of the photograph with his cloak, creating a feeling of forced perspective that is further emphasized by the camera's low angle. Not only does Young fill the foreground, but his headdress almost exceeds the limits of the image, pushing against the top center of the frame. In the right photograph Young again exceeds the frame. In the foreground his feet have partially escaped the photograph's containment. His suspenders, tinted glasses, and gimme cap unsettle the iconics of the first photograph—a portrait that at first seems to participate in the conventional "nobility" trope of traditional portraits of American Indians. The easy posture of Young, the style of his wooden chair, and the clear meeting of lawn and painted canvas backdrop serve to connect this photograph's "moment" with its picture-making event. There is a complicity between the photographer and subject—their relationship is made obvious at the same moment that the photograph "speaks back" to an established genre of American Indian portraiture.

The Neel photographs participate in a number of strategies reflecting the existing genre of photography of Native Americans. But the work supports identifying through a self-designated system of naming that does not reflect standard anthropological categorizations. Instead, it recognizes other identifying schema, including family and what Keith Basso (1996) calls "the place where one is from" (see also Clifford 1997; Blu 1980). The inclusion of interviews narrativizes and further extends the "pictures" one gains from the book, while the juxtaposition of "ceremonial" with "casual" dress confounds attempts to detemporalize the various subjects. As Neel states: "I have tried to show people as they are, with their lives in two worlds, two cultures," parallel and complicated (1992:13).

Second, there are critically important formal distinctions in *Our Chiefs and Elders*. In conventional studio portraiture painted backgrounds are usually beyond the plane of the camera's focus. They also exceed the edges of the photographic frame to present a seamless backdrop of pure, mottled, or gradual tone in the final photograph. In contrast, Neel uses a narrow painted canvas background, shooting in small spaces where it cannot drop out of focus or ensuring that the background is close to his photographic subject. The width of the background, used in combination with the medium-distance portraits he prefers, means that the background, its edges, and often the walls behind are all included in the photograph's frame, in sharp focus. The final portrait clearly implicates and indicates the processes and boundaries of photo making.

This attention to boundary and process reflects Neel's engagement with the legacy of photographers of Native Americans, perhaps most specifically with the widely known work of Edward S. Curtis.[2] Curtis's work has also served as a focus for deconstructive criticism, specifically for its rendering or erasure of "contemporary" elements in its compositions in an effort to detemporalize its subjects, to remove them from time and place. While Neel addresses this issue in *Our Chiefs and Elders*, photographer Christopher Lyman is perhaps best known for this perspective.[3]

170   Chapter 5

In making the photo-producing event an obvious and direct part of the finished photograph Neel participates in a style made prominent by commercial portrait photographers like Annie Liebowitz and Irving Penn.[4] But Neel's work is also a comment on the "erasure-of-anachronism" critiques most clearly articulated by Lyman. The artifacts of the photo-making process made visible further demonstrate the contingent mechanics of the photo-making event. They also illustrate the photograph's fusion of technology, subject, and practitioner to produce a truly "collaborative artifact" while foregrounding elements that confirm the time and place of its making.[5]

In the Neel diptychs the background and the subject's distance from it stay the same in both images. This strategic move presents a composite picture of "authentic" Indians that indicates nineteenth-century stereopticon imagery, further historicizing photographic engagement with Indians and simultaneously troubling it. For an outsider the photographs portray both a "traditional"—perhaps expected—view and a "day-to-day" view. But the photos also illustrate specific individual tribal roles as marked by special clothing or artifact. At a number of levels the portraits show the different roles that each of the individuals inhabits. This strategy shifts the subject from a place of static-tradition depiction, or incorporation into what Gerald Vizenor (1994) terms "manifest manners" and subjugation to white dominance, into a space of contemporary belonging. By extension, the juxtaposition destabilizes and temporalizes the genre of stoic American Indian portraits, creating the potential for critical engagement.

The process of "reading" photographs—as in my offered analysis of the Young photographs and those that follow—is a slippery and contradictory practice. Like the examples chosen from the museum and the casino, the choice and the interpretation of photographs for further analysis is arbitrary. As Christopher Pinney suggests, since an image that "appears to do a particular kind of work in one episteme is able to perform radically different work in another, it appears inappropriate to propose inflexible links between formal qualities and effect" (2003:3). This is also true for Curtis photographs, as seen in the variety of different reactions and analyses they continue to generate. And, as Mick Gidley (2003) warns, there is a danger of "ventriloquizing" the represented Indian subject through writing interpretations not anchored or recorded in *Indian* voices. In this chapter the photographs offered are taken from a large number of possible images; any could have been used as points or examples for further consideration. My analysis of them is necessarily located and interpretive.

Like Young, Alice R. Kirchner, the subject of figure 5.4, is at medium distance from the lens—the image records her entirely. She is shown in fairly elaborate buckskin, including boots and a bag. Kirchner is also wearing necklaces, a bracelet, and a two-feather headband. Her hair is carefully coifed, and her eyeglasses are somewhat matronly. She sits on a chair in what may be her kitchen, with a linoleum floor and wooden cabinets in the background. Her shoulders are at an angle to the camera, but she faces the camera dead-on, with her chin raised. She is lit with one broad source, and the background behind her catches some of the spill light. Her shadows are soft but dark.

The elements made obvious in Young's diptych are compressed here; the contemporaneity of the setting mixes with the style of Kirchner's dress. The unsettling that Neel achieves by pairing the Young photographs is made clear in one image, and, as if to emphasize the photograph's disconcerting quality, the horizon is skewed. A subverted horizon is evident in many of Neel's photographs here—it is a compositional device that quite literally unsettles both subject and viewer positions, as the viewer consciously or unconsciously attempts to "right" the photo subject's footing. It is a subtle way to elicit a reaction of unfamiliarity and a signal that the photograph and its subject share a sense of place distinctly different from that of the museum visitor.

The gallery presents an interesting moment in the museum's narrative, this meeting between museum visitor and pictured tribal member. The mix of the contemporary and what might be understood as the traditional participates in the

Figure 5.4 Alice R. Kirchner, from A Tribal Portrait. (Photo by David Neel)

ongoing dialogue at Mashantucket concerning self-representation, authenticity, and temporality. The tension between the "placelessness" of the painted canvas backdrop and the obvious markers of place is also key in the community's ongoing discourse of representation. And the fact that it is not only photographs but large-format black-and-white portraits that comprise the last exhibition is particularly telling. Photographs are artifacts that, more than any other, mix a sense of the evidential–the photograph as mechanically "factual" or actual record—with the evocative—the photograph as location for imagination, connection, or unfinished and uncontainable narrative.

A Short History of Photography

The creation of a stable, reusable reverse image (a photographic "negative"), useful for making a theoretically unlimited number of positive prints, was invented by William Fox Talbot in 1841. Photography shared much of the mid-nineteenth century's optimism and perspective on the process of mechanical representation. Talbot's "pencil of nature" described an intersection of technology and the natural world, a transparent, denotative transference from the visible world to the photographic record—from nature to culture—without connotative, interpretive influence. This understanding of the new technology was problematic from the beginning.

One of photography's first movements, pictorialism, sought to establish that photography was a legitimate artistic, interpretive medium and not simply a mechanical record. Pictorialists used a painterly approach and often manipulated their images by hand. Their urge and legacy, and the popular use of photographs in advertisements, albums, court records, and identification documents, continue to blur the line between photographs as interpretive objects and photographs as direct transfers, what Susan Sontag refers to as "something stenciled off the real, like a footprint or a death mask" (1973:154).

174   Chapter 5

At once record and object, photographs have a problematic relationship with the visible world. Created by the registration of reflected light from a subject, photographs do not capture subjects, they capture the light that subjects echo.[6] As records of indexical reflection, photographs have been popularly misunderstood as indexically representing reality, and the photograph has become an evidential measure of authenticity.

As visual documents recording the appearance of individual bodies, photographs have become enormously useful in registering those bodies. The registration and incorporation of the colonial subject is part of the uncomfortable history that anthropology and ethnographic photography share with the colonial project. The photograph, as a representation with the power of evidence, is also a powerful means of asserting control over its subject. Marjorie Halpin observes: "How that [subject] is controlled for the capture, and for what purpose, and how that image is received by a viewer, are, however, profoundly cultural matters" (1992:185).[7]

In the foreword to *Our Chiefs and Elders* Neel and Halpin note that the control and use of the captured subject as a viable point for critical analysis does not end in some past historical moment. As Neel states, "photography has been used since the last century to support . . . ideas of cultural superiority, to the loss of the First Nations of the world" (1992:15). Representations of American Indians in historical photographs have contributed to current (mis)understandings. David Penney, curator of Native American art at the Detroit Institute of Arts, asserts: "Photographs of American Indians illustrate scientific, ethnographic, and historical texts. They form a large part of what is thought of as knowledge and truth about American Indian people" (1994:6).

Edward S. Curtis is one of the more prolific figures responsible for this production of "knowledge," and his legacy cannot be overstated. Curtis's *North American Indian* offers "the largest anthropological enterprise ever undertaken," as Gidley (1998:3) asserts. Curtis's photographs continue to appear in current conflicts over the authenticity of contemporary images and peoples. Appearance, in the popular imaginary as well as in the more rarified circles of anthropology and photography, has long been critical to cultural perception. This is also true when considering the extensive archive of photographs of American Indians. Images made for the "preservation of the vanishing Indian" commit a problematic sleight-of-hand when they do not admit their own complicity in creating both that perceptual genre as well as a measure for authenticating current and future Native peoples. This measure frustrates and confounds by binding photographic subjects to particular representations (e.g., in appearance, activity, environment, or dress) and temporal placement (either vanishing or forever in a primordial and timeless past).

The Neel photographs at Mashantucket continue in the tradition established by his earlier work to speak directly against this binding. Combining contemporary settings with traditional dress or objects, the photographs disturb the possibilities of a timeless and placeless reading. Further, A Tribal Portrait reflects contemporary photo or art aesthetics, firmly seating the portraits as part of a current dynamics— the photographs depict living tribal members. Finally, the gallery voices complicate and "thicken" the tribal nation's self-representational project.

Some of the power of this representational process can be better understood after a brief discussion of Curtis's work. While not the central focus of this museum gallery, Curtis's legacy is important if implicit. As Gidley suggests, Curtis's project is a "resource so pervasive that it must be dealt with" (1998:282).

Curtis, a talented and exhaustive photographer, is often identified as a romantic given to certain poetic excess in rendering the subjects of his photographs and in his imagining photography able to capture a complete register of a people or humanity.[8] Part of what makes Curtis's work so compelling is the point it occupies in history. His lifework inhabits a major crossroads in photographic imaging and takes part in ongoing and heated discussions and movements attempting to define photography as art or science, as interpretive method or factual record. From his 1898 portrait of Princess Angeline (the daughter of Chief Sealth, from whom the city of Seattle took its name), to the publication of the final volume of *The North American*

Indian in 1930, Curtis built an unprecedented catalog of images of Indians. In all, he shot more than forty thousand photographs of Native North Americans.

His work paralleled an enormous shift in anthropology, from the universal cultural evolutionary stages established by Lewis Henry Morgan to the cultural relativism taught by Franz Boas. Boas also emphasized the need for "salvage ethnography": gathering information and artifacts in the face of impending cultural erasure. Like Boas, Curtis endeavored to record the "vanishing," but he also wanted to record the "vanished." His end goal: to create a comprehensive work documenting North American Indian language, history, stories, and images. Through careful framing, cropping, captioning, and propping Curtis set out to photograph the American imaginary of what the Native North American peoples *were*, at once a gesture including the past and an active interpretation and in-filling of that past. The Curtis photographs were not boundless acts of fancy as easily achieved in a studio as in the field, but they did engage an active and ongoing sense of nostalgia, an interpretive "looking backward" firmly rooted in the present.

Curtis's romantic images are often the focus of conflict over the "straight" documentary value and significance of his work. Here the idea of one image standing for an entire people is taken further. Instead of revealing one set of representations as standing for an entire group, a photo such as *The Vanishing Race—Navaho* not only gestures toward an entire people or group of nations but also indicates something that exceeds category (fig. 5.5).

Curtis's popular archive is his most substantial contribution to history, but his work also creates a space for critical engagement and a demand to look beyond the parameters of the images to engage in critical questions of representation, category, and the ethnographic imagination. These issues are familiar to photography's ongoing and unresolved position, straddling the distinctions of art and document or questions of the camera as interpretive or objective recording tool; it is a problematic written into the fabric of the technology itself. Curtis holds a powerful if tenuous place in the histories of photography and ethnology, a place subject to pressures and

Figure 5.5 *The Vanishing Race—Navaho*. Edward S. Curtis chose this image to be the opening photograph for the North American Indian portfolios. It is emblematic of his thought and work. (Library of Congress, Prints & Photographs Division, Edward S. Curtis Collection, LC-USZ62-37340)

limits, to changing sensibilities in the two disciplines and in ideas of documentary evidence and the popular imaginary.

Photography is a powerful and slippery medium in part because it can be moved through different contexts to appear in such disparate venues as *The North American Indian*, college dormitory rooms, and galleries and because its accompany-

178   Chapter 5

ing text or placement, its "surround," has enormous influence over its "read." One of the dominant impressions of Curtis's work is the vanishing Indian, taking leave of this mortal coil through warm sepia tones and partially soft focus backgrounds, dressed in Native garb, looking at once resolute and timeless, epic and damned. The setting and interpretive orbit for an object profoundly influence its meaning. Museums are powerful theaters for possible counterreadings of photoportraits, providing a number of potential public subject identities.

Cataloging creates a map of the "known" world, a record that becomes the narrative itself, displacing its object and rendering its origins invisible. One of the most striking things about Curtis and the photographers of his era is that the created "vanishing Indian" record does not acknowledge its own complicity in that process. Photographers like Curtis are often understood as marginal, at the periphery of white dominance, collecting and cataloging images in the face or just ahead of voracious white conquest. But such photographic projects played an important role in this conquest. As Gidley asserts, "the project always accepted the fact that Indian lives must inevitably be given up, and that Indian cultures must progressively be swept away, precisely to enable the triumph of 'civilization.' . . . Indeed, part of the project's cultural work may have been to show the inevitable 'truth' of this process" (2003:13). The control of the West depended on the control of its history-making processes, its ability to *represent* white domination as inevitable. The very creation of a narrative of disappearance enforces and supports the processes of disappearance. Colonial expansion depended on control of representational technologies as much as on maintaining borders, armed forces, and development.

Curtis's work feeds this problematics. He melded documentary, ethnographic, and romantic photographic practice to bring forth a singular constructive and schematic force to create the colonial Other. Representing the Other as strange solidifies the Other's difference while cementing *our* similarities (*our* being the great unseen community that occupies the looking end of this particular looking glass).

Photography and the Formation of the American Indian Subject

Photographs taken of American Indians, particularly those from the last half of the nineteenth and the first decades of the twentieth centuries, provide a rich archive of historic and iconic images. Importantly, this time period marks the beginnings of anthropology and photography and the entry of the American Indian—as object and subject—into both systems of knowledge. Photographs reflected and contributed to a concurrent ethnographic and colonial project fraught with the demarcation of power—the scientific cataloging of the Other. As anthropologist Terence Wright suggests, for "an anthropology deeply rooted in positivism, photography offered a tempting proposition: an objective vision and collection of 'facts,' facilitating systemic organization and analysis, in the service of scientific enquiry" (1992:20). More than any other photographer's, Curtis's work represents this period and provides distinct and important documentary and ethnographic evidence as popular representations that resonated with popular anthropological discourses. These included the concepts of cultural survivals, of rendering Others as exemplary icons illustrating whole peoples, and a belief in the making of an unproblematic record through representational technologies. Curtis's photographs may be read as authentic constructions representing the Indian in the white imagination and the position of the Other in discourses of science, history, and anthropology.

That some of his photographs were staged or retouched is not a new insight, but it does underscore the arbitrary nature of image making and image reception; it is a reminder of "the *contractual* element of the visual contract with reality" (Taussig 1993:70). This element is also a *contextual* element, seating the photograph within the contexts of its own production: "*What a photograph shows us is how a particular thing could be seen, or could be made to look*—at a specific moment, in a specific context, by a specific photographer employing specific tools" (Coleman 1998b:57). The arbitrariness of photographs provokes a critical assessment of photographic practice and the reliance on photographic records as what Victor Burgin calls "window[s] on the world" (1982b).

180   Chapter 5

It forces the realization, or at least the suspicion, that all photographs are more or less simulations.[9] In the gap between "more" and "less" lies the utility of photographs as documents and the implication of photographs as measures or illustrations of reality or authenticity.

Understanding the photograph as "transcriptive artifact" raises questions concerning the context of its use and its participation in a particular economy of meaning through articulation with and against other symbols, signs, settings, and text (Grady 1989). What makes a photograph such an intriguing object is its ability to slip its leash, to be recontextualized in settings, uses, or narratives distinctly different from its origins.

In this light, the Mashantucket Pequot museum is a powerful contextualizing register. Its scale, the richness of its exhibitions, and the advanced state of its technology all serve as reminders of the Mashantucket Pequots' ability to control and create their own self-representation. The museum's size and resources also reaffirm the tribal nation's financial power and its ability to successfully navigate the complex issues of identity politics and federal and state legislation. The Neel portraits' "contract with reality," then, resonates through the registers of place and tribal nationhood.

Photography's silent and frozen moment, with its particular commodity ability to be cast loose from its original contextualizing moorings, is part of a problematic medium, one with clear tensions drawn between photographs as interpretive documents and as factual records. Photographs enjoy a particular kind of circulation and an ability to transgress boundaries (e.g., of genre, discipline, language, or culture); a photograph is a curious and potentially dangerous thing. It represents a moment stripped from time, two-dimensional and invested with forced perspective, subject to aestheticized decisions involving point of view, processing, enlarging, cropping, re-presentation as a print or as a print within changing contexts. A decontextualized moment fixed by representational technology, a photograph offers the opportunity for almost limitless recontextualization. Curtis's work, for example, has gone through a number of different uses and appreciations since its publication, and the symbolic and cultural capital of the images has experienced a series of dramatic changes.[10] They now occupy a space of mixed appreciation and double-edged apprehension.

This is not solely a series of observations about the power of contextualization and the nuances of recontextualizing efforts and strategies. Image making is contradictory and transitory: a photograph confirms a moment of exposure; at the same time, it removes it from the flow of time. The photograph both inhabits and is inhabited by this moment, transforming that contact point into an iconic image that begins a life of circulation as an object. Within this extended moment (from initial exposure to finished print) is sketched the transition from subject to object, a transition that parallels anthropology's own problematic process from theory and fieldwork to text. As Elizabeth Edwards affirms, "in anthropology . . . the fragments [of ethnographic fieldwork] become moulded to a unifying account of 'culture.' So, in photography, the specific moment becomes representative of the whole and the general" (1992:8). Deciding which moments is deeply, ideologically embedded.

Photographic documents are the products of intense mediations. These processes include the reciprocity and mutual understandings between the photographer and the photographic subject, regardless of what informs these understandings or how unbalanced they may be, and between the photographed technology and the photographed site. This recalls Gidley's "double focus," which recognizes *interaction* between Curtis and his photographic subjects. The Curtis photographs are remarkable not only for their timeless quality and the pristine isolation or wilderness of their backgrounds but also for the realization that Curtis worked with a large view camera and glass plates. This invisible spectacle of production provides a possible blossoming of awareness for approaching a Curtis portrait critically. Neel's portraiture problematizes this location, this seamed gap between the mediated and the immediacy of the photoportrait.

182   Chapter 5

Knowledge, Normalization, and the Theft of Souls

The collection of photographs of American Indians that continued through the end of the nineteenth century, enacted as cataloging campaigns, photographs of delegates to Washington,[11] or Ishi photo opportunities behind his Berkeley university museum home in California, are parts of a positioned knowledge (Vizenor 1992). Some American Indians, such as Lakota leader Crazy Horse, refused to have their picture taken, thereby rejecting incorporation into an image collection controlled by the whites (Grady 1989). To lose control over one's representation and the context of one's own imaged "presence" is to lose an integral aspect of one's self. The decontextualized photograph becomes a flat visage, a soulless object in the stream of commodities participating in the conquest of the West and the domination of its Native peoples.

Inclusion within an expanding catalog of Indian photographs continued the confusion and collapse carried out under the generalizing category "Indian." Before Wounded Knee, the final massacre that ended the "Indian Wars," tribes retained particularity. Although "Indian" was a designation in use from first contact, its powers of inclusion and conclusion were checked by tribal identities. While tribes and their leaders were identified as singular bands in armed opposition to the United States over treaty violations, encroachment, and forced removal from their lands, they maintained a group of singular identities: as nations entering into compacts with the government, as delegations to Washington, and even as Indians traveling in Wild West shows. The creation of catalogs, like the end of the Indian Wars, supported the final dominance of the all-inclusive category *Indian*, a category that served to normalize an understanding of what it was to be an Indian and what such a designation demanded in terms of appearance.

The trade in photographic images supported this normalizing category, as did the location of photographic subjects outside the flow of time and embraced by a generalized sense of place, often in dramatic natural surroundings. Portraying Indians in these environments was part of fixing them within a narrative of predetermined and inevitable loss, what Eve Darian-Smith calls the "narrative of inevitable historical tragedy" (2004:17). Within the white imagination these settings contributed to a normalizing perception of the American Indian as removed from the distinctions of individual identity and national belonging: vanishing, romantic, and doomed. Like other representations, the photograph served to fill a need prescribed by its own existence. Photographs of Indians served to extend the category and depiction of the Indian subject as belonging to the past and to locate the authentic Indian *in* the past, discounting or dismissing contemporary Indians without regalia or noble poses.

The growing popularity of photography and the increased portability of photographic equipment in the first half of the nineteenth century contributed to the rapid expansion of the genre of Indian photography. Refinements in film and paper emulsions and lens optics over the years have made the camera a portable and easy-to-use recording instrument. But what precisely is it the camera records? The photograph's removal of the subject from the flow of time and space parallels the concept of an atemporal ethnographic present; it is also the source of photography's most powerful attribute. Removal from time allows the space of contemplation, permitting dialogue, recognition, and potential recontextualization. But such recontextualization is not always affirmation. Rendering the photographic subject as object, like the creation of an ethnographic Other, removes the subject from the ongoing process of his or her own representation. It is important to keep this dual aspect of *time* in the photograph in mind. A photograph can be read as a static representation of the subject at the instant of the film's exposure, but the photograph is also an ongoing and active object within the construction of knowledge that lies at the heart of viewing photographs, indeed, that lies at the heart of any participation with an act of representation. At the same time, photographs are potential sites for powerful rereadings, as documents of particular historical discourses.[12]

The photographic subject becomes object, one that enters particular and multiple fields of constructed meanings and contexts. Photo historian John Szarkowski states that the photograph "forces a concentration on the picture edge—the line that separates in from out" (1966:9). It thus enters the discursive fields of anthropology and photographic practice as a singular and intensified cultural object. Photographs are visual quotations, signs that mix a double meaning of apprehension: a way of knowing and a way of critically assessing the appearance of a recontextualized referent. As visual quotation the photograph is a point of departure, contemplation, and entry for ethnographic and photographic structures of knowledge. Photographs invoke an image that holds itself frozen and fleeting, momentarily caught in the motion of looking backward while indicating the present and the future—a point of both departure and ethnographic and historical attention. And the photograph is a perfect document for representing stasis—as image and *time*. Photographs occupy an important gap between signifier and signified, a resonant space that is filled with meaning in an effort to span this breach, to smooth the gap between "real" time and referential time. In the formation of the American Indian subject the methodologies and theoretical bases of anthropology and photography are coindicative and codependent.

Current ethnographic practice stresses an engagement with its subjects that often extends to political or social activism. The belief in any representational technology as a transparent recording medium has been brought under close, even cynical, scrutiny for some time. And the ability to imagine an ethnographic subject at the distance of "survival," closer to nature than to culture, has been the locus of extended theoretical critique. Anthropological and photographic practices, however, are still concerned with the creation of record, the (re)presentation of actual events, of someone crossing the camera or the fieldworker's observational field. With the creation of record, the specific moment becomes general, a representative of the whole. Both disciplines, as technologies that capture and deliver "reality," rely on a shared concept of the "real." This delivery does not solely depend on their respective technologies; it also depends on expectation: "in other words the photograph is perceived as 'real' or 'true' because that is what the viewer expects to see: 'this is how it should be' becomes 'this is how it is/was'" (Edwards 1992:32). The same can be said for ethnographic texts. But this realization can also be inverted; in so doing, it enters a highly charged zone of identity politics where "this is how it was" becomes "this is how it should be." This is powerful in the legacy of American Indian photographs. Romantic, nostalgic images have set tenacious conceptual precedence, supporting a "vanished" Indian as an "authentic" Indian.

Roland Barthes examined this problematic relationship between what a photograph shows and what it represents, between a denotative aspect of the image— what it *is*—and a connotative aspect—what *meaning* it conveys or illustrates. By using these two aspects he hoped to develop a way to explore, and decode, photographs. But the opposition of denotative and connotative calls for an initial understanding of the photograph as a pure object, a literal text, a purely visual image. John Tagg suggests that the reality of such an image is "Edenic fiction" (1993:188). Allan Sekula also rejects the purely denotative function of photographs, suggesting that the idea of a primitive core of meaning in a photograph, "pure denotation" devoid of all cultural determination, is folklore at best. The "folklore of pure denotation" is useful, however, to provide an "ideal type" understanding of photographs as neutral evidence, one that "elevates the photograph to the legal status of a document and testimonial . . . [and] generates a mythic aura of neutrality around the image" (Sekula 1982:87). Sekula refuses to separate the photograph from its cultural task of representation as an element in a discursive system. His observations parallel contemporary movements in poststructuralism that problematize a separation between metaphoric and literal meaning.

In performing a representational task a photograph becomes an icon *invested* with meaning. It becomes a vehicle for transmitting a message, one that exceeds its own containment. This significantly decenters the photograph as neutral document while it simultaneously opens the photograph for consideration as an object that reflects shifts in structures of knowledge. The photograph presents "merely the

186   Chapter 5

possibility of meaning" (Sekula 1982:87). What is mobilized, then, to fill this possibility? How are photographs placed within the representational contexts of anthropology and photographic practice, for example? The contextualization of an image within a discipline affects its viewing and the task it performs within a given perspective. And the investment of meaning can change direction—a photograph can be reread against the grain of its original message or context. The generic sources of the photograph place it in important initial fields of orbit. The possibility of a discrete boundary between discursive fields matters less than the meaning made from the photograph as object, how it is placed and how it is used.

Photographs of American Indians continue to form a large part of what is thought of as knowledge and truth about American Indian people; they are documents of power. A photograph appropriates its subject; in so doing it allows the viewer to enter a certain power relationship with the visible that *feels* like knowledge. To challenge this relationship, photographs of American Indians must reenter a contemporary power dynamics to be seen not as the images of archaic survivals but as part of what Clifford identifies as "an ongoing process, politically contested and historically unfinished" (1988:9).

The Neel photographs emphasize the unfinished and ongoing process at Mashantucket. They offer powerful documentary evidence of the tribal nation at a specific historical point displayed through the faces and circumstances of its people. The activity of the portraits is achieved by their ability to straddle a number of photographic genres. It is difficult to pin down precisely what the Neel photographs *are*. Documentary images? Straight portraiture? Ethnographic records? They participate in all of these categories, and as objects they blur catalog, record, and art. But their placement is key to their project—context profoundly influences use value, and the portraits perform a number of interconnected and simultaneous tasks. In large part, the power dynamics of a current moment are expressed by their placement in the final exhibition gallery. The contemporaneity of the museum and the omnipresent issues of Native identity and history that are the backbone of its exhibition plan locate the tribal nation and tribal members in the present. As photographs, the Neel portraits offer particular kinds of historical and documentary information about their subjects. But photographs are more than a medium of information. What they show, how they show it, and where they are placed are all parts of a complex interpretive—and often invisible—process.

In figure 5.6 the distinctive elements of the paired portraits from *Our Chiefs and Elders* are again compressed, and signs of Indianness—buckskin dress, boots, and jewelry—are blended with other contemporary signs that do not reflect popular notions of Indianness—the high-backed chair and white crew socks. There are elements that clearly foreground the photo-making activity from which this image is drawn: the edge of the backdrop is visible, a stand holding the canvas catches light in the otherwise dark edge of the picture, another canvas backdrop has been placed on the floor to more effectively erase the "place" of the image. The horizon line is skewed; the shadows are rich and soft. The main light is broad and directional.

Unlike images from *Our Chiefs and Elders*, this photograph focuses on a family group. Rather than a narrative of family origins and place, the group here is shown in the moment, present, as if family and connection are reckoned in a space similar to that of the image—framed together and mixing signs. It is also in contrast to Curtis's iconic style and overwhelmingly solo portraits. Compare this image to figures 5.8 and 5.11. Both images of tribal member families, they actively play with signs of popularly and not-so-popularly recognizable Indianness, shifting from regalia and buckskin to a single Mashantucket Pequot logo on a polo shirt.

In viewing the following collection of photographs it is critical to understand how they transgress a variety of anticipated signs and genres to unsettle popular understandings of Indianness, formal photoportraiture, and identifications of race and ethnicity. While a microanalysis of individual images can further problematize the formal disjunctures of the photographs, reading the group of images as a whole provides some of the exhibition's more powerful and subtle statements. What they make clear is the representation of Mashantucket Pequot identity as profoundly

mixed, exhibiting a variety of phenotypical features–including black, white, and Indian—and Indian dress and objects. They also depend on different recognitions of nature or the close security of a separate and photographed "place," one that exists only for the taking of the picture and that will disappear once the exposure is completed. While the arrangement of the photographs as individual or small family group meeting the gaze of the camera's lens (and, by extension, the imagined gaze of the museum visitor) offers singular points of possible connection or identification, the overall impression of the exhibition is one of a diverse but familiar community.

Evocation and Evidence: The Photograph as Document of Memory, Sensual Experience, and Power

The dual role of the photograph, as product and producer of Native Americans in the U.S. popular imaginary, focuses attention on the image's reception. Key to this attention is the journey from photographic event to photographic document. What are the tools for a photograph's ingestion as a representative object, and how can photo viewing be understood as an experience, a particular entrance into what Raymond Williams (1977) calls a structure of feeling? There are different ways to assess the problematic relationship between image and ideology, the experiences of expression and criticism, and what I have been calling evocation and evidence. In photographs these forces, the sensually experiential and the theoretical, contaminate one another—memory connects them. The following investigation focuses on the experience of photo reception and is mimetic of the experience of a photograph that gains attention—through association, consideration, and experience—to rapidly overspill the boundaries of its own frame.

Figure 5.6 Jean Merrill, Joy Hale, and Joshua Hale, from A Tribal Portrait. (Photo by David Neel)

It has been argued that the photograph is an analogue of physical reality and that the assigning of meaning, interpretation, is a secondary activity. However, it may be more useful to consider the photograph as an analogue of visual experience, and as such, a culturally based ordering of the world in which the signifier and the signified are read at one and the same time. (Edwards 1992:8)

Photographs experience their widest use as documents, as iconic representations of particular narratives alone, or as objects adjunct to other narratives. One popular use of the photograph is as "realistic" illustration, an integral element in an argument for attention. This emphasis depends on realizing the photograph as evidential representation. As representations claiming evidential authority, photographs are deployed in discourses of power. They become part of an information system, a vast "shadow archive" of all things photographed and organized and those waiting for categorization and use (Sekula 1989). Here photographs straddle an uneasy fence between the magic of subject acquisition and such acquisition's potential use in a system of identification, normalization, and evidence. As in Curtis's images, the photographs' tasks alter to reflect the systems that mobilize them.

Understood as evidential power or as elements of different discursive regimes, photographs are examined for what they *mean*, how they fit and are used by different narrative and power structures. To forward this understanding, however, we must make key distinctions between photographs and photography. If the former is an analogue of visual experience, a sight-reflective artifact with a specific discursive task or set of tasks, the latter may be understood as both force and practice. Tagg suggests:

Photography as such has no identity. Its status as a technology varies with the power relations which invest it. Its nature as a practice depends on the institu-

Figure 5.7   Matthew Pearson, from A Tribal Portrait. (Photo by David Neel)

192   Chapter 5

tions and agents which define it and set it to work. Its function as a mode of cultural production is tied to definite conditions of existence and its products are meaningful and legible only within the particular currencies they have. Its history has no unity. It is a flickering across a field of institutional spaces. (1993:11–12)

Photography as a mode of production creates photographs; they occupy a field of meaning decided by use and use value. To understand them we must examine the motivations, framings, and implications of their appearance within specific ideological and textual frameworks. Sontag focuses on understanding the visual document's code in relation to the text or location that surrounds or supports it. Understanding generic distinctions between different uses of the photograph maps different exercises in evocation and evidence. But an insistence on discerning and understanding the code relies on the imposition of a code-based system of meaning onto representations, which are further nuanced by their inescapable relation to sensual experience. A search for the code creates a viewing system that is dominated by semiotic perception, truncated from the sensual and essential.

Exercises to discern generic difference and to map intent and use move away from the photograph as a site for sensual experience and closer to it as a site for ideological analysis. Photographs are judged for their appearance, their surfacing within particular contexts, in light of "what dependencies they create, what antagonisms they pacify—that is, what institutions they buttress, whose needs they really serve" (Sontag 1973:178). Here photographs are fit into and read for what they indicate about particular power hierarchies. The portrait gallery at Mashantucket mixes its location in the tribal nation's representational power with the production of a sensually immersive visitor experience. The gallery's project actively plays with the space between semiotics and sensuality and engages this space as a location for active meaning and experience. As in the display environments of the museum and the casino, the Neel portraits are activated agents engaged in a complex hegemonics of represented cultural identity. They are intimately involved with the demarcation of a viewing frame and the arrangement of what it contains for the primary purpose of being viewed.

Photographs are a particular kind of narrative device, and the representations themselves must be investigated for position. The motives of the image maker and the image receiver must be brought under closer inspection, with attention paid to concepts of truthful representation, mediation, and the processing of image reception into information beyond the visual. By using this perspective, however, the image is in danger of becoming complete metaphor, no more than a visual stimulus leading to the formation of ideological sense. This might help us understand processes of representation, but the image as visual experience is elided. It is replaced with the seduction of seeing the representation not only as secondary to the original but as replacing the original. The representation, as Susan Stewart cautions, "instead of supplementing or supplanting the original . . . serves to create the original. . . . [E]ach fiction contaminates the imaginary purity of everyday life by denying the privileged authority of immediate, lived context and that context's subsequent 'authenticity' of experience" (1993:21). Mediation, understood as an interpretive distancing from an imagined "real," is a function of representation, not an effect.

But the idea of a nonmediated experiential site conceived as buttress for a use-value critique, which shifts the plane of significant experience from the event to the experience of the event's record, is equally problematic. The preliminary means to access the (original) event and the photographic record of the event involve primarily the same sense: sight. But this optic sense is just part of what we bring to viewing photographs. We also bring complex associations to making sense of what we see, based on different memories, experiences, and knowledges. While a picture may be worth a thousand words, those words are unique to every viewer and to every viewing event. And sight is not discrete—in trying to make meaning of what we see, our senses are overlapping and catalytic. Memories, necessarily involving a

194   Chapter 5

tangled mix of thought and sensual experience, offer complex and contradictory avenues to access remembered events.

If we are willing to understand the viewing of photographs as a practice that depends on a mix of activated memory and the ingestion of new knowledge or constellations of people, places, and things, how do we view a photograph, and what does the act of viewing entail? Viewing necessarily includes larger processes and extensions of memory and the utilization of different systems of knowledge and recognition. John Berger offers the idea of a radial system for presenting a photograph: the photograph doesn't represent a segment of time, captured and fixed, as much as an opportunity that leads or points from itself to an infinite variety of connections and stimulations. For Berger the presentation of a photograph must reflect this: "Words, comparisons, signs need to create a context for a printed photograph. . . . [T]hey must mark and leave open diverse approaches. A radial system has to be constructed around the photograph so that it may be seen in terms which are simultaneously personal, political, economic, dramatic, everyday, and historic" (1980a:62–63). Creating structures to allow the exercise of a radial system of potential engagements resembles current trends in museum and exhibition design, including supplementary text and objects, image grouping or juxtaposition, the use of open-ended information sources like multidirected touch-screen computer displays or audio texts, and open exhibition floor plans.

Roland Barthes's ideas on writing and intertextuality—reading as an unbounded experience and the idea of the animating or affecting image—provide additional support for thinking about radial systems, representation, display environments, and memory. Intertextual reading is an associative practice whose beginning in memory and imagination starts as a shift from text to experience. Viewing a photograph involves an initial sensual experience, an overlapping parallel with the sensual experience of viewing the (original) event itself.

As part of an effort to further contextualize photographic images, Berger suggests constructing a presentation that would allow for other possible ways of making connections with the act of viewing the photograph—other texts, narratives, photographs. This would expand the act of viewing into a larger, multiconnected, multicontextualized experience; viewing the photograph would be connected with other forms of memory provocation.

> If we want to put a photograph back into the context of experience, social experience, social memory, we have to respect the laws of memory. We have to situate the printed photograph so that it acquires something of the surprising conclusiveness of that which *was* and *is*. . . . Such a context replaces the photograph in time—not its own original time for that is impossible—but in narrated time. Narrated time becomes historic time when it is assumed by social memory and social action. (Berger 1980a:61)

Photographs connect a "frozen" moment to a narrative of history and the process of memory. This in turn reintroduces time and continuity. The concept of narrated time is critically important to approaching the final gallery of the MPMRC. And the overlapping aural experience of the taped oral histories provides a particular performance of contextualization through the use of located voices.

A Tribal Portrait II

The portrait gallery's exercise extends beyond an extensive contextualizing effort. The design, shape, and final placement of the gallery call for a shift in meditative space. As commodity objects, the photographs enjoy a currency different from the preceding artifacts of the museum, from life-cast figures to full-size village to examples of material culture. In this last gallery the presented photographs carry most of the exhibition's weight. The meaning-making process here parallels making meaning through "reading" a photograph, taking an image in and processing it by the powers of memory, imagined history, sensual experience, and visual evidence. Making sense of the images depends on a general public knowledge of "Indianness" and receptivity to that hegemonic image being turned on its head.

A radial system has been constructed in this gallery, surrounding and extending

the photographs, opening the images to be seen in simultaneously "personal, political, economic, dramatic, everyday, and historic" terms. The opening is signaled by the soundwash of tribal members' oral histories. The histories particularly ground the images without providing a one-to-one relationship between single voices and single images. More so than the group picture in the museum's opening gallery, these portraits provide an extensive and multiply nuanced group photograph of the tribal nation. Here the visitor is invited to navigate between images, creating pathways and links while traversing the room, moving from voice to whisper and back again. The voices and narratives, like the photographs, offer different articulations of sameness and difference, working between registers of nostalgia and the unsettling of nostalgic impulse.

In *Our Chiefs and Elders* Neel took great care to create interviews that respect the individuality of his sitters while simultaneously affirming their complicated multiple cultural roles and locations. The photographs are presented in the first half of the book, and the texts of the collected interviews are presented in the second half in the same sequence as the images. The reader can move back and forth between image and text, from portrait to story.

The narratives in the gallery, however, are individually disconnected. The stories told give voice to the collective experience of tribal members returning to the reservation or entering it for the first time. The voices present a generalized personal experience of Mashantucket, opening the gallery experience to the simultaneous registers and events of a radial presentation. The Neel photographs occupy the territory between evidence and evocation, all in a more conceptual archive that creates a composite picture of the Mashantucket Pequot Tribal Nation at a particular point in time. While the gallery offers a temporally located rendering of the tribal nation, it also provides a forward-looking archive, a resource for future

Figure 5.8 Arline Phelmetta and Eunice Mitchell, from A Tribal Portrait. (Photo by David Neel)

Figure 5.9 Gary Brend, from A Tribal Portrait. (Photo by David Neel)

Figure 5.10 Michael Holder and sons, from A Tribal Portrait. (Photo by David Neel)

Figure 5.11 Carolyn Colebut and Steven Colebut, from A Tribal Portrait. (Photo by David Neel)

Figure 5.12 Vernon Colebut, from A Tribal Portrait. (Photo by David Neel)

202   Chapter 5

generations of tribal members: "It's kind of difficult to describe, but just imagine finding out tomorrow that you are the cousin of an entire family of people that are total strangers to you, and then attempting to rejoin that family, if you will. So it definitely wasn't a socially comfortable thing, but still that sense of belonging that said the moment I was there that I would not leave" (voice from the Mashantucket Pequot oral history project).

As a portrait of the tribal nation, the collection makes subtle and interesting statements. The absence of any foregrounding or discussion of race is striking. Politicians, powerful developers, and local neighbors have attacked the tribal nation on the issue of racial identity since the Mashantucket Pequots began to gain financial power. The gallery shows a wide variety of tribal members, young and old, with a range of phenotypical features and characteristics. The variety of "racial characteristics" is paralleled by the variety of subjects and settings. Here in regalia, there at the kitchen table, here as a corporate portrait, there incorporating other portraits within the frame. Racial and ethnic identities—omnipresent elements in most discussions of Mashantucket Pequot representations of cultural identity or authenticity—are not explicit exhibition elements. The photographs are captioned with names only and are not further contextualized by subject origin, family, or occupation. The group of photographs resonates with a forceful underlying statement: "We are Mashantucket Pequots, each and every one of us. Although we may seem disparate, we present a group identity to the viewing world. And we don't have to explain ourselves to you." Race shifts from a field of contradiction or challenge to one of silent assertion and affirmation.

The dislocated oral histories further support this sense of group identity. Without a specific identification for the speakers or a didactic linking of voice to image, the continuous soundwash of the intermixing voices creates an aural environment in which every story describes a shared history, in which related experiences are made common through the anonymity of speaking.

The formal conceit of the portraits and the direct gaze of the subjects add another unifying element to the group of photographs. The direct gaze indicates a sitter making eye contact with the lens of the camera and with the photographer through the camera's viewfinder. The portraits' direct gaze engages the museum visitor, the viewing public, which, by this collective gaze, is rendered Other, the object of the photographed subjects' sight. This is the first space in the museum's exhibitions where the gaze of the visitor is met and returned. As the last gallery, it makes the museum's final impression. The overlay of multiple oral histories, the mixed sensation of visual and aural stimuli, and the gallery as possible final node of a multitexted, multimedia museum experience tease at radial structures and multiple contextualizations.

John Berger also argues for the extension and use of social memory, a connecting sense that unites private with public. Currently, the museum's effort is more methodological than united by a shared sense of close, extended community and social memory. The Mashantucket Pequots' comparatively recent reconstitution of their reservation community and their often antagonistic relationships with the towns and villages that surround it complicate the museum's exhibition strategies and artifacts and their ability to tap into a deep sense of belonging together. Without a shared sense of community the artifacts deployed in the museum's exhibitions, especially the photographs, are in danger of transforming represented subjects into public spectacle. This transformation depends on creating what Berger identifies as "an internal present of immediate expectation. . . . [W]ith the loss of memory the continuities of meaning and judgment are also lost to us. The camera relieves us [of] the burden of memory" (1980a:55). In this sense, memory defines a sense of knowing that is part of a continuum of judgment and identification; it is memory removed from embodiment and the senses.

Viewing a photograph is not a discrete exercise of visual sense. For Berger, the photograph displaces memory. The shape of memory invoked by looking at a photograph more closely resembles narrative in-filling. Photographs are linked to texts, possibilities of texts, radial presentations that incorporate and reflect different textual interactive levels. As such they offer the concept, most notably expounded by Bakhtin, that text does not exist as a discrete object, a stream of indivertible meaning from author to reader. Between author and reader, between the text and reading the text, exists an unbounded space of multiple possible meanings with no authoritative closure. The act of reading is an open act, the ongoing processing and creation of meaning that take the text as a jumping-off place, but it is neither limited by nor contained within it. Not only is there no closure, but the text's reading resists fixing. As the reader changes, so does the potential understanding and sense made of what is read.

Viewing a photograph resembles this process of reading, but with a different deployment of visual sense and recognition. This sense can be understood as the expansive ability of an image to exceed its obvious subject. Just as the eye begins to make sense of the scene depicted, to recognize objects and their relationships within the frame, it also begins to translate the image from a two-dimensional artifact to the three-dimensional event it conveys. Were the photograph to remain at the level of representation, it would be indistinguishable from other forms of pictorial rendering. Because of its connection with an event, its realization as the "trace" of a "real" that passed in front of the lens, the photograph achieves a distinctly different form of representation. As Edwards states above, the photograph can be appreciated as an analogue of visual experience, key to creating and supporting a culturally based ordering of the world.

The photograph as analogue becomes a vehicle of evidential history as well as a stimulus of memory. Berger points to the social use of narrated time as an indicator of historic time. Social acceptance of a particular narrative moves that narrative from the private to the public. This move parallels a photograph's journey from photographic moment to incorporation in a public narrative or discourse. Here the photograph participates in the recognition that history is a force around which narratives or representations cluster, describing and influenced by history's power without fixing or containing it. Photographs, like writing, ignite what Taussig calls "the capacity of the imagination to be lifted through representational media, such as marks on a page, into other worlds" (1993:16). Or, as Tagg reminds us, "histories are not backdrops to set off the performance of images. They are scored into the paltry paper signs, in what they do and do not do, in what they encompass and exclude, in the ways they open onto or resist a repertoire of uses in which they can be meaningful and productive. Photographs are never 'evidence' of history: they are themselves historical" (1993:12). Images can be read as trace—as "historical" documents—and as documents of memory; these two strategies for reading or understanding unite under a concept of the public imaginary.

The final gallery of the exhibitions both ends and indicates the museum's master narrative, which began with a contemporary moment quickly followed by a temporal erasure. But the narrative has also in-filled the time and place of Mashantucket. Tracking from prehistory to history, from contact to postcontact periods, and tying the personalized history of tribal members to particular points in the larger backdrop of U.S. history, the MPMRC re-creates a localized and Mashantucket Pequot–intensified narrative of the past becoming present. The portrait gallery not only provides a contemporary moment to this story's end, it reintroduces the concept of dynamic time through the medium of photography. It does so by participating in the trope of "the Indian" as photographic subject, creating a site for multiple engagements on the part of the visitor, a place for expectations and public imaginations to connect or be deflected through a personal, intensified body of images representing group identity. The photographs offer a shifting ground, a latent engagement with imagined audiences; this is their most powerful and potential point of engagement. The gallery closes a circular exhibition narrative for the MPMRC with a final reckoning with and of the Mashantucket community. The information and new set of knowledges gained through this immersive journey navigating through the galleries are called upon as visitors "meet" the tribal members "face-to-face."

A Tribal Portrait also represents a process—the growing role of the museum in the Mashantucket community. Neel initially found it difficult to get members to sit for the portraits (Neel, personal communication, 1997). Original plans for the gallery were based on one installation of photographs, and the project was not intended to continue. Although the exhibition design company established no maximum number for the gallery portraits, a minimum was suggested for exhibition by opening day. The popularity of being part of the project has grown since it started, reflecting shifts in the perception of the gallery and the museum as a community resource. The project has gained momentum, and a place has been made for ongoing participation. Neel completed the third project installment in 2002; the collection currently numbers approximately 125 finished images. (Neel is currently working on the project's fourth installment.)

The photo exhibition parallels much of the overall impact of both the museum and the casino: that context and ownership, while not necessarily bringing a change in performance or poetics, dramatically affect the politics of representational genres. The actual boundaries of the image are called into question, and interpretive frames radiate from its center. Is the edge of the representational image defined by the individual photograph? The group? The gallery setting? Ongoing battles over representational power and authorship? The Neel photos cross between the categories of documentary, ethnographic, and straight portrait as subgenres of photography (or photographic practice)—and they serve as catalog, record, and art. But their placement is key to their multiple project, and the portraits simultaneously perform a number of interconnected tasks. As counter to the vast shadow archive of photographs of unnamed Native Americans, the Neel portraits and their context reinscribe this image making with a connection to the present. And by drawing a critical comparison to work like Curtis's they contribute to the recontextualization and repatriation of a genre.

I use the term "repatriation" cautiously. The distinction I am making is that the Neel photographs—as photographs of Native Americans taken by a Native American for use in a Native American museum—participate in a project larger than the repatriation of a single photograph, where an image is reimmersed or reconfigured within forms of reckoning very different from those of its inception (see, e.g., Clifford 1997; Horse Capture 1993). The repatriation of a genre speaks to a reconfiguration of the role of photography within a distinctly Native mode of production.

But the Neel portraits, like much of the rest of the museum and the casino, walk a fine line between reaffirming and subverting the canon of representations of American Indians. In many ways the portraits participate in and depend on the same iconics as Curtis photographs, and they betray some of the same distanced and objectified positioning. But the Neel tribal portraits also provide an excellent example of strategic challenge to popular hegemonic notions of Indianness and race. This is accomplished in part through their incorporation and subversion of traditional canons in Native American portraiture.

The comparative and recontextualizing practice exemplified by the final gallery indicates the design strategy of the MPMRC. As part of Mashantucket Pequot self-representation and self-identification the photographs stake a certain claim on our attention and make a collective statement about group and individual identity. Part of this statement is seen in the variety of people that the tribal nation embraces as member-citizens. The mutability of "Pequot" and "Mashantucket Pequot" identifications has been a constant idea throughout the museum—from the introduction to Paleo-Indian ancestors, through periods of Native settlement to contact, from the decimations of disease and war, to a long period of Euro-colonial and post-Euro-colonial challenges. The exhibitions feature Mashantucket Pequot abilities to appropriate and resist elements of dominance as central themes of the overall narrative. While the majority of the exhibition galleries map social and cultural changes, the final gallery presents a collection of the contemporary results and survivors of those changes.

In the portrait gallery what goes without saying because it comes without saying is the wide range of racial, ethnic, and professional markers made visible in the photographs. As a group the portraits make a contemporary statement affirming tribal membership and community belonging. As photographs the Neel portraits offer particular kinds of historical and documentary information about their subjects. But photographs are more than a medium of information. What they show and how and where they show it are all parts of a complex interpretive—and often invisible—process.

Throughout the exhibition galleries the museum has attempted to create an *inhabited* rendition of tribal history through the use of life-cast figures and life-scale exhibitions. The mixing of interior and exterior, the use of the reservation as omnipotent presence and exhibition "partner" seen through the windows of the galleries, and the shifting location of the visitor—between spectator and exhibition animator—unsettle "fixed" representation by keeping alive a dynamic connection to the present.

The portrait gallery works in this space of dynamic time by presenting images of living tribal members. The portraits reinvigorate the historic progression of life on the reservation by introducing the contemporary to the visitor experience. As the oral histories provide a shared *remembered* history, the portraits give that history an individual face. While they indicate each other as a group and destabilize essential notions of "Indianness," the portraits provide a progression of possible singular connections for the visitor, mixing elements of personal, historic, and cultural markers and offering multiple routes for recognition. In this consideration the photographs, like the museum, become charged contact zones, and the arrested points of view become points of negotiation.

Conclusion

The last twenty-five years have seen enormous changes in Native America, realized in both local and national contexts; one of the most profound expressions of change has been in tribally created or directed narratives of self-identification and representation. Many Native Americans are fighting for—and in some instances newly winning—the right to their own stories, to be in charge of their own definitive narratives. The representational space that many Native people occupy or influence has been seized as a key strategic location with far-reaching implications, and the ability to create and promote historical and ethnographic narratives that counter or unsettle existing dominant histories is very powerful. It has the potential to transform the concept of "Indians" and "Indianness" in the popular imaginary and to force the recognition of other histories, other ways of reckoning the past and the contemporary. Such representations can affect a large visiting, mostly non-Native public. They can also provide rich archives and identity affirmation for Native people.

As owners of the largest and most profitable Indian casino in the world, the Mashantucket Pequots have the financial power to design and create any kind of representational space they wish. To the largest extent, representational practice at Mashantucket oscillates between the two most public spaces—the museum and the casino. While the historical and identity narratives at the museum may be more coherent and complete, those at the casino enjoy a much larger audience and may thus have the greater opportunity to influence public opinion (subtly or not); casinos present a significant opportunity to display public identities.

210   Conclusion

But the right to tell your own story is complicated if your tribal history includes near annihilation, termination, large-scale diasporas, and a vibrant renaissance that embraces tribal self-definition as a political and cultural goal. The representation practices at Mashantucket are not solely pointed outward. The reservation repopulation effort initiated by Skip Hayward and the tribal council in the 1970s created a unique community of many disparate individuals and families. Tribal members use the resources of the museum and research center to investigate genealogies and to discover and further establish how and what they are as a tribal community and a tribal nation. The authoritative narrative provided by the museum supports this kind of investigation.

In part the museum achieves this authority through appropriating and reinscribing existing mainstream representational discourses of local, colonial, and national history, discourses that have historically been used to tell decidedly different stories about Native Americans and Mashantucket Pequots. Included in these discourses and influential in the public imaginary concerning Indians is photography of Native Americans. The photographs in the museum provide a compelling example of how existing methodologies and narratives can be (re)invested with new meaning or direction to build new kinds of public identities. These identities have repercussions in popular understandings, but they are also critical to ideas of federal recognition and Native sovereignty.

As John Tagg suggested above, a photograph can be understood as a "flickering across a field of institutional spaces" (1993:12), and only a study of this field can yield the photograph's potential products and meanings. This calls for an investigation of the productive field between reference and performance and, in Mashantucket (and elsewhere), the articulation and strategic use of this space in the play between the referential "fact" of federal recognition and tribal nation identification and the publicly performed "experience" of that identity as represented in reservation displays and historical narratives.

The representational project at Mashantucket is created in a number of different levels, some best understood as differences in levels of sharpness or distance, some as levels of kind. Moving between these different levels of representation—from the casino to the museum, for example, to animatronic figures and life-cast villagers—offers a method for understanding the nuances of Mashantucket Pequot self-identification and self-representation. Mashantucket offers a number of immersive environments, and each environment uses a variety of representational methods and technologies.

This investigation navigates and inhabits the tense landscape between the evidential and the experiential, backtracking across spaces of fact and legislation, accelerating to describe rich and lived spaces, caught in the blue shimmering light of newscasts, the sound of the spill in the casino, the birdsong and murmuring voices of the museum. The strategic occupation of this landscape is tangential for all involved—for the Mashantucket Pequots who are mapping their history and, through historical reckoning, their origins and identity; for the variety of visitors to the museum, brushing the overlays of their own historical and contemporary understanding of Indianness and Mashantucket Pequotness against the density of exhibitions and architecture; and for the casino patrons, moving between spaces of distraction, entertainment, and gaming, experiencing the Indian thematic space of Foxwoods.

This book has been structured as an experiential immersion, ratcheting in ever-tightening focus to get at the "observable grain" of the Mashantucket spaces of representation and to finally center on the images in the closing gallery. Berger's radial system for presentation offers a useful means to approach the practice of representation at Mashantucket as a whole—each artifact, building, representation, and industry offers a complex set of interconnected influences and understandings. A radial reading includes the expansion of context and contextualization, the saturation and overlap of space and time, and the products and industries of identity representation. The casino and the museum meet most fully at this point to create a porous boundary of cross-contamination.

212   Conclusion

This investigation traverses three different intersections or fields of experience. First, it critically explores the relationship between the performative and referential meanings of "Indian." The first is found in the representational conceits for the casino and the museum and how Indianness is performed for popular consumption in the reservation's public spaces. The second refers to the practical struggle for recognition, experienced as a navigation of formal legal category and establishment. This relationship has been discussed in terms of a dialectic between evidence and evocation, between meaning as an assembly of evidential data—visual, aural, spatial, and textual—and meaning as felt or evoked through using this assembled data as the foundation for a sensual immersion through visual, aural, spatial, and textual performances. The casino is a particularly rich site for this kind of interplay, but the relationship made obvious there is no less foundational than that in use at the museum. It is important to remember, however, that the bingo hall and the eventual casino were the Mashantucket Pequots' primary public representational spaces for more than ten years, before the museum and research center opened.

Second, this investigation recognizes that while the casino uses the relationship between the inside and the outside as part of its overall thematic, the museum emphasizes this interplay as critical for its entire narrative, experienced as the relationship between the architectural shell and the reservation surround. This same surround serves as an active element in a number of exhibitions and galleries, spaces rich with active play between poetic performance and referential significance. The final exhibition in the museum crystallizes these strategies and relationships within genres of photography—both American Indian photography and the Neel portrait project create documents that are evidential and evocative, referential and poetic.

Third, the investigation acknowledges that the Mashantucket Pequots' skillful use of appropriation is crucial to Mashantucket Pequot projects of representation and public-dependent industry. Both the casino and the museum appropriate industries, technologies, knowledges, and existing archives and genres for rereading and incorporation. Appropriation is a kind of poetics, a way of generating new meaning in existing referential relationships through shifts in position, emphasis, and performance, and Mashantucket is rife with examples of such shifts. Here, as an engine to the representational and moneymaking projects of the reservation, appropriation can be understood as a powerful means of production.

Cultural production and reproduction are necessarily linked to the practices of "cultural industries," both those marked as culturally specific—like Indian gaming—and those whose industry is the production or explication of cultural difference. The latter is exemplified by a museum that speaks to and represents practices of national, ethnic, and cultural identity that are powerfully informed by the subtext of authentication. The practice of appropriation speaks to the relationship between the hegemonic and the counterhegemonic, between strategies designed to stabilize or destabilize traditional practices and discourses. The use of photography to unsettle existing discourses concerning Indians as photographic subjects and the use of photography at the reservation as documentary medium in such different venues as museum exhibitions or public relations materials embody this relationship.

The tension between hegemonic and counterhegemonic representation plays through the entire Mashantucket project of identity. Perhaps most acutely sensed in the tribal nation's spaces of representation, particularly in the relationships between understandings of Indianness and Mashantucket Pequotness, it is also an integral aspect in understanding the politics of Mashantucket. For example, while some Native activists would maintain that taking part in the system of federal recognition or state compacts for gaming compromises a true sovereignty for Native America, others recognize that one path to political power follows existing structures of law and legislation. Such power can be realized by reading this structure oppositionally, looking for cracks and fissures that can be used to tactical advantage.

One eerie embodiment of this tension as a particular element of the museum

214 Conclusion

and research center's main narrative is the commissioning and use of life-casts in the exhibitions. The composite figures stand as imagined actors in an "accurate" portrayal of Mashantucket Pequot history. At the same moment that the museum is particularizing this story, its technologies are drawing from a generalized "Indian"—in thematic and physical type—through the use of these figures. The use of a generalized Indianness is indicative of an active play with a hegemonic referential system. That the figures in Life on the Reservation are based on life-casts of Mashantucket Pequot tribal members and that those before are not further complicates reading Pequotness from its lifelike replication.

Poetics and hegemonics as well as stabilization and destabilization are linked at the reservation through a productive against-the-grain reading of historical and contemporary Indianness. The creation of counterhistories depends on the existence of a structure from which to depart or to reconfigure. The Mashantucket Pequots work within existing structures both to uphold them, as with federal recognition, and to subvert them. Simultaneously, they work within existing performative genres as well—photography, museums, and casinos—to recast them or to create new performances with new emphases.

Finally, Mashantucket offers a space to investigate the concept of "imagining the nation." In Anderson's referential framework for nationality the lived experience of being a citizen was an act of imagination, an in-filling of this framework with a performance of national belonging. This sense of belonging was both inclusive and exclusive, both figured within the national boundary and figured against the boundaries of other nations. Representational and informational media enforce and enact this sense of a national imaginary. The museum and the casino together offer a prime site for understanding the revitalized formation of a national community and how public spaces of representation—both formal and vernacular—are mobilized to support the parameters of community as an inclusive and exclusive construct.

This book's flickering light embraces the difference between pragmatics—the tangible as law or legislation—and the representational-poetic—the fabulous story told by the museum and the casino. While the Mashantucket Pequots have a secured legal identity as a tribal nation, they still spend a lot of time and money creating projected representations designed to confirm themselves as Native Americans and Mashantucket Pequots, recognizing that this public terrain is a key battlefield for articulating tribal and Indian identities.

This struggle over public terrain is emblematic of contests across Native America, reacting to centuries of images and understandings forged in the public sphere. Indian gaming has effectively accelerated and energized this contest by supplying new sources of capital for engaging in this struggle. Since gaming depends on a large patron base, Indian gaming has also provided new public forums for self-representation. Museums, as both a contemporary growth industry and a traditionally recognized theater for "authentic" historical narratives, have become a parallel enterprise for many Native peoples. But comprehending the complex institutional spaces at Mashantucket provides understandings and raises questions not limited to Native America. The relationships at Mashantucket indicate the ongoing interplay between the politics and poetics of self-representation.

Native America, at the beginning of the twenty-first century, is actively participating in two quickly expanding industries—casinos and museums. And the relationship between these two different types of business is mutually dependent and supporting. Museums have long been identified as spaces for representation, for telling particular stories with particular meanings, and Indians have been popular objects of these museum stories for a long time. Their appearance in museums has often supported or extended other popular notions of Indians, those gained through films and television, photographs, books, and popular culture: Indians, once noble, are vanishing or vanished, doomed in the face of relentless "progress." But popular public perception of Native America has gone through enormous changes since the passage of the 1988 Indian Gaming Regulatory Act. The phenomenal growth of Indian gaming has placed Indians increasingly in the news. As part of this coverage mainstream press has devoted attention to issues important to Native Americans, including tribal sovereignty, public identity, politics, economic power, lobbying ability, representation, and education about Indians past and present.

One measure of the recognized importance of representation for Native America can be understood in the 2004 opening of the National Museum of the American Indian (NMAI) in Washington, D.C. The NMAI represents an enormous achievement for American Indians. Native Americans are now primarily responsible for making critical decisions concerning museum narratives about Native Americans, designed to convey particular viewpoints and influence public opinion in our national capital. Construction and operation funds for the NMAI came from monies allocated by Congress, but significant donations came from tribes and tribal nations involved in Indian gaming; the Mashantucket Pequots were one of the first to pledge funds for the museum's construction. But these contributions are not simply a factor of economics. While casinos generate significant funds, they also increase the national profile of Indians and things Indian. Casinos and museums offer new public venues for the exploration of different thematic interpretations of Indian identity or "Indianness," and they have become corresponding enterprises for many tribal nations. On the one hand, the large amount of capital often necessary for building museums can be found in successful casinos, and many tribes and tribal nations use gaming profits to create cultural storehouses and display spaces. Native people have long recognized that their histories—both as distinct peoples and as parts of the history of the United States—have not been adequately told in mainstream U.S. and natural history museums.[1]

On the other hand, museums supply powerful cultural capital, representations of Indian peoples that validate and firmly place them on the land (in sovereign Indian space), in history (as a significant part of the past, both pre- and postcontact), and in the present (as ongoing dynamic peoples with distinct cultural identities). Indian museums and cultural centers articulate and authenticate Native cultures and histories at precisely the moment when questions about authenticity are an active part of challenges raised against Indian gaming. At the same moment Indian casinos, through their displays and exhibitions and their significant ability to raise revenue, work to make the strange familiar. The operation of Indian casinos helps to normalize the facts of Indian gaming, particularly its Native ownership or management and the recognition of casino gaming as a quotidian part of a number of Native (and other) economies. And the success of Indian gaming provides a highly visible example of Native American survival and persistence.

Foxwoods and the MPMRC offer a way to recognize the growing power of Native economies and communities. This power recognizes, insists on, and realizes the ability to construct self-representations as key to telling a different kind of history in a different kind of space.

Notes

Introduction

1. I use this term here and elsewhere as a way to collectively describe the many self-governing Indian communities throughout the United States.

2. The 2004 opening of the National Museum of the American Indian provides the highest-profile example of this possibility.

Chapter 1. Coming to Ground

1. See Newman (1993:A2). In 1992 the state's gross domestic product had dropped almost 1.4 percent, the steepest decline for any state in the country. In 1993 Connecticut measured the highest rate of job losses in the nation.

2. *Seminole Tribe of Florida v. Butterworth*, 658 F.2d 310, 313 (5th Cir.), *cert. denied*, 455 U.S. 1020 (1981), established that bingo fell under state statutes classed as regulatory rather than prohibitory, opening the door to high-stakes bingo games on reservations across the country. Florida challenged the *Seminole* decision, and in 1987 the Supreme Court ruled that the tribe's interest in promoting gaming for their economic good outweighed the state's interest in regulating these games.

3. *California v. Cabazon Band of Mission Indians*, 480 U.S. 202, 218 (1987) established that once a state has legalized any form of gambling, Indian tribes within that state can offer the same game on trust land without any state interference or restriction. The IGRA created rules for offering those games and making compacts with the states.

4. From the National Minority AIDS Education and Training Center, www.nmaetc.org/cultural/NativeAmerican.asp, accessed June 8, 2004.

5. *Indian Gaming Regulatory Act*, Public Law 100-497, 100th Cong., October 1988, 11.

6. The phrase "domestic dependent nation" was introduced in the Supreme Court decisions *Cherokee Nation v. Georgia* in 1831 and *Worcester v. Georgia* in 1832 to describe and circumscribe the particularities of Native sovereignty and self-determination.

Chapter 2. Tribal Renaissance

1. The Narragansetts were rivals with the Pequots for the domination of territory and trade with the Europeans, and the Eastern Niantics were allied with the Narragansetts (Cave 1992:512).

2. See Pasquaretta (2003) for an excellent discussion of historically shifting and strategic readings of the past as part of contemporary Mashantucket Pequot political identity.

3. Indeed, vestiges of this system of overseers continued until the early 1970s (Hauptman 1990:76).

4. This reduction of reservation land through state auction was to become a pivotal point in the later 1975 suits for return of land and for federal recognition.

5. The act was designed to transfer reservation lands from communal property to private property and to decrease both tribal landholdings and recognized tribal populations. Following the act, Native American landholdings fell nationally (between 1887 and 1934) from 138 million to 48 million acres.

6. During the Mashantucket Pequots' most aggressive repopulation efforts tribal membership was decided using this standard. In 1996 the tribal council voted to change the parameters for membership and recognized all existing members as fully Mashantucket Pequot.

7. These rolls listed about thirty-five names (Hileman 1993:B4).

8. The Indian Trade and Intercourse Act was first used in challenge for eastern tribes by the Oneida Indian Nation in 1970. In 1985 the Supreme Court ruled in favor of the Oneidas.

9. *Joint Tribal Council of the Passamaquoddy Tribe v. Morton*, 528 F.2d 370 (1st Cir. 1975).

10. The colitigants were the Passamaquoddy Tribe, the Penobscot Indian Nation, and the Houlton Band of Maliseets.

11. See *Mashantucket Pequot Indian Claims Settlement Act*, 25 U.S.C. Title 1751–60 (1994).

12. Foxwoods was the only gambling site in Connecticut until 1996, when the Mohegan Sun opened. By 1997 combined revenue for the two casinos was nearly $1.5 billion. This represents roughly 38 percent of what the twelve Atlantic City casinos posted for revenues in the same year (Sinclair 1993).

13. My use of this problematic term "contingent independence" echoes the legal concept of "domestic dependence" in describing Indian reservations and nations. Its contingency depends on a use of common structures of figuring power and politics, a defensive nationalism against a greater political force.

14. I am not able to give this discussion the room it deserves for a complete investigation. For an excellent analysis of how these categories historically signify and change among the Lumbee see, for example, Blu (1980).

Chapter 3. "The Wonder of It All"

1. A dedicated copy of the statue was also prominently featured at the 2002 Salt Lake City Winter Olympics as part of its "American" history theme.

2. A drum is a group of singers and drummers around a specific drum.

3. Although the time sequence here may seem foreshortened, the construction schedule for Foxwoods was intensely accelerated. Foxwoods reflected innovations in casinos being built with a more conventional construction schedule (and hence later opening dates).

4. Personal communication with New England Design, the design company responsible for the interior look and feel of Foxwoods.

5. Writing texts is ultimately an ideological practice. It depends on memory and recognition of author and reader whose genesis is in a system of value and belief.

6. For an intriguing discussion of Indian gaming and an understanding of the stakes see Pasquaretta (2003), which also provides an analysis of wagering as an intersection of Native and Euro-American peoples and socioeconomic policies.

7. From http://dictionary.oed.com/, accessed July 18, 2002.

8. Like Atlantis on Paradise Island in the Bahamas or Excalibur in Las Vegas, for example.

9. From www.foxwoods.com, accessed July 2002.

10. Personal communication with Katherine Spilde, senior research associate for the Harvard Project on American Indian Economic Development, July 2002.

Chapter 4. "Discover a Nation in Your Own Backyard"

1. The title for this chapter served as the advertising slogan for the 1998 opening of the MPMRC.

2. From "Architectural Facts," www.mashantucket.com, accessed July 2002. Polshek Partnership Architects were also included in the project architects for the National Museum of the American Indian and are the principal architects for its Cultural Resources Center.

3. Graham made her first appearance in this book as one of the Indians in the attic of the Connecticut River Museum (see chap. 1).

4. See www.mashantucket.com, from the website's document "Melding Landscape and Culture," accessed March 2002. See also Ceci (1990:48–64).

5. Few Pequot artifacts have been preserved, and the NMAI's collection does not hold many. Museums in Great Britain and Germany have more substantial collections of Pequot artifacts, and the MPMRC is pursuing purchasing or exhibiting items from those institutions.

6. Personal communication with Kevin McBride, the MPMRC director of research.

222 Notes to Pages 117–174

7. From the Foxwoods office of public relations.

8. The MPMRC often had a difficult time getting its proposed budget approved by the tribal council in a timely manner. This was partly due to the museum and research center's ever-expanding costs. It was not unusual for the budget approval to be held up even three months after the end of the fiscal year.

9. Concerning intertextuality see, for example, Bakhtin (1981, 1984) and Briggs and Bauman (1992).

10. Clifford explores the University of British Columbia Museum, the Royal British Columbia Museum, the Kwagiulth U'mista Cultural Centre in Alert Bay, and the Kwagiulth Museum at Cape Mudge.

11. Personal communication with Lauri Halderman and Mike Hanke of Design Division, Inc., 1997. See also Nash (2001).

Chapter 5. A Tribal Portrait

1. David Neel was not familiar with any of the oral history texts while shooting his project, and the oral histories were collected before the photo project had been finalized.

2. See Neel (1992:16). Indeed, Curtis represents a figure that all Indian photographers must deal with in their own understanding and practice. For Neel and for this book Curtis offers one powerful means to consider how the photographing and representing of Native Americans has long reflected, indicated, and participated in structures of power and knowledge in the United States.

3. See also Faris (1996). Debates of Curtis images as sites for fakery or affirmation are many— some see the examples that Lyman critiques as potentially tainting the entire body of work as inauthentic; others state that the sample he works from is relatively small or that the images serve as important cultural source material, regardless of the full story of their origin (see Lyman 1982; Coleman 1998a, 1998b; Horse Capture 1993; Faris 1996; Scherer 1975; Gidley 1998).

4. See Penn (1974); Neel cites this project, "World in a Small Box," as influential for his work.

5. In a large and very real sense all photographs are the products of collaboration between photographer and subject. There are, of course, different levels of collaboration. See Coleman (1998a).

6. This simply describes how photographs begin as latent images on the film plane. Many equate photographs with exposing film, regardless of the processes necessary to bring latent image to print or the photographer's motivations in exposing the film.

7. Halpin is curator of ethnology at the University of British Columbia's Museum of Anthropology.

8. See the work of German photographer August Sander from the 1920s and 1930s, for example, or Edward Steichen's Family of Man exhibition for New York's Museum of Modern Art in 1955. See also Penn (1974) and Avedon (1996), which also participate in this effort to create representative human catalogs.

9. I use this concept cautiously—the theory of simulacra adds a certain perspective to the discussion of photographic images. But I hesitate to designate photographs as simulacral constructions. In practice, photographs are representative constructions. To put too much emphasis on their identity as simulations would be to diffuse an ability to talk about them as they are: highly charged and resonant images that affect the viewer through a panoply of registers and associations.

10. Curtis's images have also slowly risen in value on the art photo market over the last thirty years while increasingly carrying the burden for colonial imaging and the imposition of traditional and period-accurate representation through theatrical means.

11. Images like this are extensive (see Scherer 1975; Lippard 1992; Bush and Mitchell 1994).

12. See Clifford (1997). See also Lippard (1992) for an extended multiple exercise of this photo-reading strategy and Barthes (1981) for a discussion of the phenomenological and semiotic extensions of such a viewing practice.

Conclusion

1. That the representation of Native peoples has often been relegated to natural history museums, where they share uncomfortable if unquestioned proximity to insects, plants, and dinosaurs, has further distorted their place in both history and the "natural order" of all living things.

Bibliography

Alonso, Ana Maria. 1988. "The Effects of Truth: Re-Presentations of the Past and the Imagining of Community." *Journal of Historical Sociology* 1 (1): 33–57.

Ames, Michael. 1992. *Cannibal Tours and Glass Boxes: The Anthropology of Museums*. Vancouver: University of British Columbia Press.

Anderson, Benedict. 1983. *Imagined Communities*. London: Verso Editions.

Appadurai, Arjun. 1986. *The Social Life of Things*. New York: Cambridge University Press.

Appadurai, Arjun, and Carol A. Breckenridge. 1992. "Museums Are Good to Think: Heritage on View in India." In *Museums and Communities: The Politics of Public Culture*, ed. Ivan Karp, Christine M. Kreamer, and Steven D. Lavine, 34–55. Washington, D.C.: Smithsonian Institution Press.

Avedon, Richard. 1996. *In the American West*. New York: Harry N. Abrams.

Bachelard, Gaston. 1969. *The Poetics of Space*. Boston: Beacon Press.

Bakhtin, Mikhail. 1981. *The Dialogic Imagination*. Trans. Caryl Emerson and Michael Holquist. Austin: University of Texas Press.

————. 1984. *Problems of Dostoevsky's Poetics*. Trans. Caryl Emerson. Minneapolis: University of Minnesota Press.

Barthes, Roland. 1977. *Image, Music, Text*. New York: Noonday Press.

————. 1981. *Camera Lucida: Reflections on Photography*. New York: Farrar, Straus and Giroux.

Basso, Keith. 1996. "Wisdom Sits in Places: Notes on a Western Apache Landscape." In *Senses of Place*, ed. Steven Feld and Keith H. Basso, 51–90. Santa Fe, N.M.: School of American Research Press.

Baudrillard, Jean. 1994. *Simulacra and Simulation*. Ann Arbor: University of Michigan Press.

Beinert, Peter. 1999. "Lost Tribes: Native Americans and Government Anthropologists Feud over Indian Identity." *Lingua Franca* 9 (4): 32–41.

Benedict, Jeff. 2000. *Without Reservation: The Making of America's Most Powerful Indian Tribe and Foxwoods, the World's Largest Casino*. New York: HarperCollins.

Benjamin, Walter. 1969. "The Work of Art in the Age of Mechanical Reproduction." In *Illuminations*, ed. Hannah Arendt, 217–51. New York: Shocken Books.

226   Bibliography

———. 1980. "A Short History of Photography." In *Classic Essays on Photography*, ed. Alan Trachtenberg, 199–216. New Haven, Conn.: Leete's Island Books.

———. 1982. "The Author as Producer." In *Thinking Photography*, ed. Victor Burgin, 15–31. London: Macmillan.

Berger, John. 1980a. *About Looking*. New York: Pantheon Books.

———. 1980b. "Understanding a Photograph." In *Classic Essays on Photography*, ed. Alan Trachtenberg, 291–94. New Haven, Conn.: Leete's Island Books.

Berkhofer, Robert F. 1978. *The White Man's Indian*. New York: Vantage Books.

Biolsi, Thomas. 2005. "Imagined Geographies: Sovereignty, Indigenous Space, and American Indian Struggle." *American Ethnologist* 32 (2): 239–59.

Biolsi, Thomas, and Larry J. Zimmerman, eds. 1997. *Indians & Anthropologists: Vine Deloria Jr. and the Critique of Anthropology*. Tucson: University of Arizona Press.

Blu, Karen. 1980. *The Lumbee Problem: The Making of an American Indian People*. New York: Cambridge University Press.

Bodinger de Uriarte, John. 1995. "Fantastic Narrative, Material Strategy: Foxwoods Casino and the Mashantucket Pequot Tribal Nation." M.A. report, Department of Anthropology, University of Texas at Austin.

———. 2001. "About Face: Approaching a Dialogue of Images and Display." *Museum Anthropology* 25 (1): 11–19.

———. 2003. "Imagining the Nation with House Odds: Representing American Indian Identity at Mashantucket." *Ethnohistory* 50 (3): 549–65.

———. 2005. "Casinos & Museums: Changing the Public Face of Native America." *Tribal Government Gaming*: 8–10.

Bodinger de Uriarte, John, and Pauline Turner Strong. 2000. "Edward S. Curtis: Ethnology and the (Negative) Romantic." Paper presented at the Thornton F. Bradshaw Seminar in the Humanities, Claremont, Calif., October 7.

Bourdieu, Pierre. 1977. *Outline of a Theory of Practice*. New York: Cambridge University Press.

———. 1984. *Distinction: A Social Critique of the Judgment of Taste*. Cambridge, Mass.: Harvard University Press.

———. 1990. *Photography*. Stanford, Calif.: Stanford University Press.

Briggs, Charles L., and Richard Bauman. 1992. "Genre, Intertextuality, and Social Power." *Journal of Linguistic Anthropology* 2 (2): 131–72.

Brow, James. 1988. "In Pursuit of Hegemony: Representation of Authority and Justice in a Sri Lankan Village." *American Ethnologist* 15 (2): 311–27.

———. 1990. "Notes on Community, Hegemony, and the Uses of the Past." *Anthropological Quarterly* 63 (1): 1–6.

———. 1996. *Demons and Development: The Struggle for Community in a Sri Lankan Village*. Tucson: University of Arizona Press.

Buck-Morss, Susan. 1991. *The Dialectics of Seeing*. Cambridge, Mass.: MIT Press.

Burgin, Victor. 1982a. "Introduction." In *Thinking Photography*, ed. Victor Burgin, 1–14. London: Macmillan.

———. 1982b. "Looking at Photographs." In *Thinking Photography*, ed. Victor Burgin, 142–53. London: Macmillan.

———. 1986a. "Re-reading *Camera Lucida*." In *The End of Art Theory*, 71–92. Atlantic Highlands, N.J.: Humanities Press International.

———. 1986b. "Seeing Sense." In *The End of Art Theory*, 51–70. Atlantic Highlands, N.J.: Humanities Press International.

Bush, Alfred L., and Lee Clark Mitchell. 1994. *The Photograph and the American Indian*. Princeton, N.J.: Princeton University Press.

Campisi, Jack. 1990. "The Emergence of the Mashantucket Pequot Tribe, 1637–1975." In *The Pequots in Southern New England: The Fall and Rise of an American Indian Nation*, ed. Lawrence M. Hauptman and James D. Wherry, 117–40. Norman: University of Oklahoma Press.

———. 1991. *The Mashpee Indians: Tribe on Trial*. Syracuse, N.Y.: Syracuse University Press.

Cave, Alfred A. 1992. "Who Killed John Stone? A Note on the Origins of the Pequot War." *William and Mary Quarterly*, 3d ser., 49 (3): 509–21.

Ceci, Lynn. 1990. "Native Wampum as a Peripheral Resource in the Seventeenth-Century World-System." In *The Pequots in Southern New England: The Fall and Rise of an American Indian Nation*, ed. Lawrence M. Hauptman and James D. Wherry, 48–64. Norman: University of Oklahoma Press.

Chambers, Ross. 1991. *Room for Maneuver: Reading (the) Oppositional (in) Narrative*. Chicago: University of Chicago Press.

Chappell, Kevin. 1995. "Black Indians Hit Jackpot in Casino Bonanza." *Ebony* 50:46–52.

Chen, David W., and Charlie Le Duff. 2001. "Bad Blood in Battle over Casinos." *New York Times*, October 28, A1.

Cheyfitz, Eric. 1991. *The Poetics of Imperialism: Translation and Colonization from "The Tempest" to "Tarzan."* New York: Oxford University Press.

Clifford, James. 1986. "On Ethnographic Allegory." In *Writing Culture: The Poetics and Politics of Ethnography*, ed. James Clifford and George Marcus, 98–121. Berkeley: University of California Press.

———. 1987. "Of Other Peoples: Beyond the 'Salvage' Paradigm." In *Discussions in Contemporary Culture*, ed. Hal Foster, 121–30. Seattle: Bay Press.

228 Bibliography

———. 1988. *The Predicament of Culture: Twentieth-Century Ethnography, Literature, and Art*. Cambridge, Mass.: Harvard University Press.

———. 1991. "Four Northwest Coast Museums: Travel Reflections." In *Exhibiting Cultures: The Poetics and Politics of Museum Display*, ed. Ivan Karp and Steven D. Lavine, 212–54. Washington, D.C.: Smithsonian Institution Press.

———. 1997. "Four Northwest Coast Museums: Travel Reflections." In *Routes: Travel and Translation in the Late Twentieth Century*, 107–45. Cambridge, Mass.: Harvard University Press.

Clifton, James. 1990. *The Invented Indian: Iconoclastic Essays*. New Brunswick, N.J.: Transaction Publishers.

Coleman, A. D. 1998a. "Edward S. Curtis: The Photographer as Ethnologist." In *Depth of Field: Essays on Photography, Mass Media, and Lens Culture*, 132–57. Albuquerque: University of New Mexico Press.

———. 1998b. "The Image in Question: Further Notes on the Directorial Mode." In *Depth of Field: Essays on Photography, Mass Media, and Lens Culture*, 53–61. Albuquerque: University of New Mexico Press.

Comaroff, John, and Jean Comaroff. 1992. *Ethnography and the Historical Imagination*. Boulder, Colo.: Westview Press.

Crampton, Norman. 1992. *The 100 Best Small Towns in America*. Old Tappan, N.J.: Prentice-Hall.

Curtis, Edward Sheriff. 1968. *Visions of a Vanishing Race*. Boston: Houghton Mifflin Co.

———. 1972. *Portraits from North American Indian Life*. New York: Promontory Press.

———. 1976a. *The Portable Curtis*. Berkeley: Creative Arts Book Co.

———. 1976b. *Selected Writings of Edward S. Curtis*, ed. Barry Gifford. Berkeley: Creative Arts Book Co.

———. 1977. *The Vanishing Race*. New York: Taplinger Publishing Co.

———. 1993. *Native Nations: First Americans as Seen by Edward S. Curtis*. Ed. Christopher Cardozo. Boston: Little, Brown.

Darian-Smith, Eve. 2004. *New Capitalists: Law, Politics, and Identity Surrounding Casino Gaming on Native American Land*. Belmont, Calif.: Wadsworth/Thompson Learning.

Deloria, Philip J. 1998. *Playing Indian*. New Haven, Conn.: Yale University Press.

Deloria, Vine. 1974. *Behind the Trail of Broken Treaties*. Austin: University of Texas Press.

———. 1982. "Introduction." In *The Vanishing Race and Other Illusions: Photographs of Indians by Edward S. Curtis*, by Christopher M. Lyman, 11–13. Washington, D.C.: Smithsonian Institution Press.

———, ed. 1985. *American Indian Policy in the Twentieth Century*. Norman: University of Oklahoma Press.

Deloria, Vine, and Clifford Lytle. 1984. *The Nations Within: The Past and Future of American Indian Sovereignty*. New York: Pantheon Books.

Dirks, Nicholas B., ed. 1992. *Colonialism and Culture*. Ann Arbor: University of Michigan Press.

Dobrzynski, Judith H. 1997. "Profits from Foxwoods Casino Help an Indian Tribe Reclaim Its History." *New York Times*, September 1, A1.

Dorst, John. 1989. *The Written Suburb: An American Site, an Ethnographic Dilemma*. Philadelphia: University of Pennsylvania Press.

————. 1993. "A Walk through the Shooting Gallery." *Museum Anthropology* 17 (3): 7–13.

————. 1999. *Looking West*. Philadelphia: University of Pennsylvania Press.

Duncan, James, and David Ley. 1993. "Representing the Place of Culture." In *Place/Culture/Representation*, ed. James Duncan and David Ley, 1–21. New York: Routledge.

Durham, Jimmie. 1992. "Geronimo!" In *Partial Recall: Photographs of Native North Americans*, ed. Lucy R. Lippard, 55–58. New York: New Press.

"An Eagle's Eye on the Big Picture." 1994. *ConnStruction* 32 (4): 41.

Edwards, Elizabeth, ed. 1992. *Anthropology and Photography, 1860–1920*. New Haven, Conn.: Yale University Press.

Erikson, Patricia Pierce. 2002. *Voices of a Thousand People: The Makah Cultural & Research Center*. Lincoln: University of Nebraska Press.

Fabian, Johannes. 1983. *Time and the Other: How Anthropology Makes Its Object*. New York: Columbia University Press.

Faris, James C. 1996. *Navajo and Photography: A Critical History of the Representation of an American People*. Albuquerque: University of New Mexico Press.

Forbes, Jack D. 1990. "The Manipulation of Race, Caste, and Identity: Classifying Afroamericans, Native Americans, and Red-Black People." *Journal of Ethnic Studies* 17 (4): 1–51.

Gates, Henry Louis, Jr. 1992. *The Signifying Monkey*. New York: Oxford University Press.

Gidley, Mick. 1998. *Edward S. Curtis and the North American Indian, Inc.* Cambridge: Cambridge University Press.

————. 2003. *Edward S. Curtis and the North American Indian Project in the Field*. Lincoln: University of Nebraska Press.

Goffe, Leslie. 1999. "Hitting the Genetic Jackpot: How Native Blood Paid out for Some African Americans." *Utne Reader*, May–June, 76–78.

Grady, Dennis. 1989. "The Devolutionary Image: Toward a Photography of Liberation." *SF Camerawork* 16 (2–3): 28–31.

Greenblatt, Stephen. 1991. "Resonance and Wonder." In *Exhibiting Cultures: The Poetics and Politics of Museum Display*, ed. Ivan Karp and Steven D. Lavine, 42–56. Washington, D.C.: Smithsonian Institution Press.

————. 1992. *Marvelous Possessions: The Wonder of the New World*. Chicago: University of Chicago Press.

230 Bibliography

Halpin, Marjorie. 1992. "Afterword." In *Our Chiefs and Elders*, by David Neel, 183–89. Vancouver: University of British Columbia Press.

Handler, Richard, and Eric Gable. 1997. *The New History in an Old Museum: Creating the Past at Colonial Williamsburg*. Durham, N.C.: Duke University Press.

Handler, Richard, and Jocelyn Linnekin. 1984. "Tradition, Genuine or Spurious." *Journal of American Folklore* 97 (385): 273–90.

Harmon, Alexandra. 1998. *Indians in the Making: Ethnic Relations and Indian Identities around Puget Sound*. Berkeley: University of California Press.

———. 2002. "Wanted: More Histories of Indian Identity." In *A Companion to American Indian History*, ed. Philip J. Deloria and Neal Salisbury, 248–65. Malden, Mass.: Blackwell Publishers.

Hauptman, Lawrence M. 1990. "The Pequot War and Its Legacies." In *The Pequots in Southern New England: The Fall and Rise of an American Indian Nation*, ed. Lawrence M. Hauptman and James D. Wherry, 69–80. Norman: University of Oklahoma Press.

Herzfeld, Michael. 1987. *Anthropology through the Looking Glass: Critical Ethnography in the Margins of Europe*. Cambridge: Cambridge University Press.

Hess, Alan. 1993. *Viva Las Vegas: After Hours Architecture*. San Francisco: Chronicle Books.

Hileman, Maria. 1993. "Rebirth of a Nation." *New London Day*, December 12, B4.

Hobsbawm, Eric, and Terence Ranger, eds. 1983. *The Invention of Tradition*. New York: Cambridge University Press.

Holder, John. 1994. "Narrative from the Rainmaker." *Pequot Times* 3 (2): 3.

Horse Capture, George P. 1993. "Foreword." In *Native Nations: First Americans as Seen by Edward S. Curtis*, ed. Christopher Cardozo, 13–17. Boston: Little, Brown.

Houlihan, Patrick T. 1991. "The Poetic Image and Native American Art." In *Exhibiting Cultures: The Poetics and Politics of Museum Display*, ed. Ivan Karp and Steven D. Lavine, 205–11. Washington, D.C.: Smithsonian Institution Press.

Jaimes, Annette. 1996. *The State of Native North America: Genocide, Colonization, and Resistance*. New York: Oxford University Press.

Jakobson, Roman. 1960. "Closing Statement: Linguistics and Poetics." In *Style in Language*, ed. Thomas Sebeok, 350–77. New York: Wiley & Sons.

Jakobson, Roman, and Moris Halle. 1965. "The Metaphoric and Metonymic Poles." In *Fundamentals of Language*, ed. Moris Halle, 76–82. The Hague: Mouton.

Jameson, Fredric. 1984. "Postmodernism, or the Cultural Logic of Late Capitalism." *New Left Review* 146:53–92.

Jennings, Francis. 1975. *The Invasion of America: Indians, Colonialism and the Cant of Conquest*. Chapel Hill: University of North Carolina Press.

Johansen, Bruce A. 2001. "Betting on Gaming: New York State Turns to Sovereignty as Economic Rotor." *Native Americas, Akwe:kon's Journal of Indigenous Issues* 18 (3–4): 28–31.

Johnson, Kirk. 1992. "Betting in Harmony with Nature." *New York Times*, January 29, B1.

Johnson, Tim. 1995. "The Dealer's Edge: Gaming in the Path of Native America." *Native Americas, Akwe:kon's Journal of Indigenous Issues* 12:20–21.

Karp, Ivan. 1991. "Culture and Representation." In *Exhibiting Cultures: The Poetics and Politics of Museum Display*, ed. Ivan Karp and Steven D. Lavine, 11–24. Washington, D.C.: Smithsonian Institution Press.

Kirshenblatt-Gimblett, Barbara. 1991. "Objects of Ethnography." In *Exhibiting Cultures: The Poetics and Politics of Museum Display*, ed. Ivan Karp and Steven D. Lavine, 386–443. Washington, D.C.: Smithsonian Institution Press.

————. 1998. *Destination Culture: Tourism, Museums, and Heritage*. Berkeley: University of California Press.

Kopytoff, Igor. 1986. "The Cultural Biography of Things: Commoditization as Process." In *The Social Life of Things: Commodities in Cultural Perspective*, ed. Arjun Appadurai, 64–91. New York: Cambridge University Press.

Kreps, Christina F. 2003. *Liberating Culture: Cross-Cultural Perspectives on Museums, Curation, and Heritage Preservation*. New York: Routledge.

Kroft, Steve. 1994. "Wampum Wonderland." *60 Minutes*, CBS, September 18.

————. 2000. "Wampum Wonderland." *60 Minutes II*, CBS, May 23.

LaCroix, Celeste C. 1999. "Wealth, Power, and Identity: A Critical Reading of Competing Discourses about the Mashantucket Pequots and Foxwoods." PhD diss., College of Communication, Ohio University.

Lawlor, Mary. 2005. "Identity in Mashantucket." *American Quarterly* 57 (1): 153–77.

Lightman, David. 1993. "Trump Criticizes Pequots, Casino; Trump Says Indian Gaming Vulnerable to the Mob." *Hartford Courant*, October 6, A1.

Linnekin, Jocelyn. 1991. "Cultural Invention and the Dilemma of Authenticity." *American Anthropologist* 93 (2): 446–49.

Lippard, Lucy R., ed. 1992. *Partial Recall: Photographs of Native North Americans*. New York: New Press.

Lyman, Christopher M. 1982. *The Vanishing Race and Other Illusions: Photographs of Indians by Edward S. Curtis*. Washington, D.C.: Smithsonian Institution Press.

Marx, Karl. 1978 [1852]. "The Eighteenth Brumaire of Louis Bonaparte." In *The Marx-Engels Reader*, ed. Robert C. Tucker, 594–617. New York: W. W. Norton & Co.

McBride, Kevin. 1990. "The Historical Archaeology of the Mashantucket Pequots, 1637–1900." In *The Pequots in Southern New England: The Fall and Rise of an American Indian Nation*, ed. Laurence M. Hauptman and James D. Wherry, 96–116. Norman: University of Oklahoma Press.

232 Bibliography

Morris, C. Patrick. 1992. "Termination by Accountants: The Reagan Indian Policy." In *Native Americans and Public Policy*, ed. Fremont J. Lyden and Lyman H. Lagters, 63–84. Pittsburgh: University of Pittsburgh Press.

Nagel, Joanne. 1996. *American Indian Ethnic Renewal*. New York: Oxford University Press.

Nash, Alice. 2001 [2000]. "Still Pequot after All These Years." *Common-Place* 1 (1). www.commonplace.org/vol-01/no-01/lessons. Accessed March 15, 2002.

National Indian Gaming Association. 2004. *An Analysis of the Economic Impact of Indian Gaming in 2004*. www.indiangaming.org. Accessed August 1, 2004.

Neel, David. 1992. *Our Chiefs and Elders: Words and Photographs of Native Leaders*. Seattle: University of Washington Press.

Newhall, Beaumont. 1982. *The History of Photography: From 1839 to the Present*. New York: Museum of Modern Art and Little, Brown.

Newman, Anne. 1993. "Connecticut Fights to Halt Worst Rate of Job Losses in US." *Wall Street Journal*, February 10, A2.

Overton, Penelope. 1993. "Tribe's Non-Indian Neighbors Feel Threatened." *New London (Connecticut) Day*, December 15, B4.

Pasquaretta, Paul. 1994a. "On the 'Indianness' of Bingo: Gambling and the Native American Community." *Critical Inquiry* 20 (Summer): 694–714.

————. 1994b. "Tricksters at Large: Pequots, Gamblers, and the Emergence of Crossblood Culture in North America." PhD diss., Department of English, State University of New York at Stony Brook.

————. 2003. *Gambling and Survival in Native North America*. Tucson: University of Arizona Press.

Penn, Irving. 1974. *Worlds in a Small Room*. New York: Grossman.

Penney, David W. 1994. "Images of Identity: American Indians in Photographs." In *Images of Identity: American Indians in Photographs*, 4–20. Detroit: Detroit Institute of Arts. Published in conjunction with the exhibition Images of Identity: American Indians in Photographs shown at the Detroit Institute of Arts.

Pinney, Christopher. 1992. "The Parallel Histories of Anthropology and Photography." In *Anthropology & Photography: 1860–1920*, ed. Elizabeth Edwards, 74–95. New Haven, Conn.: Yale University Press.

————. 2003. "Introduction: 'How the Other Half . . . '" In *Photography's Other Histories*, ed. Christopher Pinney, 1–14. Durham, N.C.: Duke University Press.

Quin, Douglas. 1999. "Nature by Design: Soundscape in the Museum." PhD diss., Union Institute, Cincinnati, Ohio.

Rabinow, Paul. 1984. *The Foucault Reader*. New York: Pantheon Books.

Root, Deborah. 1997. "'White Indians': Appropriation and the Politics of Display." In *Borrowed Power: Essays on Cultural Appropriation*, ed. Bruce Ziff and Pratima V. Rao, 225–33. New Brunswick, N.J.: Rutgers University Press.

Rugoff, Ralph. 1995. "Gambling with Reality: The New Art of Las Vegas." In *Circus Americanus*, 3–7. New York: Verso.

Salisbury, Neal. 1982. *Manitou and Providence: Indians, Europeans, and the Making of New England, 1500–1643*. New York: Oxford University Press.

———. 1990. "Indians and Colonists in Southern New England after the Pequot War: An Uneasy Balance." In *The Pequots in Southern New England: The Fall and Rise of an American Indian Nation*, ed. Laurence M. Hauptman and James D. Wherry, 81–95. Norman: University of Oklahoma Press.

Scherer, Joanna C. 1975. "You Can't Believe Your Eyes: Inaccuracies in Photographs of North American Indians." *Studies in the Anthropology of Visual Communication* 2 (2): 67–79.

Scully, Diana. 1995. *Maine Indian Claims Settlement: Concepts, Context, and Perspectives*. Maine Indian Tribal State Commission.

Sekula, Allan. 1982. "On the Invention of Photographic Meaning." In *Thinking Photography*, ed. Victor Burgin, 84–109. London: Macmillan

———. 1987. "Reading an Archive." In *Blasted Allegories: An Anthology of Writings by Contemporary Artists*, ed. Brian Wallis, 114–27. Cambridge, Mass.: MIT Press.

———. 1989. "The Body and the Archive." In *The Contest of Meaning: Critical Histories of Photography*, ed. Richard Bolton, 343–89. Cambridge, Mass.: MIT Press.

Sequoya, Jane. 1993. "How (!) Is an Indian?: A Contest of Stories." In *New Voices in Native American Literary Criticism*, ed. Arnold Krupat, 453–73. Washington, D.C.: Smithsonian Institution Press.

Sinclair, Sebastian. 1998. "Go-Go Times Roll on for Foxwoods, Mohegan Sun." *Indian Gaming Business: A Quarterly Supplement to International Gaming & Wagering Business* (May): 8–9.

Sontag, Susan. 1973. *On Photography*. New York: Anchor Books, Doubleday.

Spicer, Edward. 1994. "The Nations of a State." In *American Indian Persistence and Resurgence*, ed. Karl Kroeber, 27–49. Durham, N.C.: Duke University Press.

Spilde, Katherine A. 1999. "Indian Gaming Study." *Anthropology Newsletter* 4 (4): 11.

Spivak, Gayatri. 1990. *The Post-Colonial Critic: Interviews, Strategies, Dialogues*. New York: Routledge.

Starna, William A. 1990. "The Pequots in the Early Seventeenth Century." In *The Pequots in Southern New England: The Fall and Rise of an American Indian Nation*, ed. Laurence M. Hauptman and James D. Wherry, 33–47. Norman: University of Oklahoma Press.

Stewart, Kathleen. 1988. "Nostalgia–A Polemic." *Cultural Anthropology* 3 (3): 227–41.

———. 1996. *A Space on the Side of the Road: Cultural Poetics in an "Other" America*. Princeton, N.J.: Princeton University Press.

234 Bibliography

Stewart, Susan. 1993. *On Longing*. Durham, N.C.: Duke University Press.

Stocking, George W. 1985. *Objects and Others: Essays on Museums and Material Culture*. Madison: University of Wisconsin Press.

Strong, Pauline Turner. 1999. *Captive Selves, Captivating Others: The Politics and Poetics of Colonial American Captivity Narratives*. Boulder, Colo.: Westview Press.

————. 2002. "Transforming Outsiders: Captivity, Adoption, and Slavery Reconsidered." In *A Companion to American Indian History*, ed. Philip J. Deloria and Neal Salisbury, 339–56. Malden, Mass.: Blackwell Publishers.

Strong, Pauline Turner, and Barrik Van Winkle. 1993. "Tribe and Nation: American Indians and American Nationalism." *Social Analysis*, no. 33:9–26.

————. 1996. "'Indian Blood': Reflections on the Reckoning and Refiguring of Native North American Identity." *Cultural Anthropology* 11 (4): 547–76.

Szarkowski, John. 1966. *The Photographer's Eye*. New York: Museum of Modern Art, distributed by Doubleday.

Tagg, John. 1993. *The Burden of Representation*. Minneapolis: University of Minnesota Press.

Talbot, William Henry Fox. 1969. *The Pencil of Nature*. New York: Da Capo Press.

Taussig, Michael. 1993. *Mimesis and Alterity*. New York: Routledge.

Todorov, Tzvetan. 1984. *The Conquest of America*. New York: Harper Perennial.

Vizenor, Gerald. 1990. *Crossbloods*. Minneapolis: University of Minnesota Press.

————. 1992. "Ishi Bares His Chest: Tribal Simulations and Survivance." In *Partial Recall: Photographs of Native North Americans*, ed. Lucy R. Lippard, 65–71. New York: New Press.

————. 1994. *Manifest Manners: Postindian Warriors of Survivance*. Hanover, N.H.: Wesleyan University Press.

Waldrep, Shelton. 1999. "Story Time." In *Inside the Mouse*, 72–97. Durham, N.C.: Duke University Press.

Wax, Murray L. 1997. "Educating an Anthro: The Influence of Vine Deloria Jr." In *Indians & Anthropologists: Vine Deloria Jr. and the Critique of Anthropology*, ed. Thomas Biolsi and Larry J. Zimmerman, 50–60. Tucson: University of Arizona Press.

Weaver, Jacqueline. 1994. "The Mashantucket Miracle Lives On." *ConnStruction* 33 (1): 36–62.

Weber, Max. 1958. *From Max Weber: Essays in Sociology*. Ed. C. Wright Mills, trans. Hans H. Gerth. New York: Oxford University Press.

Weschler, Lawrence. 1995. *Mr. Wilson's Cabinet of Wonder*. New York: Pantheon Books.

Williams, Raymond. 1977. *Marxism and Literature*. New York: Oxford University Press.

Wolf, Eric R. 1982. *Europe and the People without History*. Berkeley: University of California Press.

Wright, Terence. 1991. "The Fieldwork Photographs of Jenness and Malinowski and the Beginnings of Modern Anthropology." *Journal of the Anthropological Society of Oxford* 22 (1): 41–58.

————. 1992. "Photography: Theories of Realism and Convention." In *Anthropology & Photography: 1860–1920*, ed. Elizabeth Edwards, 18–31. New Haven, Conn.: Yale University Press.

Index

activism: political, 19–20

African Americans: identity and, 56–57

allegory, 70; ethnographic, 89–90; MPMRC as, 126–27

anthropology: colonialism of, 22

Apes, William, 144, 146

appropriation, 10–11, 212–13

archaeology, 103, 105

artifacts, 32, 39, 221n5; in Foxwoods Casino, 69, 94; in MPMRC, 109, 110–13, 114–17

"Assessing NAGPRA-Related Inventories: Toward a New Methodology," 25–26

authentication, 38

authenticity, 53; invention vs., 51–52; as Mashantucket Pequot, 61–62, 91–92

Bell, Theresa Hayward, 24, 34, 152

Benedict, Jeff: *Without Reservation: The Making of America's Most Powerful Indian Tribe and Foxwoods, the World's Largest Casino*, 50

Billie, James, 45

bingo: high-stakes, 15, 45–46

biographical vignettes: of reservation life, 144–46

Black Indians, 56–57

blood quantum, 44, 57, 58

Brend, Gary, 198(fig.)

Bringing the People Home exhibit, 155–56; trailer home display in, 157–60

Brown, Michael, 48

budget: MPMRC, 26–27, 128

California v. Cabazon Band of Mission Indians, 15, 46, 219n3

Campisi, Jack, 25

capitalism: commodity, 91

Carter, Gary, 57

Carter, Joey, 56

casinos, 93, 215–16, 217; Foxwoods as standard for, 75–76; themed, 70–73. *See also* Foxwoods Resort Casino

Cassacinamon, Robin, 43, 144, 146

Child Development Center, 106, 142

Cinetropolis, 96, 97(fig.)

citizenship: national, 11

civilization, 41, 47

Club Newport International casino, 99

Colebut, Carolyn, 200(fig.)

Colebut, Steven, 200(fig.)

Colebut, Vernon, 201(fig.)

colonialism, 22

colonization: European, 40–41

236 Index

community, 29; and identity, 60–61; Mashantucket, 23, 48
compression, 73–74
concourse: at Foxwoods, 78–83
Connecticut, 32; economy, 13, 16, 219n1; Indian gaming and, 46, 220n12; Pequot reservations and, 43–44
Connecticut Alliance against Casino Expansion, 50
Connecticut River Museum (CRM), 4, 27–28, 36–37
Connecticut River Valley, 28, 42
conquest: European, 40–41
consensus building: museum, 35–36
contextualization: of artifacts, 112
continuity: tradition and, 33–34
copper: symbolic importance of, 88
cordwood sales, 44
creation stories, 125
CRM. *See* Connecticut River Museum
Crow, Hugh, 51
Cultural Resources Center, 105
culture, 90, 213
Curtis, Edward S.: photography of, 7, 169, 171, 174–78, 180–81, 206, 207, 222nn2–3, 223n10
Custer Died for Your Sins: An Indian Manifesto (Deloria), 22

dance competition, 49
DDI. *See* Design Division, Inc.
Deloria, Vine: *Custer Died for Your Sins: An Indian Manifesto*, 22
Democratic Party, 49
Design Division, Inc. (DDI), 4, 24, 94, 159

development: Mashantucket Pequot, 53–54
dioramas: MPMRC, 129–38
display environments, 8, 116
documentation: photographic, 181

economic development: Indian gaming and, 15–16, 45–46, 47, 49
economy, 13; reservation, 14–15, 44
Ellal, Martha Langevin, 44
ethnography, 70, 181; as allegory, 89–90
Essex (Conn.), 27–28
ethnohistory, 105
Europeans, 42; colonization by, 40–41; and Pequot political organization, 29–30
Everett, John, 87–88
exhibits, 155; design of, 141–42; maintenance of, 127–29; MPMRC, 108–10, 113–15, 118–20, 122–25, 129–37, 144–53; resonance of, 138–39

families: political battles among, 151–52
fantasy: themed casinos as, 71, 73, 74
farmstead: MPMRC exhibit of, 147–50, 152, 153–54
Festival of Green Corn (Schemitzun), 49
Fort at Mashantucket Project, 103, 105
"Fort at Mashantucket: Second Phase, The," 25
Foxwoods bingo hall, 46
Foxwoods Resort Casino, 3, 4, 6, 14, 33, 40, 47, 49, 60, 63, 69, 85(fig.), 121, 209, 211, 217, 220n12, 221n2; casinos in, 98–100; Cinetropolis, 96–97; cultural authenticity and, 91–92; design thematics of, 71, 72, 74–77, 86–91, 93–94; as MPMRC exhibit,

118–20; pedestrian concourse of, 78–83, 94–98; as public space, 8, 9; *Rainmaker* installation at, 64–68; as representational space, 10–11, 16–17, 212

gambling business, 47–48
gaming. *See* Indian gaming
gaming compacts, 11
gated community: Mashantucket as, 6, 23
Gates, Merrill E., 47
Gathering Space, 108, 109(fig.)
General Allotment Act, 44, 220n5
General Court of Connecticut, 43
George, Austin, 144, 145(fig.)
George, Peter, 144, 146(fig.)
Goodwin, Michael, 105
Graham, Gail, 105, 221n3
Grand Pequot Tower, 8, 13–14, 63, 64(fig.), 77, 99, 108, 122; pedestrian concourse to, 96, 97–98
grant proposals, 24, 25–26
Great Cedar Casino, 98–99
Great Cedar Hotel, 77
Great Cedar Swamp, 40, 75, 87, 144

Hale, Joshua, 188(fig.)
Hale, Joy, 188(fig.)
Hard Rock Cafe, 77, 99
Hayward, Richard "Skip," 23, 24, 44, 45, 56, 67, 94, 152, 210
Hayward family, 152
hegemonics, 36, 53, 214; Indian designation in, 32–33; representation and, 8–9
heritage: construction and production of, 127, 135–36

Historic Preservation Fund Grants to Indian Tribes, Alaska Natives, and Native Hawaiian Organizations, 25
history, 71, 140; Foxwoods exhibits on, 94–96; objects in, 116–17; Pequot placement in, 124–25; photographs as, 195, 204–5, 208; in *Rainmaker* installation narrative, 65, 67, 69
history making, 18–19
hog farming, 44
Holder, John: *The Rainmaker* installation, 67–68
Holder, Michael, 199(fig.)
Houser, Alan, 100; *The Sacred Rain Arrow*, 67, 94

Ice Age: narrative of, 65, 69, 123
identity, 12, 24, 30, 33; community, 60–61; cultural, 4, 51–52; Indian, 32, 49–50, 58–59; Mashantucket Pequot, 3, 8, 9–10, 34, 39, 49, 62, 101, 151–52, 186–87, 202, 205–6, 207–8, 213; public, 5, 29; racial, 18, 34; self-represented, 19–21; tribal, 55–56, 182
IGRA. *See* Indian Gaming Regulatory Act
image making, 181
imaginary, 6, 9, 30, 69
imagination, 11, 214
Indian(s), 10, 216; as Foxwoods theme, 74–75, 84; as hegemonic description, 32–33; identity as, 29, 49–50, 58–59, 69; as photographic subject, 175–81, 206–7
Indian gaming, 59, 217, 220n12; classes of regulated, 15–16; economic development and, 45–46, 49; growth of, 215–16; industry impacts of, 47–48; MPMRC exhibit on,

238   Index

118–20; regulating, 46–47, 219n2; success
of, 4–5

Indian Gaming Regulatory Act (IGRA), 15–
16, 46, 119, 215, 219n3

Indianness, 9, 18, 43, 49, 61–62, 151–52,
209, 212, 216; in Foxwoods, 75, 76, 93; in
photographic portraits, 161, 195, 208

Indiantown, 25, 103, 105

"Indiantown: Survey and Inventory of a
Transitional Community," 25

Indian Trade and Intercourse Acts, 44–45,
220n8

industry: oppositional, 47–48

intelligent selfishness, 46–47

intermarriage: and identity, 25

invention: vs. authenticity, 51–52; cultural,
52–53

*Joint Tribal Council of the Passamaquoddy Tribe v.
Morton*, 45

King Philip's (Metacom's) War, 25

Kirchner, Alice R., 171, 172(fig.)

knowledge, 5, 182; structures of, 36, 185, 186

Kroft, Steve, 43, 50–51, 54

Lake of Isles Boy Scout camp, 51

land, 121, 220n5; Mashantucket Pequot,
43–44, 51, 220n4, 220n6; ownership, 121;
recovery of Indian, 44–45

landscape: MPMRC and, 103

language: Pequot, 141–42

Las Vegas: theme casinos in, 72–73

life casts: in MPMRC exhibits, 129–30, 131–
37(figs.), 214

Life on the Reservation exhibit, 155–56, 214;
description and photos of, 144–53

local, the: in museum displays, 142–43

looking at, 8, 9

Luciani, Al, 67

Lyman, Christopher, 169

maple syrup manufacturing, 44

Mashantucket, 6, 43, 101, 121; as Foxwoods
theme, 74–75; self-reference, 31–32;
self-representation, 33–34; views from
Foxwoods of, 78–79; visitor experience at,
30–31

Mashantucket Pequot Gaming Enterprise, 46

Mashantucket Pequot Indian Claims
Settlement Act, 45

Mashantucket Pequot Museum and Research
Center (MPMRC), 3, 4, 7, 8, 28, 34, 35,
49, 60, 94, 104(fig.), 209, 211, 217, 221n5,
222n8; administration for, 24–25; as
allegory, 126–27; design for, 26, 103, 221n2;
exhibit maintenance in, 127–29; exhibits in,
113–15, 118–20, 122–25, 129–38, 141–42,
143–53, 155–56, 157–60; farmstead exhibit
in, 153–54; layout of, 108–10; narratives at,
38–39; objects in, 110–13, 115–17; poetics
of, 120–21, 154–55; political structure of,
26–27; portrait gallery in, 162–73, 205–6;
public spaces in, 105–8; as representational
space, 10–11, 16–17, 214–15; role of the
local in, 142–43; visitor experiences at,
138–39, 156–57

Mashantucket Pequotness, 43, 61, 75, 76, 101

Mashantucket Pequot Reservation, 13, 32,
43, 51, 103, 121, 210, 220n6; exhibits on,

144–53; land as representation on, 84, 86; land on, 44–45; representational space on, 16–17

Mashantucket Pequot Tribal Nation, 3, 4, 18, 44, 48, 156, 202, 209, 210; appropriation by, 212–13; authenticity of, 91–92; development projects, 53–55; federal recognition of, 11, 49; grant proposals for, 24, 25–26; identity of, 8, 23, 29, 34, 38, 50, 56–57, 60, 61–62, 101, 186–87, 205–6, 207–8; and MPMRC, 26–27, 127, 222n8; museum exhibit of, 108–9, 123; representation of, 214–15; self-definition of, 101–2; tribal identity of, 9–10

Mashpee Meetinghouse, 147(fig.)

Mason, John, 42

"Massacre at Mystic Fort" narrative and exhibit, 94–96

McBride, Kevin, 25, 68

meaning: production of, 121–22

mediation, 193

memory, 193–94; photographs and, 203–4

Merrill, Jean, 188(fig.)

Metacom, 25

Mitchell, Eunice, 196(fig.)

Mohegan reservation, 13

Mohegans: and Pequots, 42–43

Mohegan Sun Casino, 13, 47, 220n12

MPMRC. *See* Mashantucket Pequot Museum and Research Center

museums, 5, 223n1; as allegory, 126–27; authenticity and, 216–17; as colonial practice, 139–40; consensus building in, 35–36; at Foxwood Resort Casino, 63, 94–

96; tourism and, 135–36; tribal-controlled/ Native, 113, 161, 215–16

Mystic: Pequot village at, 42, 108, 110(fig.)

Mystic River drum, 68, 221n3

NAGPRA. *See* North American Graves Protection and Repatriation Act

Narragansetts, 42, 43, 220n1

narrative(s), 9, 12, 106; cultural and tribal, 88–89, 91; Massacre at Mystic Fort, 94–96; MPMRC, 38–39, 123–25; photographs as, 193, 195, 197, 202; poetics in, 120–21; in portrait gallery, 163–64, 165–67; *Rainmaker* installation, 65, 67, 69; themed casinos as, 71–72; Yankee, 79–83

National Museum of the American Indian (NMAI), 34, 49, 219n2, 221n2

National Park Service, 25

Native American Rights Fund, 44

nature: as Foxwoods theme, 86–87; and Indian photographs, 182–83

Neel, David, 222n1; portraits by, 7, 167–73, 175, 181, 186–89, 195–203, 205–7, 212

New England: European settlement of, 40–41; Foxwoods animatronic tribute to, 79–83

New England Design, 87–88

Niantics, 42

NMAI. *See* National Museum of the American Indian

Noank, 43, 108

North American Graves Protection and Repatriation Act (NAGPRA), 5, 25–26

nostalgia, 89, 91, 141–42

objects: photographic, 183–84. *See also* artifacts

objects of cultural patrimony, 5

observation tower (MPMRC), 8, 103, 104(fig.), 123

Occum, Samson, 103, 145

Ocuish, Hannah, 144

opposition: Indian gaming as, 47–48

oral history project, 159–60

Other: representation of, 178, 183

Our Chiefs and Elders (Neel), 167, 168, 169, 174, 197

Pasquaretta, Paul, 55

Pearson, Matthew, 190(fig.)

Pequot-English alliance, 25

Pequot language: loss of, 141–42

Pequot reservation, 43

Pequots, 77, 220n1; European colonization, 40–42; historical narrative of, 94–96, 124–25; and Mohegans, 42–43; political organization, 29–30

Pequot Society gallery, 141–42

Pequot Village exhibit, 140; description and photos of, 129–37; experiencing, 143–44

Pequot War, 28, 40, 42, 144

performance, 3, 10, 70; of Indianness, 61–62, 212; *Rainmaker* installation as, 64–69

Perry, John, 57

Phelmetta, Arline, 196(fig.)

photodocumentary project, 25

photographs/photography, 7, 10, 20–21, 36–37, 222nn5–6, 223n9; as creation of record, 184–85; Curtis's, 174–78, 222nn2–3, 223n10; as documents, 189–95; as evidential history, 204–5; Indian, 22, 179–83; meaning of, 185–86; memory

and, 203–4; Neel's, 167–73, 186–89, 196–201(figs.); portrait, 8, 161, 162–67, 202–3; role of, 210, 212; subjects of, 183–84

pictorialism, 173

Plouffe, Elizabeth George, 44, 94, 96, 109

poetics, 33, 126, 214; of location, 120–21; of MPMRC, 154–55; as production of meaning, 121–22

politics: MPMRC, 26–27; Pequot, 29–30

portraits: Neel's, 167–73, 181, 188(fig.), 190(fig.), 192–93, 196(fig.), 198–201(figs.), 202–3; photographic, 7, 8, 94, 174–78; tribal, 63, 161, 162–67, 212

postmodernity, 31

power: photographs as, 191–92

public spaces, 5, 8, 9, 11–12

race, 49, 161; and Mashantucket Pequot identity, 56–57, 151–52

Rainmaker, The (statue), 64, 221n1; development of, 67–68; imagery of, 69, 84; show centered around, 65–67

Rainmaker Casino, 63, 99

Rainmaker Square, 67–68

records: photographs as, 184–85

representation(s), 19, 31, 70, 105, 178, 193; casino and museum as, 10–11, 90, 151; in Foxwoods, 89–90; hegemonic, 8–9; of Indians, 5–6, 84; levels of, 210–11; of Mashantucket Pequots, 214–15; public spaces of, 11–12

reservations, 220nn4–5; as compression centers, 73–74; economic revitalization of, 14–15

resonance: of MPMRC exhibits, 138–39

Sacred Rain Arrow, The (Houser), 67, 94
savagery, 41
Schemitzun (Festival of Green Corn), 49
Sebastian, Stewart, 84
self-definition, 55, 101
self-determination, 23, 47, 55
self-identification, 18, 20, 43, 59
self-reference, 31–32
self-representation, 4, 6, 12, 180; challenges to, 23–24; conflict in, 37–38; Mashantucket, 33–34, 75, 215
Seminole Tribe of Florida v. Butterworth, 15, 45, 219n2
sense of place: in MPMRC, 105–6; photographs and, 182–83
shows: thematic, 65–67, 79–83
60 Minutes reports, 48, 50–51, 54–55
slot machines, 46, 98–100; as historical objects, 117, 118–20
sovereignty, 5, 11, 34, 47, 55, 58, 213
Stargazer casino, 99
storytelling: exhibits as, 155
Studio EIS: life-cast figures, 129–30
Sunsimons family: and farmstead exhibit, 148, 152
survivance, 55, 59

theater, 9; exhibits as, 136, 138
thematization, 135–36
tourism: and museums, 135–36
tradition, 35, 61; construction of, 52–53, 77; continuity and, 33–34; invention of, 29, 153
Treaty of Hartford, 43, 95, 96
tribal membership: defining, 44

tribal nations: as domestic dependents, 60, 220n13; federal recognition of, 3, 11, 58–59; public identity of, 9–10
Tribal Portrait, A, 162–65, 175; examples from, 172(fig.), 188(fig.), 190(fig.), 196(fig.), 198–201(figs.); organization of, 195, 197; and tribal identity, 205–8
tribes: designation and identification of, 5, 55–56, 182
Trump, Donald, 46, 49, 57
Tubridy, Kevin, 88
Tureen, Thomas, 44–45

Uncas, 42
Underhill, John, 42, 95, 108

Vanishing Race–Navaho, The (Curtis), 176, 177(fig.)
violence: European, 41
visitor experience, 30–31, 115, 127
volunteerism, 20

wampum, 108
wealth: Indians and, 50
whites: in Foxwoods Casino narratives, 82–83
Winthrop, John, 95
Without Reservation: The Making of America's Most Powerful Indian Tribe and Foxwoods, the World's Largest Casino (Benedict), 50
Witness, The (film), 144

Yankees: Foxwoods thematic narrative of, 79–83
Young, Nathan, 167–68, 171

About the Author

John Bodinger de Uriarte is an assistant professor of anthropology at Susquehanna University, where he teaches courses in visual anthropology, public culture, Native America, and museum studies. His articles have appeared in *Ethnohistory, Museum Anthropology,* and *Tribal Government Gaming.* Bodinger de Uriarte, a native of California, completed his PhD in cultural anthropology at the University of Texas at Austin in 2003. His field research in Mashantucket included working as a contract consultant for Design Division, Inc., the exhibition design firm for the Mashantucket Pequot Museum and Research Center (MPMRC). In this capacity he produced photographs for exhibitions and researched and wrote panel texts. He also worked as a grant proposal writer for the Mashantucket Pequot Tribal Nation and as an intern for the MPMRC. Other professional experience includes working as curator for the Connecticut River Museum in Essex, Connecticut, and as grants and special projects officer for The Wolfsonian–FIU in Miami Beach.

Before entering graduate school, Bodinger de Uriarte also worked as a documentary, editorial, and advertising photographer in San Francisco for more than ten years. His photographs have been exhibited in galleries in Boston, San Francisco, Austin, and Santa Barbara.